creating Keepsakes™

Journaling Solutions
FOR SCRAPBOOKS

07

The World's Smallest

JeDi

This was your first year Trick-or-Treating, and your Grandma Carol made this utterly perfect Jedi costume for you. It was a huge hit wherever we went (light saber clipped onto your belt, hood drawn over your face), not only with the costume, but with that sweet tooth of yours. Every time we got a piece of candy for your bucket, you'd sit down and pull it out and eat it right there. Hey, for one night a year, you can be sweet in every way, right?

A LEISURE ARTS PUBLICATION

Creating Keepsakes

Editor-in-Chief
Jennafer Martin

Founding Editor
Lisa Bearnson

Managing Editor
Lara Penrod

Creative Editor
Megan Hoeppner

Senior Editor
Kim Jackson

Senior Online Editor
Amber Ellis

Contributing Editor
Melanie King

Editor
Lori Fairbanks

Online Editor
Erin Weed

Associate Editors
Dorathy Gilchrist, Joannie McBride

Editorial Assistant
Ahtanya Johnson

Contributing Writers
Lori Anderson, Brittany Beattie, Rebecca Cooper,
Mandy Douglass, Maurianne Dunn, Ali Edwards,
Becky Higgins, Vanessa Hoy, Jen Jockisch,
Elizabeth Kartchner, Laura Kurz, Jana Lillie,
Jennifer McGuire, Britney Mellen, C.D. Muckosky,
Amanda Probst, Celeste Smith, Jessica Sprague,
Heidi Swapp, Tracy White

Art Director
Erin Bayless

Senior Designers
Neko Carillo, Maren Ingles

Contributing Designer
Gaige Redd

Photography
American Color, Symoni Johnson,
Vertis Communications

Published by Leisure Arts, Inc., 5701 Ranch Drive, Little Rock, Arkansas 72223-9633.
501-868-8800. www.leisurearts.com.

This product is manufactured under license for Creative Crafts Group, LLC., Creative
Crafts Group company, publisher of Creating Keepsakes® scrapbook magazine.
©2011. All rights reserved.

Library of Congress Control Number: 2011922657
ISBN-13/EAN: 978-1-60900-244-2

Creative Crafts Group, LLC.

President and CEO
Stephen J. Kent

VP/Group Publisher
Tina Battock

Chief Financial Officer
Mark F. Arnett

Corporate Controller
Jordan Bohrer

VP/Publishing Director
Joel P. Toner

VP/Production & Technology
Derek W. Corson

VP/Consumer Marketing
Dennis O'Brien

Leisure Arts

Editor-in-Chief
Susan White Sullivan

Director of Designer Relations
Cheryl Johnson

Special Projects Director
Susan Frantz Wiles

Senior Prepress Director
Mark Hawkins

Imaging Technician
Stephanie Johnson

Prepress Technician
Janie Marie Wright

Publishing Systems Administrator
Becky Riddle

Mac Information Technology Specialist
Robert Young

President and Chief Executive Officer
Rick Barton

Vice President and Chief Operations Officer
Tom Siebenmorgen

Vice President of Sales
Mike Behar

Director of Finance and Administration
Laticia Mull Dittrich

National Sales Director
Martha Adams

Creative Services
Chaska Lucas

Information Technology Director
Hermine Linz

Controller
Francis Caple

Vice President, Operations
Jim Dittrich

Retail Customer Service Manager
Stan Raynor

Print Production Manager
Fred F. Pruss

If you've ever been stumped when trying to write down the memories behind your photos, you're not alone. Even the most experienced scrapbookers—and writers—can get stumped from time to time. Words are sometimes hard to find, or they don't seem adequate to capture the powerful feelings behind the photos.

That's why the editors at *Creating Keepsakes* magazine have gathered together some of the most inspiring—and easy to follow—journaling solutions around in this book. Inside you'll find hundreds of ideas to both write and format your journaling to tell your stories in creative ways that capture your thoughts and feelings with ease. Whether you've just started scrapbooking and want to know where to start journaling or have been scrapbooking for years and are looking for new approaches, in these pages you'll find what you need to help you get beyond those writing stumbling blocks to share your memories with style and meaning.

JENNAFER MARTIN
Editor-in-Chief
Creating Keepsakes magazine

Journaling Solutions for Scrapbooks

contents

WE LOVE
WE WORK
WE LIKE
WE DREAM
WE LIVE

We will have baths that fit the rest of our updated house.

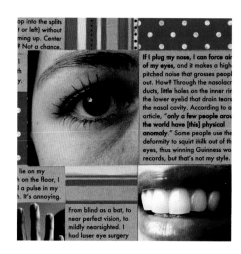

CHAPTER 1

Write from the Heart

Think back for a moment, would you? Do you have a particular Christmas gift that you received as a child that you still remember? That you possibly even still have? I tried this and can honestly only remember one gift distinctly. The others are a bit of a blur.

The one gift I remember is my dad's stamp collection. He gave it to me when I was eleven and included this note. The fact that my dad actually took the time to write a note and knew what was in the present, itself, was significant. The fact that he would share something so treasured was even more so. My dad is a fairly private and quiet sort of guy, so this glimpse into his life was a rare treat, something that truly made an impression. Did I take up stamp collecting myself? For awhile. Do I still have and treasure this collection? You betchya! I haven't added anything to it in years, but I do hope to one day get it all organized so I can share it with my sons. It remains one of my favorite gifts of all time.

So. Thinking about all this, I've been considering whether the gifts we're giving our sons are ones they'll remember. I hope some of them are. I know now that I'll be more aware of this in the future. Here's to gifts...

WORTH REMEMBERING

EVERY GOOD WRITER begins with the basics: who, what, why, when, and where. But in your personal scrapbooks, you want to expand beyond these essentials to capture the stories and emotions behind your life's experiences. Here you'll find the inspiration you need to get started, as well as great tips on how to use voices and perspectives (in addition to your own) to help tell your story with a new point of view. You'll also find inspiration for creating scrapbook layouts about life's big events and the little details in between. Plus, scrapbook experts will help you learn to love and use your own handwriting on layouts for a personal touch that future generations will cherish.

zach

second born...28 years old...three kids...
married two years...moving to Colorado...
works in telecommunications...fond of his toys

me

eldest...32 years old...three kids...married
almost 11 years...living in CO...scrapbooking
& homeschooling...wearing new boots

journaling

Even for those of us who never seem to be at a loss for words, journaling can sometimes present a special challenge. We want our sentiments to be heartfelt but not sappy, funny but not forced, accurate but not ordinary. Many of us don't think of ourselves as writers. We love the creativity of scrapbooking but are stumped when it comes to the accompanying text. In this section, you'll discover dozens of ideas for personalizing your pages with the power of words.

...rding to Asher:

...d boil eggs

...glasses (not like the ones
...wear on your face)

...water in the glasses &

...the dye

...something to hold the egg &

...the egg in the glass

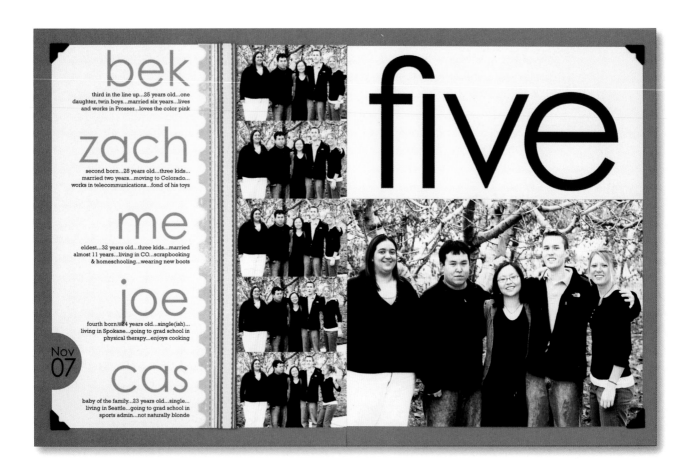

AMANDA'S SOLUTION ^

Use the "outtakes" from the photo shoot and create captions about your family members. Often these are the most accurate portrayals of people. For my layout, I used one outtake for each person pictured and added fun facts about that person.

Five *by Amanda Probst.* **Supplies** *Cardstock:* Prism Papers; *Patterned paper and ribbon:* Making Memories; *Photo corners:* Scrapbook Adhesives by 3L; *Fonts:* Century Gothic and Rockwell.

> "Creativity involves breaking out of established patterns in order to look at things in a different way."
>
> —*Edward de Bono*

"Mom! He's kissing me again...."
"But, she's so cuuuuute! I can't help it!"

"Mom said to kiss you back, so there!
"Okay" (chuckles)

"Do you love me Emma?"
"Ummm...yes! I think..."

"Do you love me Ryan?"
"Yes....with all my heart cutie pie."

"Ryan's gonna marry me when I get big."

"No, I'm not! Brothers and sisters can't get married!"

Love wears many different faces around here - especially between the two of you! Ryan, you find your little sister irresistible and always have a hug or a kiss at the ready for her. Of course, Emma, you usually find this quite annoying, especially as you are getting older and asserting your independence more and more. I'm not too worried though I know how much the two of you love each other, icky kisses and grumpy faces or not.

JANUARY 2008

THE LOOK OF LOVE

LINDA'S SOLUTION ⌃

I had these great photos of my kids, and I realized that capturing random bits of conversation between the two of them on my layout would not only support my journaling, but also enhance the photos. Years from now, I want them to remember the funny things they said, exactly the way they said them.

The Look of Love *by Linda Rodriguez.* **Supplies** *Software:* Digital Image Pro 9.0, Microsoft; *Digital paper:* Laced Love Paper Pack and Mailroom No. 1 Paper Pack by Katie Pertiet; *Digital letters:* Messy Stamped Alpha 2 by Katie Pertiet; *Digital tree:* Love Grows No. 1 Brushes-n-Stamps by Katie Pertiet; *Digital tag and pin:* Botanist No. 19 Kit by Katie Pertiet; *Digital flowers:* Pretty Please Kit by Mindy Terasawa; *Font:* Teletype.

TIFFANY'S SOLUTION ⌄

What works for me is to use the everyday slang and nicknames and informal language I use in conversation. Lots of times I just write like I would speak to my daughter—I find my voice sounds the most natural that way. Watching for moments that are unrehearsed and unplanned and recording those moments or feelings often makes for special journaling opportunities.

The Princess and a Pauper *by Tiffany Tillman.* **Supplies** *Software:* Photoshop Elements CS3, Adobe Systems; *Digital paper:* Crumpy Crumpled Black by Emily Merritt; *Digital frog accent:* Froggieland by Tiffany Tillman; *Digital journaling template:* Journal Box 1 by Anna Aspnes; *Paint:* Created by Tiffany Tillman; *Fonts:* Artistamp Medium (title) and Georgia (journaling).

Alrighty, so on Sunday we were celebrating our 4 1/2 year anniversary (yeees, we celebrate stupid little things like that), and after dinner I was just lounging about on the couch (as I am wont to do) when I suddenly heard Leonard Cohen singing *Hallelujah*, one of my all-time favourite songs, and I saw Bobby walking into the room looking really confused and carrying something around his neck. (I know it seems really unromantic to take pictures at a moment like this, but shuddup, how could I not take pictures of that dog?!) Bobby kept wandering around looking downright scared until JK picked him up and carried him over to me. I, however, was not as confused as Bobs, so I started crying immediately. I unwrapped and opened the box and inside was the perfect ring. JK got down on one knee asked me if I wanted to marry him, and of course I said yes!

It was so cute with Bobby as the ringbearer - I call him Smeagol when we're out on walks because he looks very Gollum-like when he gets excited about sniffing something, so of course he has to be the one with The Ring!

Blog entry, September 25, 2005

engaged

INGUNN'S SOLUTION ⌃

To make my journaling feel more personal, I often copy it straight from my blog or write it as if I were writing in my diary. I love using this casual style of writing because it really captures a lot of my personality and how I express myself. This type of journaling doesn't seem like a chore because it just feels like I'm describing the event to a friend.

Engaged *by Ingunn Markiewicz.* **Supplies** *Cardstock:* Bazzill Basics Paper; *Patterned paper:* BasicGrey; *Chipboard letters:* Heidi Swapp for Advantus; *Font:* Calibri; *Other:* Butterfly sequins and embroidery floss.

ALLISON'S SOLUTION ^

First of all, it doesn't matter! You are you, and your voice is important. But for a change of pace every now and then, have your family help. For my layout, I asked each of my family members to share their favorite memory of my baby's first day. I loved how they each said something completely different. Instead of just having my story of the day, I have six little stories of what my family experienced. This technique is great for event layouts because you can get several different perspectives on one event.

Favorite Memories from 5.9.08 *by Allison Davis.* **Supplies** *Cardstock:* Bazzill Basics Paper; *Patterned paper:* Scenic Route; *Chipboard:* BasicGrey, Rusty Pickle (hearts) and Heidi Swapp for Advantus (letters); *Felt hearts:* Fancy Pants Designs; *Paint:* Making Memories; *Glimmer spray:* Glimmer Mist, Tattered Angels; *Coaster:* Imagination Project; *Ink:* ColorBox, Clearsnap; *Fonts:* CK Journaling Condensed and Times New Roman.

look closer >>

Years from now, how special will it be for Allison's son to read his family's reactions to meeting him for the first time?

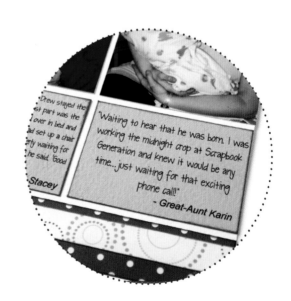

KELLY'S SOLUTION ^

Create your own journaling tags! It's an easy way to fit everything you want to say in an organized fashion that enhances the design of the page. Just cut your cardstock into small tags and handwrite your thoughts on as many as you need. Place them on your layout and attach them with brads. Here, I varied the length of the tags for more visual interest.

Prime House *by Kelly Purkey.* **Supplies** *Cardstock:* Bazzill Basics Paper; *Patterned paper:* American Crafts (black and white), Chatterbox (teal wood grain) and SEI (stripe); *Star tag:* Li'l Davis Designs; *Chipboard photo corners:* Heidi Swapp for Advantus; *Punches and decorative-edge scissors:* Fiskars; *Rub-ons, brads and pen:* American Crafts.

KELLY'S SOLUTION ^

Tough times with your family? Everyone experiences them. Scrapping about the not-so-rosy parts is a great way to be real, to capture where you are in your life. It's important to document the problems you face so future generations can see how you worked through them.

Welcome Back! *by Kelly Noel.* **Supplies** *Cardstock:* Bazzill Basics Paper; *Patterned paper, buttons, ribbon and rub-ons:* American Crafts; *Stickers:* American Crafts and Making Memories; *Font:* Kayleigh.

TIFFANY'S SOLUTION ⌃

On this layout, my journaling tells the story, but it also serves a very important design function. Lita's head, the swirly title and the line of brown dots all lead the eye to the right, so placing the journaling so it's centered horizontally (in line with the other features) on the right side of the layout and right-justifying it creates balance.

The Writer *by Tiffany Tillman.* **Supplies** *Software:* Photoshop CS3, Adobe Systems; *Digital paper:* Ledger Sun Prints by Katie Pertiet; *Digital swirl:* Purple Swirl by Kim Christensen; *Digital stamp:* Seuss Stamp by Michelle Coleman; *Digital label:* Stand Up by Sara Carling; *Digital cardboard:* Boyfriend by Holly McCaig; *Digital frames:* Simplicity by Holly McCaig; *Digital staples:* Dog Gone Cute by Mindy Terasawa; *Digital brushes:* Essentials by Tiffany Tillman; *Fonts:* Georgia (journaling) and Impact.

IRMA'S SOLUTION ^

I often have trouble coming up with creative ways to display journaling, too. For this page, I arranged journaling spots as a decorative border. As a result, my text became part of the page's decoration rather than dominating and taking attention away from the focal-point photo.

Irma's A-List *by Irma Peredne.* **Supplies** *Cardstock:* Bazzill Basics Paper; *Lace cardstock:* KI Memories; *Patterned paper and glitter stickers:* me & my BIG ideas; *Vellum and border stickers:* K&Company; *Journaling spots:* Heidi Swapp for Advantus; *Gaffer tape:* 7gypsies; *Paper flowers, staples and trim:* Making Memories; *Rhinestone brads:* Creating Keepsakes; *Mini flowers:* Prima (white) and Target (gem); *Chipboard letter:* Fancy Pants Designs; *Stickers:* Li'l Davis Designs (red), Jo-Ann Scrap Essentials (epoxy); *Rub-on stitches:* Die Cuts With a View; *Embroidery floss:* DMC; *Paint:* Delta Creative.

DENINE'S SOLUTION ^

Of course you can! Create a home for your journaling in the center of the page and crop your pictures tightly (to about 2 ½" x 2 ¾"). Adhere the photos around the journaling to frame your story.

Good People by Denine Zielinski. **Supplies** *Software:* Photoshop Elements 4.0, Adobe Systems; *Cardstock:* Bazzill Basics Paper; *Patterned paper:* My Mind's Eye (blue) and Scrappin' Sports (brown); *Brads:* Stemma, Masterpiece Studios; *Felt flowers:* Creative Imaginations; *Buttons:* BasicGrey; *Embroidery floss:* DMC; *Foam letters:* American Crafts; *Digital swirl brushes:* Rhonna Swirl 5 by Rhonna Farrer and Skinny Mini Swirlies by Mindy Terasawa; *Fonts:* Modern No. 20 and Cream Puff.

> "Never be too big to ask questions; never know too much to learn something new."
>
> —Og Mandino

EMILY'S SOLUTION ^

I almost always use my own handwriting for journaling. I love the personal touch it adds to my layouts. For this page, I used crochet trim to create an oval that leads the eye to the heart of the picture and placed my title stickers inside the oval frame. Then I wrote my journaling inside the oval, creating a unified design.

In Love *by Emily Falconbridge.* **Supplies** *Patterned paper:* BasicGrey; *Rub-ons and letter stickers:* Making Memories; *Stamp:* Autumn Leaves; *Other:* Crochet trim and pen.

AMANDA'S SOLUTION ^

For these egg-dying photos, I decided to let my sons do the journaling for me and simply asked them to explain how to dye Easter eggs. Not only do I have a great record of the day, but I captured their personalities and thoughts as well.

How to Dye Easter Eggs *by Amanda Probst.* **Supplies** *Cardstock:* Prism Papers; *Journaling sheets:* Making Memories; *Chalk pencils:* Koh-I-Noor Gioconda; *Corner rounder:* EK Success; *Pen:* Precision Pen, American Crafts; *Font:* CK Evie.

Punch buggy, don't punch me.

Mom, it's "punch buggy green, no punch backs" - you gotta say it right or it doesn't count.

Awwww, Mommy, that's not fair! I didn't see it.

But that's the point, honey. I saw it first so I said it first. Punch buggy don't punch back.

MOM! C'mon, it's "punch buggy green, no punch backs," so now yours doesn't count.

Well, that makes no sense whatsoever. Why ...

OOOOOOH, MINE, MINE THEN! PUNCH BUGGY GREEN, NO PUNCH BACKS, MOMMY!

Ugh, please don't scream. And did you just kick me?

I can't reach to punch you, Mommy.

Oh, ok sweetie.

PUNCH BUGGY BLUE, NO PUNCH BACKS!

Is it really necessary to body slam me while I'm driving? Can we stick to simply punching?

It was just a touch, Mom! Geez, you need to lighten up. You're becoming a wimp.

You CAN'T be serious? Me? A wimp? Are you out of ...

PUNCH BUGGY RED, NO PUNCH BACKS!

Ow! Wait a minute, I don't think ...

Gotta pay attention, Mom.

No fair! I didn't see it. MOMMY, SHE'S NOT PLAYING FAIR.

It is too fair. I saw it first. Not my poblem you're a shrimp.

MOMMY!!

OK, no name calling, new rule. And let's try to use our indoor ...

PUNCH BUGGY BLACK, NO PUNCH BACKS!

MOMMY! I GOT IT FIRST IT'S MINE! I GOT IT! I BEAT YOU!

OK ENOUGH - let's play statues! Who's with me?

ANDREA'S SOLUTION ⌃

Trying to convey conversation involving multiple speakers can get tricky and very convoluted if you constantly refer to who's speaking. On my layout, I used different colors to represent each speaker. As you read the conversation, it becomes readily apparent who is saying what to whom, without ever having to use the words "she said."

Punch Buggy *by Andrea Chamberlain.* **Supplies** *Software:* Photoshop CS2, Adobe Systems; *Stock-car photo:* Stockxpert; *Digital floral swirl brushes:* Brusheezy; *Digital swirl brushes:* Carrie Stephens; *Fonts:* Weezer and Broadway.

After a miserable couple of weeks of "Juneuary", we fled east in search of the sun. Just beyond the creepy, faux-Bavarian town of Leavenworth lies a plethora of beautiful trails, and we chose the eight mile round trip to the emerald gem that is Colchuck Lake. This hike also gave us the chance to scope out my big challenge for this summer - Aasgard Pass. Beyond that steep, long pass flanked by the jagged spires of Dragontail Peak lies the Enchantments; the beautiful alpine paradise of lakes and tarns that I have been hearing about ever since I started hiking in Washington. Due to a strict permit system, we will only be allowed to camp here at Colchuck (a gorgeous destination in itself), then climb 2,200 feet over one mile (eep!) up Aasgard Pass | 06.14.08

INGUNN'S SOLUTION ︿

A trick I use to spice up my albums is to connect layouts and events together so that when you're looking through the album, you really feel like you're reading a narrative of our lives. On this layout, instead of just writing, "We went to Colchuck Lake today. It was a beautiful hike and we saw lots of pretty wildflowers," I revealed my anxiety about a challenging hike we would be doing in that area later in the summer. A few pages later in the album, you can read about how I successfully overcame my challenge.

Gateway to the Enchantments *by Ingunn Markiewicz.* **Supplies** *Patterned paper:* Fancy Pants Designs; *Fonts:* Bodoni MT, Calibri and Suzie's Hand.

ALLISON'S SOLUTION ⌃

When my grandma held my newborn son for the first time, she was so cute, and the way she spoke to him was hilarious and sweet. I was beyond excited when I learned that my mom had captured that moment in this photograph. My son is now three, and it took me that long to get the page done because I didn't know what to say. I loved the picture, but any journaling I came up with just didn't seem right. I finally figured out that my grandma's actual comments were perfect, so I got out the home video and transcribed them word for word.

Hello *by Allison Davis.* **Supplies** *Cardstock:* Bazzill Basics Paper; *Patterned paper:* KI Memories; *Cardstock stickers:* Crate Paper; *Chipboard:* BasicGrey (quotation marks), Fancy Pants Designs (flourish) and me & my BIG ideas (heart); *Paint:* Making Memories; *Ink:* ColorBox, Clearsnap; *Fonts:* Times New Roman and 2Peas Fancy Free.

My **2** brothers and me. **3** of us out of our family of **5**

Mike is **11** months younger than me. Matt is **8** years.

But somehow my little brothers are both at least **7** in. taller than me?!

2 brilliant doctors-to-be. Who will support their **1** artsy sister.

We live over **70** miles apart. With Matt in the middle.

We've shared **2** houses, **5** cars, **6** Disney vacations, & **0** pets.

And I know they'll be there for me for the next **80** more.

three *Of* us.

KELLY'S SOLUTION ⌃

We took lots of photos at my brother's graduation, but this one was special because it included my brothers and me—just the three of us. I decided to focus my journaling around numbers. The important numbers about our relationship help tell the story behind the photo.

Three of Us by Kelly Purkey. **Supplies** *Cardstock:* Bazzill Basics Paper; *Patterned paper:* Heidi Grace Designs (green argyle and yellow), KI Memories (orange) and Scenic Route (green dots); *Stamp:* Studio Calico; *Ink:* StazOn, Tsukineko; *Stickers:* American Crafts, Heidi Grace Designs and Making Memories; *Epoxy stickers:* Cloud 9 Design, Fiskars; *Border punch, star punch and circle cutter:* Fiskars; *Font:* American Typewriter.

look closer »

Check out how Kelly's use of number stickers adds dimension and style to her layout.

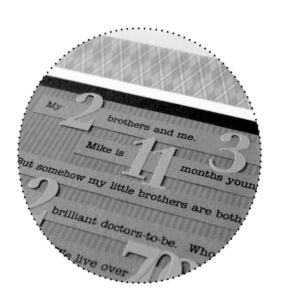

EMILY'S SOLUTION ⌃

Try printing your journaling on your 8 ½" x 11" printer, "breaking up" the journaling and placing your title and decorative touches between the two sections, like I did here. I actually think it adds to the design to have text on a contrasting color of cardstock both above and below my title.

Fall *by Emily Magleby.* **Supplies** *Cardstock:* Bazzill Basics Paper; *Patterned paper:* Tinkering Ink; *Flower:* Prima; *Brad and letter stickers:* Making Memories; *Circle punch:* Fiskars; *Font:* CK Becky; *Other:* Thread.

Nine-and-a-half. It's such an awkward age to be, half way between nine and ten. Still a child, but desperately wanting to be older. Already starting to develop a bit of that "teenage girl" attitude. You're asking about wearing makeup and crazy about shopping for clothes. Not so interested in playing with dolls and toys anymore, but wanting to hang out with friends, listen to music and talk on the phone. Fortunately, you're also very compassionate, sweet and helpful. You'll still play board games and hug us in public (even though sometimes you are too busy to stop and do it!) I am confident that when you do actually hit the dreaded age of thirteen, you'll do just fine. Don't rush to get there though!

LISA'S SOLUTION ^

One idea is to journal your thoughts about your subject's current age. Highlight where he or she is in life, what he or she is doing, and some of his or her favorite things. It will be a great keepsake!

9.5 *by Lisa Habisreutinger.* **Supplies** *Software:* Photoshop CS, Adobe Systems; *Digital cardstock:* Naturally Krafty Paper by Katie Pertiet; *Digital paper:* Sweet Cherry Pie by Nancie Rowe Janitz; *Digital stamped letters:* Hand Stamped Alpha by Michelle Coleman; *Digital stitching:* Karen Lewis; *Font:* Bliss.

SUZY'S SOLUTION ⌃

After adding two 4" x 6" photos and the large sun to my page, I wasn't sure where to put my journaling. Then it occurred to me that I could journal on the orange rays coming out of the sun. The sun is a strong focal point on the layout, so I knew the journaling wouldn't get lost if I added it there. I hand-wrote my journaling on each ray with a white gel pen and then wrapped the end of each ray around a pencil to curl it.

Kayak Fun *by Suzy Plantamura.* **Supplies** *Patterned paper:* Bo-Bunny Press (yellow), Scenic Route (orange for sun) and We R Memory Keepers (orange, stripe and turquoise); *Trim:* Fancy Pants Designs; *Chipboard letters:* Maya Road; *Foam letters and rub-ons:* American Crafts; *Brads:* Making Memories; *Stickers:* Scenic Route; *Paint:* Delta Creative; *Ink:* Clearsnap; *Other:* Rickrack and thread.

look closer >>

Suzy's inventive journaling solution is also a great design feature!

LINDA'S SOLUTION ⌃

This layout is about my son and our discovering that he has Tourette's syndrome, a tic disorder. Originally I wanted a more subtle and clever way to create a title than just incorporating the word "Tic" somewhere on the page. I started trying to think of words that had the three letters "Tic" in them, hoping I could find one I could highlight as my title. The more I looked, the more words I found that were in some way reflective of my son's personality. In the end, I decided to use most of the words I found, capitalizing the "Tic" in each word and using the words as a design element on my layout.

TIC *by Linda Rodriguez.* **Supplies** *Software:* Digital Image Pro 9.0, Microsoft; *Digital paper:* Schwartz MonoBlendz (black) by Anna Aspnes; Bandana Basics No. 2 (red and yellow) and Naturally Krafty No. 3 by Katie Pertiet; *Digital date stamps:* Christy Lyle; *Digital stitched frames:* Anna Aspnes; *Font:* AL Singsong.

The Little Things by Sara Winnick. **Supplies** *Patterned paper:* Cosmo Cricket; *Tag:* October Afternoon; *Rub-ons:* Little Yellow Bicycle; *Letter stickers and heart:* American Crafts; *Chipboard letters:* Pink Paislee; *Punches:* EK Success; *Brads:* American Crafts and Making Memories; *Stamp:* FontWerks; *Ink:* Ranger Industries; *Adhesive:* Scrapbook Adhesives by 3L; *Other:* Button, thread and pen.

For some of us, journaling comes naturally and the words seem to flow onto the page (or journaling spot). But for others, journaling is the most difficult part of the creating process. Try asking yourself a few questions about the photos or the story you are trying to tell before putting pen to paper. For her "The Little Things" layout, Sara Winnick crafted her journaling after looking through her photos and observing the connections her husband made with his family. If you're someone who thinks "I don't have anything to say," start small and finish big by asking yourself these questions:

1. Why do I love these photos? Is it the lighting, the location, the person in the photos? Does the photo tell a story of an event or an occasion I want to write about?

2. If I were to pick up these photos in 10 years, what would I want to know about these photos as I looked at them?

3. How do these photos make me feel?

HERE IS ANOTHER TIP FOR OVERCOMING JOURNALING HANG-UPS:

 Do you feel like you don't have enough to say to fill an entire journaling block? Try filling some of the open space with small embellishments and accents so you don't feel obligated to write in the entire area.

Capture the who, what, when, where, and how

Journalists refer to these as the 4-Ws: the who, what, when, and where (with a little how thrown in for good measure) are the basics of every news story written. They can also be the basis for the journaling on your next layout. And as Stacy Cohen aptly demonstrates, you can stick to those basics, capture all the details, and still create eye-catching journaling.

Take a tip from Stacy and use the 4-Ws right in your journaling as the subheads. Or leave the who, what, when, and where off and just answer the questions. You'll be amazed at how much information you can capture just by defining those four things.

DESIGN TIP: Stacy used canvas alphabet letters and burlap to mat her photos because they reminded her of the purses, totes, hats, and blankets found at the souvenir shop. Read on for more about using embellishments to enhance your journaling.

who: Rebecca and Danielle

what: While on vacation in Mexico, the girls did what they do best: shop for souvenirs. They had a ball picking out trinkets from the little shops. But as you can see from the expression on Rebecca's face, she got tired of me taking so many photos.

when: December, 2007

where: Ensenada, Mexico

how: We got there via a cruise ship. Ensenada was one of several stops on the cruise.

Olé by Stacy Cohen. **Supplies:** Cardstock: Bazzill Basics Paper; Patterned paper: Lily Bee Design; Chipboard: BasicGrey; Canvas: Li'l Davis Designs; Epoxy stickers and hemp: Darice; Paint: Shimmerz; Ink: Ranger Industries; Font: Georgia; Adhesive: Helmar; Other: Buttons and burlap.

Use your own handwriting

There are very few of us in the world who love our handwriting. But it's easier to tell a complete story when we're writing it down ourselves. If you always use a computer to capture your journaling, try using your own handwriting and see if the words flow more freely. I know, you're already cringing, thinking, "But I hate my handwriting." Once you've captured your story, slip it into an inconspicuous spot on your page, like Stacy Cohen did.

On her "Amore" layout, Stacy hid her handwritten journaling on a card she slipped behind the top photo of her and her husband. The pull tab she added lets the viewer know the journaling is there, but Stacy doesn't have to look at her handwriting every time she looks at the page. "Knowing that my journaling was going to be hidden behind a photo on this page, I didn't worry about whether or not my handwriting was perfectly neat. It was very freeing," Stacy commented.

JOURNALING TIP: Handwrite your journaling in pencil first to make sure everything is the way you want it and it all fits. When it's just the way you want it, go back over it with pen and erase the pencil.

Amore *by Stacy Cohen. Photography by Melissa Walker-Scott. Supplies: Carstock:* Bazzill Basics Paper; *Patterned paper, chipboard, and flourish:* Prima; *Stickers:* Making Memories; *Tab:* Melissa Frances; *Glitter glue:* Ranger Industries; *Spray ink:* Shimmerz; *Ink:* Clearsnap; *Adhesive:* Tombow.

Free write

Not sure where to begin your story? Set a timer for 10 or 15 minutes, and then just begin to write. Don't worry about where you start, just begin with the first thought you have about the event you're scrapbooking. When the timer goes off, stop writing. You can go through and review what you've captured and just use the sentences you really like. You'll be amazed at how much you can capture in 10 or 15 minutes. Deena Wuest used this exercise for the journaling on her "Fear Less" layout. The result was a tribute to how much her young daughter is teaching her about being fearless.

An easy way to incorporate this on your next layout is to get with several family members or friends and get them talking. Record their memories as they come and use those as your journaling. You can get them talking by asking questions such as

• What do you remember most about . . .?

• What would you like to be able to forget?

• Why was this so fun?

• How do you remember these events taking place?

Fear Less *by Deena Wuest.* **Digital Supplies:** *Software:* Adobe; *Patterned paper:* Katie Pertiet and Mindy Terasawa; *Stickers:* Mindy Terasawa; *Frames and alphabet:* Katie Pertiet; *Font:* Avant Garde.

Write to someone

Structuring your journaling as a letter or note to someone else can often make the words come easier. Writing as if someone specific will be reading your journaling will help you convey all of the information you'd want that person to know about why you've chosen this topic to scrapbook. Kim Watson commented, "I found it so easy to write the letter, as if I knew my mum would be reading it." You can write directly to a person, complete with a salutation and signature, like Kim did, or just write as if you're leaving someone a quick note.

Because Kim's layout is about a Skype lunch her mother and son shared, she created her scrapbook page to resemble a blog post, complete with a banner title, clean graphic lines, and an avatar. Her journaling was a natural fit in the center of her "blog" page, putting even more emphasis on the letter to her mom. Look for ways you can design your layout that will help make your journaling feel more natural. **ck**

Lunch by Kim Watson. **Supplies:** Cardstock: American Crafts and Bazzill Basics Paper; Patterned paper: Jenni Bowlin Studio, Lily Bee Design, My Mind's Eye, and Studio Calico; Stickers: Adornit-Carolee's Creations and Little Yellow Bicycle; Chipboard and rub-ons: American Crafts; Metal accent: Advantus; Punch: EK Success; Paper piercer: Close to My Heart; Adhesive: American Crafts, Scrapbook Adhesives by 3L, and Tombow; Other: Buttons and thread.

ONE BOY,
ONE GIRL
by Laura Kurz

Use a song as inspiration.

Laura used the song played at her wedding rehearsal years ago as the starting point for this page. Isn't it amazing how a simple song can trigger so many memories and warm fuzzies? I also love how this transparency page is two-sided so that when it's slipped into a page protector, it's already complete on both sides.

a new journaling *perspective*

I took 1,892 photos last July. Really. This perhaps ridiculous number of photos helped me tell many stories and create plenty of layouts. In doing so, though, I realized that these stories were lacking in one primary area: perspective. I'd wager that, like mine, most of your layouts are written in your own voice. They tell the story through your eyes. For this month's layout, I wanted to focus instead on what was important in the eyes of my husband and sons.

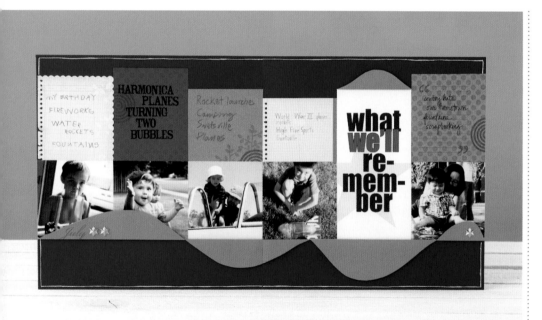

What We'll Remember *by Amanda Probst.* **Supplies** *Cardstock:* Prism Papers; *Notebook journaling pages:* Making Memories; *Brads:* Creative Impressions; *Rub-on letters:* American Crafts; *Stamps:* Cornish Heritage Farms (dotted background) and Hero Arts; *Ink:* Close To My Heart and VersaMark, Tsukineko; *Pens:* Precision Pens, American Crafts; Uni-ball Signo, Newell Rubbermaid (white); *Font:* Impact, Microsoft; *Other:* Pencil.

SO, RATHER THAN simply telling what *I* thought were the most important parts of July, I decided to ask my family members what *they* remembered most about the month. I had them each select four favorite memories and jot them down. (Asking for a fixed number of items in simple list format, by the way, is a very easy way to get started.) I then selected a photo that went with one of the favorite memories and put it all together. Take a moment to ask your loved ones to write down what they remember. (Feel free to "help" little ones!) I love that I was able to include their handwriting and look forward to including these other perspectives in future layouts!

7 Quick Prompts

Admittedly, asking simply for favorite memories in a given month is a bit generic. Instead, consider asking about:

- A favorite outing (include a memory from each family member)

- A favorite meal that month (include recipes if desired)

- Something each person learned during the month

- Favorite outfits that month (can't you just see the fun photos that could go with this layout?)

- What each person liked best about being where you were

- Quick favorites (color, song and more) of each person for the month

- Each person's wish list during the month

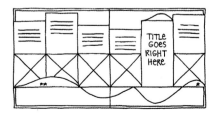

BY AMANDA PROBST

Scrapbook the Written Words

Everyone loves receiving cards and notes from kids, but too often they end up buried in a pile and forgotten. Bring them out of those piles or keepsake boxes and showcase them on scrapbook pages for fun, authentic pages that illustrate a kid's point of view. Include them on a layout, as Laura Vegas did with her daughter's "I'm Sorry" note, or include a scan or photograph of them on your pages.

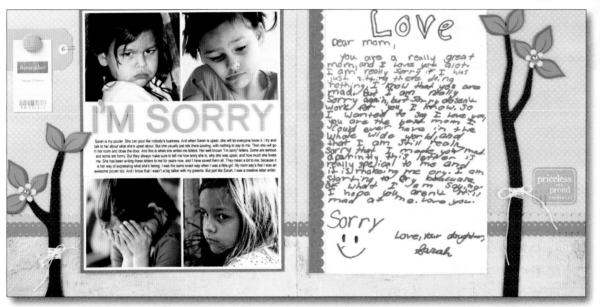

I'm Sorry by Laura Vegas. **Supplies** Cardstock: American Crafts (white) and Paper Reflections (kraft); Patterned paper: BasicGrey (yellow) and Bo-Bunny Press (blue); Border strips: Doodlebug Design; Sticker and tags: Creative Imaginations; Brad: Bazzill Basics Paper; Acetate letters: Heidi Swapp for Advantus; Chipboard accent: KitoftheMonth.com; Silver accents: Michaels; String: Coats & Clark; Embossing template and die-cutting machine: Provo Craft; Punch: Stampin' Up!; Font: Arial Narrow; Adhesive: EK Success and Therm O Web; Other: Staples.

Capture Those Quotable Words

What expressions or catch phrases do the kids in your life say? Since remembering them all at once can be both difficult and daunting, we recommend writing them down as you notice them, little by little. Here are a few ideas to help you write those quotable words for future scrapbook pages:

 Notebooks. Carry a small notebook to jot down quotable sayings. For a personal touch, cover the notebook with scrapbook supplies, like Julia Nomichith did on here.

 Message boards. Keep a small chalkboard or dry-erase board on the fridge to write down little sayings as they happen at home. Jot them down or photograph them before they're erased.

Voice recorders. Bring a small digital or tape recorder with you as you go about your day, and record expressions. Then listen to them later when you scrapbook.

 Web solutions. Update your Facebook, MySpace or Twitter accounts with a fun word or saying you overheard, and refer to it later as a springboard for a page.

Enjoy the Little Things notebook by Julia Nomichith. **Supplies** Notebook: Target; Stamps, rub-ons, ink, embossing powder, flower and adhesive: Stampin' Up!; Ribbon: Stampin' Up! and Wal-Mart.

have your spouse write your journaling

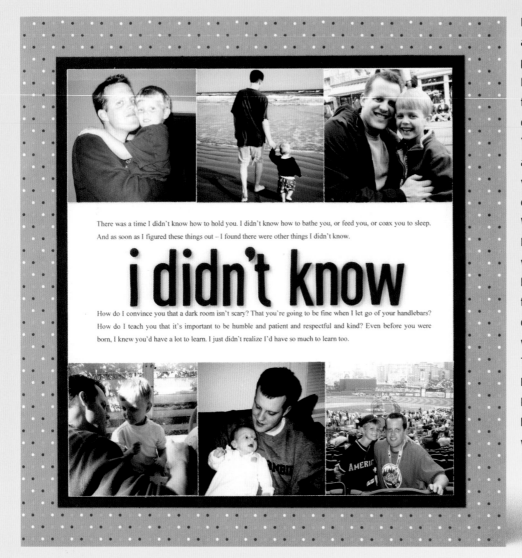

There was a time I didn't know how to hold you. I didn't know how to bathe you, or feed you, or coax you to sleep. And as soon as I figured these things out – I found there were other things I didn't know.

i didn't know

How do I convince you that a dark room isn't scary? That you're going to be fine when I let go of your handlebars? How do I teach you that it's important to be humble and patient and respectful and kind? Even before you were born, I knew you'd have a lot to learn. I just didn't realize I'd have so much to learn too.

materials patterned paper (Heidi Grace Designs) • foam letter stickers (American Crafts) • Times New Roman font • *12 x 12 page by Beth Proudfoot, Lebanon, NJ*

Beth had an advantage with this prompt. Her husband Kevin is a writer-turned-creative-director at a New York City ad agency, and he actually volunteered to journal on a layout for her. While looking through Beth's scrapbooks, he was impressed that her feelings for their two sons were so well documented, and he wanted to do the same. This is the first layout Beth has designed with Kevin's words, and she hopes many more will follow.

how to trick a husband into journaling

1. Use your feminine wiles (whatever that means to you).
2. Barter with him: "You write some of your feelings down on paper, and I'll keep my feelings to myself for a whole week!"
3. Hold the remote control for ransom.
4. Replace his razor and shaving cream with a journaling pen and some cardstock.
5. Follow him around with a tape recorder, asking him how he feels about the kids/dog/latest vacation.

"I love being married. It's so great to find that one special person you want to annoy for the rest of your life."
—*Rita Rudner*

12-25-86

Dear Amanda,

This is my stamp collection book that I had when I was your age. In it are some stamps that I had collected, but there is still room for many more. Stamp collecting can be a very fun hobby. There are other sources where you can get stamps. At special stores, letters and the U.S. Post Office. Take care of this collection add to it and have fun.

Merry Christmas

Dad

Think back for a moment, would you? Do you have a particular Christmas gift that you received as a child that you still remember? That you possibly even still have? I tried this and can honestly only remember one gift distinctly. The others are a bit of a blur.

The one gift I remember is my dad's stamp collection. He gave it to me when I was eleven and included this note. The fact that my dad actually took the time to write a note and knew what was in the present, itself, was significant. The fact that he would share something so treasured was even more so. My dad is a fairly private and quiet sort of guy, so this glimpse into his life was a rare treat, something that truly made an impression. Did I take up stamp collecting myself? For awhile. Do I still have and treasure this collection? You betcha! I haven't added anything to it in years, but I do hope to one day get it all organized so I can share it with my sons. It remains one of my favorite gifts of all time.

So. Thinking about all this, I've been considering whether the gifts we're giving our sons are ones they'll remember. I hope some of them are. I know now that I'll be more aware of this in the future. Here's to gifts…

WORTH REMEMBERING

{ WORTH REMEMBERING }
by Amanda Probst

Include a handwritten note.

What were some of your favorite gifts you received growing up? This note, by itself, was significant to me—significant because my dad took the time to write it and because it was intended to be passed along with a treasured collection. Here, I focused on the note but also included photos from the collection and actual stamps.

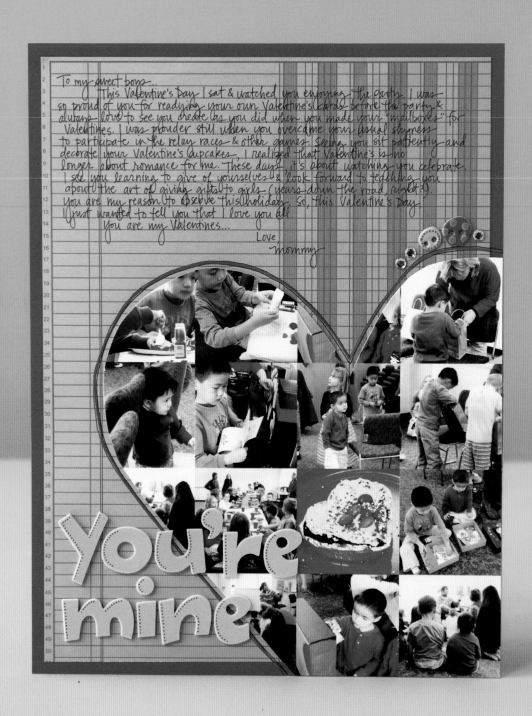

To my sweet boys...
        This Valentine's Day I sat & watched you enjoying the party. I was
so proud of you for readying your own Valentine's cards before the party &
always love to see you create as you did when you made your "mailboxes" for
Valentines. I was prouder still when you overcame your usual shyness
to participate in the relay races & other games. Seeing you sit patiently and
decorate your Valentine's cupcakes, I realized that Valentine's is no
longer about romance for me. These days, it's about watching you celebrate.
I see you learning to give of yourselves & look forward to teaching you
about the art of giving gifts to girls (years down the road, right?).
You are my reason to observe this holiday. So, this Valentine's Day
I just wanted to tell you that I love you all.
You are my Valentines...
                                        Love,
                                          mommy

you're mine

{ YOU'RE MINE }
by Amanda Probst

Write a love letter.

It doesn't have to be a mushy love letter, but write one. This one is to my
boys, describing how they've influenced my perspective on Valentine's Day.

Words to Live By

Scrapbook the messages that touch lives

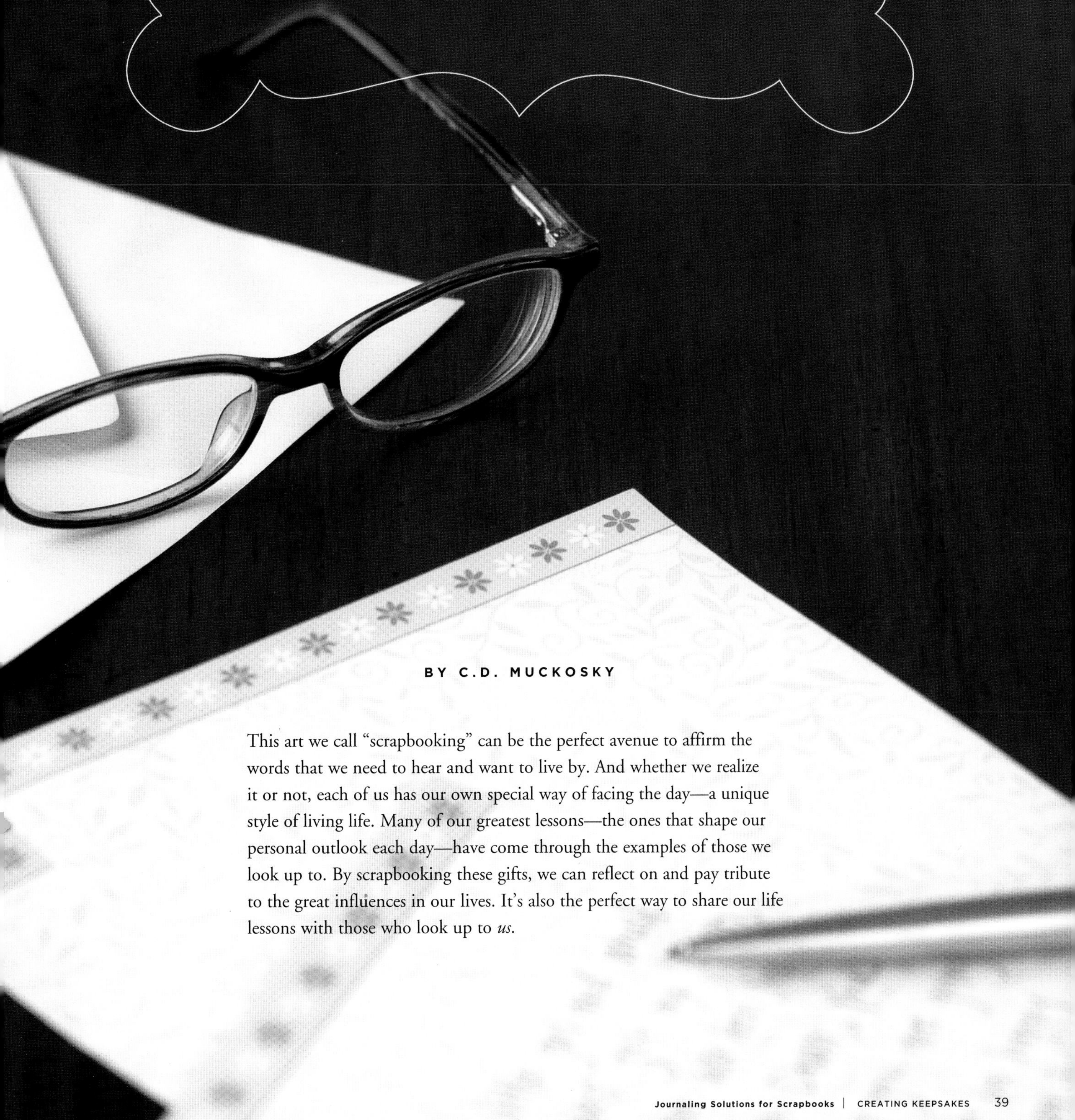

BY C.D. MUCKOSKY

This art we call "scrapbooking" can be the perfect avenue to affirm the words that we need to hear and want to live by. And whether we realize it or not, each of us has our own special way of facing the day—a unique style of living life. Many of our greatest lessons—the ones that shape our personal outlook each day—have come through the examples of those we look up to. By scrapbooking these gifts, we can reflect on and pay tribute to the great influences in our lives. It's also the perfect way to share our life lessons with those who look up to *us*.

Happy Is What You Make It by C.D. Muckosky. Photos by Krista Domres. **Supplies** *Transparent overlays:* Hambly Studios; *Crochet butterfly:* Maya Road; *Letter stickers:* American Crafts; *Kraft word stickers:* Making Memories; *Colored pencils:* Prismacolor, Newell Rubbermaid; *Red gems:* My Mind's Eye; *Black pen:* Sakura; *Other:* Cotton bands, cardboard, buttons and embroidery floss. *Idea to note:* I used a sunny shaped overlay and bits of yellow accents to reinforce the feeling of happiness in my page design.

Passed on Through Generations

When I was a little girl and would let life's small troubles get me down, my mom would pull me into her lap and gently say, "Christie-Dawn, YOU decide what kind of day you are going to have. You can *choose* to be happy no matter what comes your way today, or you can decide to sit and grumble. But either way, it is a *CHOICE*." Not only with gentle words but also by how she's lived, my mom has really shaped the outlook that I have today. Thanks to her I *do* choose to live life with a smile and find the good in each day.

It's not only thanks to her, though, that I learned that lesson—it's a gift that has been passed through generations of women in my family. It's an outlook on life that my mom was taught as a girl by my grandmother, and it's something that I now tell my girls. What a happy legacy.

I grew up listening to the recital of Vedic hymns at home. Even when I was too young to understand the hymns, I used to be enchanted by them. There was one phrase in those hymns that I really liked and chanted it with my dad. The words were 'Charaiveti Charaivate'.

When I grew a little older, my dad explained what 'Charaiveti' means. Just as plants and trees move toward light, we should move forward as our eyes and feet face forward. Movement is life and we should make constant efforts to keep moving forward no matter what obstacles stand in our way as stagnation brings decay. Dad's explanation was forever engraved in my young mind. He read to me several pieces of literature that supported this Vedic concept. He never let me forget just how important it is to keep on keeping on.

keep moving forward

As time went on, I came face to face with many of life's inevitable and unique challenges, some of which seemed practically insurmountable. During those times, my family and friends gave me advice, encouragement and support. And in some quiet moments, dad whispered to me, 'Charaiveti' and I recited to myself, 'Charaiveti Charaivate Charan Vai Madhu Vindate'.

Those words and the conviction with which my dad uttered them were very empowering. They never failed to encourage and give me new hope. They taught me endurance and acceptance, replaced complacence with new goals and gave me the strength to persevere against odds. Even though these are not my dad's own words, to me he became the vehicle of the mantra that I learned to live by.

Keep Moving Forward
by Mou Saha. **Supplies** *Cardstock:* Frances Meyer; *Letter stickers:* American Crafts (title) and Making Memories (mini); *Rub-ons:* Chatterbox (blue borders) and Hambly Studios (turquoise photo corner); *Chipboard accent:* K&Company; *Brad:* Die Cuts With a View; *Embroidery floss:* DMC; *Paint:* Delta Creative; *Font:* American Typewriter, *www.fonts.com.*

Life Words from Parents

Our parents play a truly special role in shaping how we handle life and deal with obstacles that come our way. For Mou Saha, reflecting on the messages that her parents taught her was a process of both laughter and of tears. She chose to focus on a lesson from her dad that has become one of her life's most powerful influences. The resulting layout is a beautiful tribute to a caring and wise father, and it will become a priceless gift to *her* children and grandchildren someday.

9 Things to Teach Your Children *by Maryanne Hawes.* **Supplies** *Chipboard book:* Maya Road; *Paint:* Making Memories; *Rub-ons:* BasicGrey and Hambly Studios; *Letter stickers:* American Crafts; *Die-cutting machine:* Craft Robo.

Lessons to Teach Our Children

Words are important to Maryanne Hawes's family. Family members love to read and write them, and they've discovered that words put together carefully can change lives. Maryanne's great little book holds nine lessons that she wants to teach her children to embrace. I love that this book is not filed away in a bookshelf or hidden in a drawer—it sits on a shelf in the kitchen where the children can flip through it often. The book also reminds Maryanne of how she wants to guide her children.

"I love to teach my children that however complicated and challenging life may seem at times, we can soon get back on the road to happiness and fulfillment by remembering what really matters in life. A few carefully chosen words can point us in the right direction."
—*Maryanne Hawes*

dream BiG

From wishes made to dreams fulfilled,
celebrate hopes and goals in your scrapbooks

WHEN I STARTED WORKING for *Creating Keepsakes*, a friend gave me a bookmark with this quote from Henry David Thoreau: "Go confidently in the direction of your dreams!" She felt it was appropriate, considering the situation—working for a magazine is definitely a dream of mine! I love that quote, and I love the idea of scrapbooking about the goals I've been able to see accomplished in my life, along with those I still have yet to achieve.

At this time of year when most of us set or renew goals, enlivened hopes and dreams come to the forefront of our thoughts. What are you doing this year to accomplish those dreams? What do you still wish for? Scrapbook it! Future generations will love knowing your hopes, dreams and goals—and how they change from year to year. Here are five great tips to help you record them most meaningfully and easily in your albums.

Recording those dreams is definitely the first step to achieving them! >>

BY MAURIANNE DUNN

a practical look

Setting goals will help you accomplish a dream. To avoid feeling overwhelmed by multiple goals, group them into a single dream instead, with the individual goals as subsets. Then scrapbook about your dream and the goals you've set to accomplish it.

Paula created this layout about her dream for the new year—to reclaim her life—and the goals she thought would lead to accomplishing that dream. She included general ideas and specific ways to accomplish each goal.

great **idea:** At the end of the year, create a follow-up layout that shows your progress on your goals.

take care

drink water
get LASIK
exercise
more

enjoy now

savor my time
with the kids,
they won't be little forever

make time
to read again

read

focus

make time to do
what I want to do

Two Thousand Seven   2007

I'm not one for making resolutions on January 1st, but this year was different. I've been in baby mode for so many years that I focused on just getting through that and now that the fog is starting to lift I've been thinking of where I want my life to go. I'm still going to be living in kid-land, because that's my life now, but I've decided that it's time to reclaim part of me that was lost when I became a mom. I used to read, be knowledgeable about music and movies and current events. I used to talk about things other than children. I used to be fit (or at least fitter than I am now) and generally took better care of myself. This year I'm working on reclaiming the person that I used to be, while still focusing on my job, which is taking care of my kids. I've got a plan, I've got the motivation, I'm going to...

reclaim me
A Plan for my Life

Reclaim Me *by Paula Gilarde.* **Supplies** *Software:* Adobe Photoshop CS2, Adobe Systems; *Cardstock:* Daylily Paper Pack (white) and Classic Cardstock Paper Pack (black) kits by Katie Pertiet; *Drop shadow action:* Katie Pertiet; *Year in the Life template:* Kellie Mize; *Ribbon:* Sundae Festival by Leora Sanford; *Scallop:* Apron Strings by Leora Sanford; *Fonts:* Impact and Century Gothic, Microsoft Word. *Note:* All digital elements were downloaded from *www.designerdigitals.com.*

careers through the years

Like every little kid, when I was young, I used to dream of what I would one day become. What career path I would choose.

When I was ten and my grandfather was sick, I would rub lotion on his back every day to make him feel better. He called me his little nurse, and I started thinking of a nursing career. I waned from this idea several times through the years, but when it came time to choose a college track, nursing is exactly what I chose. It always made me feel good to think that Poppy was looking at me from heaven. His little nurse all grown up. Of course, because of my injuries, this career has been put on hold. The doctors won't let me return to it yet. Someday, hopefully, I know I made a great nurse; it was one of the few things in my life that I felt I did really well. Someday I'll use that stethoscope again.

When I was in school, I dreamt of becoming a teacher. Most little kids probably do at some point in their lives. Teachers were cool. Teachers had power. Part of me still lives this dream. While my days as Gabe's room mother has taught me that I can, in no capacity, be an elementary school teacher, I still consider the possibility of teaching at a nursing school some day.

When we visited Mr. Greg, my Sunday School teacher and family friend, I dreamt of becoming an architect just like him. I would spend my teenage days drawing house plans to scale. Every house had a pool. It fed my crafty side. Now, instead of drawing houses, I create scrapbook pages. While it is not a career in the truest sense at this point, I have been very blessed doing this, and I would certainly love to see it become a full-time thing in the future.

When I grew up, a new career presented itself: a stay-at-home mom. I can honestly say this is one career path I never considered as a child. I always assumed that I would work outside of the home. As a nurse, I had four days a week off, so I was 1/2-way to SAHM status, anyway. However, disability forced me into it, and I have enjoyed it. Spending more time with the kids is a blessing. At this point I don't know how much longer it will last. The disability is over, and I have to think about what I am going to do to help support our family. But for now, the title of SAHM suits me just fine.

Careers through the Years *by Tracey Odachowski.* **Supplies** *Cardstock:* Bazzill Basics Paper (blue) and Wausau Paper (white); *Patterned paper and stickers:* KI Memories; *Ink:* VersaMark, Tsukineko; *Cutting machine:* Wishblade, Xyron; *Fonts:* Impact (title) and Century Gothic (journaling), Microsoft Word.

then & now

Most children have lofty goals of what they want to be when they grow up. I did! How has your childhood dream of a career or future life changed as you've grown up? And just because you've grown up doesn't mean your dream can't still happen. Check out Tracey's take on her careers through the years—and what she still hopes for in the future.

great idea:

Scrapbook what your child wants to be when he or she grows up. Later in life, the child will love looking at those childhood dreams!

the dream fulfilled

Have you ever wished for something for a long time and then it finally happened? Or maybe a dream turned out different from what you expected, but you realize that it turned out how you wanted it to all along . . . or even better?

Preserve those good memories by creating a layout about them! It's always nice to look back on those happy, successful times—and to remember that you can accomplish great things, because you can. Kelly talks about life turning out very different from what she'd originally planned, but it turned out better than she had imagined.

This Is So Much More by Kelly Lautenbach. **Supplies** *Cardstock:* Bazzill Basics Paper; *Patterned paper:* 7gypsies and Anna Griffin; *Letter stickers:* American Crafts and Making Memories; *Chipboard swirls:* Technique Tuesday; *Photo-collage template:* Janet Phillips, It Kit Studio; *Notch tool:* BasicGrey; *Fonts:* Fling, downloaded from the Internet; Palatino Linotype, Microsoft Word.

a step outside of yourself

Scrapbook the dream of a sibling, spouse, parent or grandparent. Sometimes the stories of a dream—fulfilled or unfulfilled—portray character and personality more than anything else. When you understand the greatest desire of someone, you understand who that person is. Tiffany created this layout about her father and his dream to be an EMT. It's amazing what insight you gain when you see goals and dreams from a different perspective!

The EMT by Tiffany Tillman. **Supplies** *Software:* Adobe Photoshop CS3, Adobe Systems; *Patterned paper:* Anna Aspnes, www.designer-digitals.com; *Yellow dots:* Kim Christensen, www.scrapartist.com; *Paper tears:* Jen Caputo, www.scrapbookgraphics.com; *Flourish stamp:* Flower Flourish Brushes kit by Jesse Edwards, www.designerdigitals.com; *Title studs and wave trim:* Organic kit by Shabby Princess, www.theshabbyshoppe.com; *Fonts:* Impact (title) and Times New Roman (journaling), Microsoft Word.

secret yearning

Do you have a book manuscript under your mattress that you've never dared to send to a publisher? Or do you have daydreams about singing and dancing on Broadway? Scrapbook that secret yearning—no matter how unrealistic it may seem. Friends and family will love to see what you've always wanted to do but never dared tell about. (And if you're still not ready to share it, you can hide the layout under the bed with the manuscript as well! It will be our little secret.) Check out Jill's charming layout on wanting to be a farmer's wife. **ck**

Want to Be a Farmer's Wife *by Jill Hornby.* **Supplies** *Patterned paper:* Crate Paper, Heidi Grace Designs and Scenic Route; *Die cuts:* Daisy D's Paper Co.; *Rub-ons:* American Crafts and Heidi Grace Designs; *Scalloped-edge scissors:* Fiskars; *Punch:* Brick by Brick, Fiskars; *Soft star charm:* Love, Elsie for KI Memories; *Font:* Splendid 66, downloaded from *www.dafont.com;* *Other:* Staples and thread.

mom & *me*

Time spent with Mom is priceless—from childhood to adulthood, the memories will never fade because of the love that each memory represents. Every activity, every conversation, every hug and every "I love you" expressed between mother and child holds infinite value.

Mother, Circa 1975 *by Lisa Kisch.* **Supplies** *Patterned paper, flowers and button:* Making Memories; *Rub-ons:* BasicGrey and FontWerks; *Ink:* ColorBox, Clearsnap; *Letter stickers:* BasicGrey and Making Memories; *Software:* Picasa.

Haven't recorded those precious expressions of your mother relationships on a layout yet? Now's the time with one of these seven ideas and inspirational layouts. You may have heard the ideas before, but *have you actually done them yet?* This is the month to make it happen!

1 **Find a heritage photo of you with your mother and create a decorative layout for her home.**

BY BRITTANY BEATTIE

5 ways to remember a loved one

If you've lost someone dear to you, find peace with a memorial layout

For me, May brings fond memories of the Memorial Days I spent with family while growing up. I think of visiting the local cemetery with my dad. We would leave hand-cut peonies in tinfoil-wrapped jars on the graves of family members, most of whom I'd never met.

I haven't been home to do that in years, and I've missed it. This year, though, is different. This is the first year that even the possibility of doing that is gone. You see, my dad died unexpectedly last August. This year, it's his grave I'll want to visit.

I know I'm not the only one who will be missing a loved one this Memorial Day. I hope I'm also not the only one scrapping about it. For many, scrapping about a lost loved one can be painful and overwhelming. You don't know where to start, and even thinking about it churns up emotions you'd rather not dwell on. But scrapping about loved ones can also be therapeutic and even fulfilling. I know it has been for me. Memorial Day is an opportune time to stop and remember, to celebrate and commemorate.

While having a grand plan for your layout is great, it's not necessary. This is one of those times when the most important thing is to simply get started. I hope these layouts inspire you as they have inspired me, and I hope you find some peace in the process.

by Amanda Probst

Hey there, Dad. I know you're able to read this and it makes me feel better talking to you. You always were more of a listener anyhow (and a good one at that). :) I know, also, that you're watching over all of us and are still with us in spirit. Sometimes I can even hear your voice in my head…telling me to stop fussing with something or just chuckling that chuckle that was so yours. I tell the boys stories about you and am working on recording many of them so that my kids will be able to tell their kids who you were. I miss you, obviously. Through these things, though, I keep you with me.

But. There's something missing. Something that makes me long for a time machine. Aside from actually being able to prevent you from going out on the tractor that fateful day, what I wish for most is simply a picture…of the two of us. I've found plenty of photos of the two of us when I was little, and they truly warm my heart. As I got older, the pictures became fewer. In recent years, they're non-existent. This pains me. I was appalled to discover that the most recent photo of just the two of us was taken SEVEN years ago. Seven. How is that possible given the sheer quantity of photos that I take?! I suppose that's the answer right there. I'm almost always behind the camera. I'm working on that. In the meantime, I am devastated that I don't have that picture…that I won't have any more photo opportunities with you. Even though I can picture you in my head, I can't share that image with the boys, with others. I so wish I could.

I know that some people won't understand this particular ache. I'm such a visual person…photos and stories are such a big part of my life. So, this lacking hits me hard. I want to throw my arm around you while we're sitting watching the Seahawks and have someone snap a picture of us laughing. I want to blitz directly at you while we're playing touch football on Thanksgiving and have the moment captured on film. I want to simply walk through the orchard with you and freeze that experience in a picture. I want to sit with you as you cut up apples for your famous apple pie and get a photo of you scolding me for snitching. I want just to stand right beside you and have us smile and say "cheese." I want these missing photos.

You're probably shaking your head at me with that wistful grin, maybe even shrugging your shoulders as if to say, "what can you do?" I know there's nothing I can do to get these photos now. I don't have to like it. I just wanted you to know.

Missing Photos *by Amanda Probst*. **Supplies** *Cardstock:* Prism Papers; *Frames:* Ormolu Etsy Shop, www.etsy.com; *Chipboard letters:* Heidi Swapp for Advantus, Li'l Davis Designs, Making Memories and Rusty Pickle; *Pen:* Precision Pens, American Crafts; *Paint:* Plaid Enterprises; *Fonts:* CK Painterly, www.scrapnfonts.com; Rockwell, Microsoft.

Journal to Your Loved One

For my memorial layouts, I initially had a very tough time with the journaling. I just couldn't seem to find my voice. Finally, I had one of those "a-ha!" moments. I simply started writing what was in my head . . . and in my heart. I wrote as if I were talking *to* my dad. For me, this serves two purposes. First, it allows me to journal much more freely, more like a conversation. Second—and more important—it comforts me and helps me feel that I'm still communicating with my dad.

"This is one of those layouts I just knew I'd have to do. This regret hit me very early and has stuck with me. As a scrapbooker, I think of all the pictures I didn't take and all those I now won't have, and it hurts. Somehow, admitting this regret helped me recapture some favorite memories and made the regret easier to carry. It motivates me to do a better job of taking photos of my relationships from here on out."

—AMANDA PROBST

Include Your
Children's Memories

Lisa's layout is one that immediately inspired me. I love that she used her daughter's artwork and involved her in this process. Often, discussing loss with our children can be uncomfortable. Actively including them in the scrapbooking process is a perfect solution, one that lends itself to gorgeous layouts and gives you a wonderful starting point.

I Miss Noona *by Lisa Swift.* **Supplies** *Cardstock:* Bazzill Basics Paper; *Patterned paper:* Doodlebug Design and KI Memories; *Stickers:* Mustard Moon; *Pen:* Uni-ball Signo, Newell Rubbermaid; *Button:* Autumn Leaves; *Rubber charms:* KI Memories; *Rub-ons:* American Crafts; *Felt border:* Fancy Pants Designs; *Font:* Decker, Internet; *Other:* Thread and flowers.

Imagine What You'd
Do with One More Day

This layout has me itching to make my own! Elizabeth took what most of us probably have thought about and turned it into a stunning layout. She explained what she'd do with one more day with her dad. Sometimes letting our imagination run and actually acknowledging our wishes can be very therapeutic.

One More Day *by Elizabeth Kartchner.* **Supplies** *Cardstock:* Prism Papers; *Letter stickers and buttons:* American Crafts; *Patterned paper:* American Crafts and BasicGrey; *Word stickers and metal tab:* 7gypsies; *Clear acrylic clock:* Heidi Swapp for Advantus; *Rub-ons:* Daisy D's Paper Co.; *Fonts:* 2Peas Essential (highlighted words in journaling), www.twopeasinabucket. com; Traveling Typewriter, Internet (journaling); *Other:* Pen and thread.

The Stuff That Matters *by Tania Willis.* **Supplies** *Cardstock:* Prism Papers; *Patterned paper:* Karen Foster Design and Tinkering Ink; *Letter stickers:* American Crafts and Sonburn; *Stamps:* Inque Boutique; *Rub-ons, star brads, embroidery floss and brads:* Karen Foster Design; *Ink:* Clearsnap; *Adhesive:* Gem-Tac, Beacon Adhesive; *Fabric:* Scrapworks; *Glitter:* Art Institute.

Look Back on Journal Entries

Tania took this journaling directly from a journal entry she wrote the day she brought home some of her mom's possessions after she passed away. The days following a loved one's death are often a jumble of emotions and demands, so keeping a journal can definitely be a blessing. Similarly, creating a layout about that time can help bring closure.

Our Little Tradition *by Allison Davis.* **Supplies** *Cardstock:* Bazzill Basics Paper; *Patterned paper:* BasicGrey (brown striped), Daisy D's Paper Co. (green) and Sandylion (red dot); *Photo overlay:* Rusty Pickle; *Letter stickers:* American Crafts ("little"), Fancy Pants Designs ("tradition") and Rusty Pickle ("our"); *Word stickers:* EK Success; *Tag sticker:* Daisy D's Paper Co.; *Felt heart:* Fancy Pants Designs; *Ink:* ColorBox Fluid Chalk, Clearsnap; *Font:* American Typewriter, Internet.

Pick a Favorite Memory

Making layouts like this helped Allison make sense of things after her dad's passing. She's come to appreciate her relationship with him and her memories of him. This layout is of a favorite memory, which is a great (and easy) place to begin. **ck**

shoe *stories*

Take a look in your closet. How many pairs of shoes do you see? Are you crazy about shoes (like I am), with a pair for every aspect of your life? Do you have a pair that evokes memories every time you see or wear it?

How do your shoes demonstrate the different roles you play in your life?

Whether you have one pair or twenty, there's bound to be at least one pair of shoes that speaks volumes about who you are. So when it comes to your scrapbook, answer the following questions and let your shoes tell the stories. >>

Finding the Balance *by Britney Mellen. Photos by Candice Stringham.* **Supplies** *Software:* Adobe Photoshop CS3, Adobe Systems; *Patterned paper and ribbon:* Amelie Kit by Lynn Grieveson, *www.designerdigitals.com; Frame:* Whirly Girls Frames Brushes-n-Rub Ons by Rob and Bob Studios, *www.designerdigitals.com; Fonts:* CK Gutenberg, *www.scrapnfonts.com;* I Love Derwin, Internet.

BY BRITNEY MELLEN

*What do your shoes
say about your
aspirations
or values?*

Practical *by Jill Hornby.* **Supplies** *Patterned paper:* Autumn Leaves, KI Memories and Making Memories; *Rub-ons and flower:* Heidi Swapp for Advantus; *Stamps:* Autumn Leaves; *Ink:* Close To My Heart; *Letter stickers:* BasicGrey; *Dimensional accents:* KI Memories; *Chipboard:* Love, Elsie for KI Memories; *Corner-rounder punch:* Fiskars; *Other:* Thread.

*Do you have a
pair of shoes that
reminds you of
a certain time in
your life?*

I Love the '80s *by Emily Magleby.* **Supplies** *Cardstock:* Bazzill Basics Paper; *Patterned paper:* My Mind's Eye; *Flower:* me & my BIG ideas; *Corner-rounder punch:* EK Success; *Fonts:* CK Becky, www.creatingkeepsakes.com; CK Jessica, www.scrapnfonts.com. **ck**

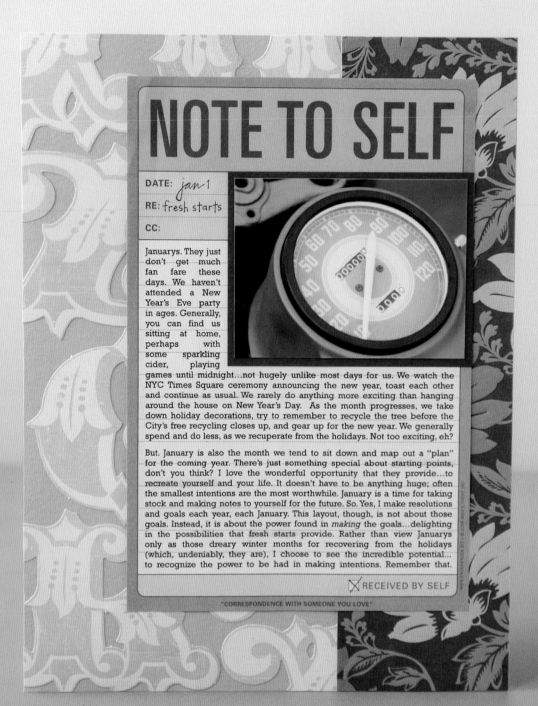

NOTE TO SELF

DATE: jan 1

RE: fresh starts

CC:

Januarys. They just don't get much fan fare these days. We haven't attended a New Year's Eve party in ages. Generally, you can find us sitting at home, perhaps with some sparkling cider, playing games until midnight...not hugely unlike most days for us. We watch the NYC Times Square ceremony announcing the new year, toast each other and continue as usual. We rarely do anything more exciting than hanging around the house on New Year's Day. As the month progresses, we take down holiday decorations, try to remember to recycle the tree before the City's free recycling closes up, and gear up for the new year. We generally spend and do less, as we recuperate from the holidays. Not too exciting, eh?

But. January is also the month we tend to sit down and map out a "plan" for the coming year. There's just something special about starting points, don't you think? I love the wonderful opportunity that they provide...to recreate yourself and your life. It doesn't have to be anything huge; often the smallest intentions are the most worthwhile. January is a time for taking stock and making notes to yourself for the future. So. Yes, I make resolutions and goals each year, each January. This layout, though, is not about those goals. Instead, it is about the power found in *making* the goals...delighting in the possibilities that fresh starts provide. Rather than view Januarys only as those dreary winter months for recovering from the holidays (which, undeniably, they are), I choose to see the incredible potential... to recognize the power to be had in making intentions. Remember that.

☒ RECEIVED BY SELF

"CORRESPONDENCE WITH SOMEONE YOU LOVE"

{ NOTE TO SELF }
by Amanda Probst

Delve deeper than making goals.

Making goals is wonderful. I do it all the time. But, beyond recording what those goals are and when you meet them, take a moment to consider just how powerful the act of making goals is.

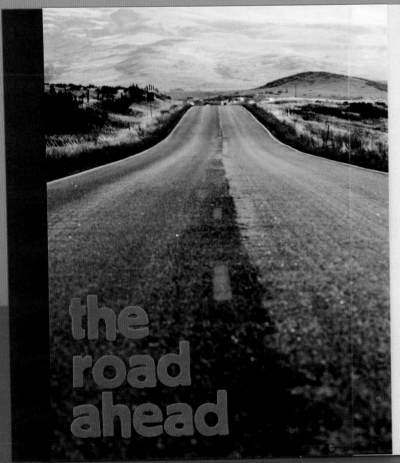

We do a lot of our "big" talks in the car. This was no exception. I don't remember exactly when it was (I want to say spring of 2004). I do remember, though, driving along this road north of Fort Collins...admiring the scenery and discussing our reasons for wanting to homeschool. More importantly, we were listing what we wanted for our children. I compiled that list and made out this mission statement of sorts, with the intention of framing it to hang in our home as a reminder. I've yet to do that, though I've carried it with me in my calendar routinely. Regardless, we *have* adopted homeschooling into our lives and the plan is to continue doing so. This mission statement still holds true today and will, I think, help guide us into the future.

By choosing to homeschool, we hope to...

- Foster a lifetime love of learning

- Provide the tools and atmosphere to encourage our children to think critically

- Cultivate loving, helpful and healthy relationships between our sons and ourselves

- Enable our children to obtain information they require (through knowing how to read well and knowing where and how to find needed information)

- Enable our children to communicate effectively with others both orally and in writing

- Provide a broad general knowledge base from which our children can draw as needed

- Instill the math knowledge required for daily life, as well as an awareness, if not a working knowledge, of how higher math shapes the world

- Encourage qualities of self-confidence and responsibility in our children for their choices and their actions

- Promote a sense of respect for the community and an attitude of service

- Enjoy and cherish the time we have with our children...learning alongside them

{ THE ROAD AHEAD }
by Amanda Probst

Write a mission statement.

This is one of those layouts where the journaling came first. Because the words are so essential, I didn't want to take the focus away from them with a distracting photo or a number of embellishments. Rather, I added a single photo that ties in nicely with the story. Simple, but the words are what's important here.

I DON'T HAVE ANY SPECIFIC CHILDHOOD MEMORIES OF VALENTINE'S DAY. WAIT. I DO REMEMBER ALL THE LITTLE VALENTINES EXCHANGED DURING SCHOOL...MAKING SPECIAL MAILBOXES AND WRITING OUT CARDS FOR CLASSMATES. NOTHING SPECTACULAR, BUT I SUPPOSE IT WAS A NICE EXCUSE TO HAVE SOME CANDY, AND I DID ENJOY MAKING THOSE ART PROJECTS. I NEVER WAS ONE OF THOSE GIRLS VERY INTO PINK AND FRILLS AND HEARTS, THOUGH, SO VALENTINE'S DAY HAS JUST NEVER APPEALED TO ME MUCH. BEFORE NATHAN, I DON'T KNOW THAT I WAS EVER EVEN DATING DURING VALENTINE'S SO I MISSED OUT ON THAT ASPECT OF IT AS WELL. I GUESS THE BEST THAT CAN BE SAID OF VALENTINE'S DAY IS THAT IT MANAGED TO BRING A LITTLE EXCITEMENT TO OUR OTHERWISE FAIRLY SEDATE FEBRUARYS. COME TO THINK OF IT, FEBRUARYS REALLY WERE PRETTY EMPTY OF EVENTS...BETWEEN SPORTS SEASONS, AFTER END/START OF TERMS...NO RELIABLE REASON TO BE BUSY. GUESS THERE HAVE TO BE MONTHS LIKE THAT.

{ FEBRUARYS }
by Amanda Probst

Tell a story, even if there's not much to tell.

Okay, this isn't the most exciting layout ever. The important thing, though, is that I wrote down how I felt about the month of February growing up. It's part of the larger picture of my childhood. For me, some months just weren't as exciting as others. But if I didn't say so, future generations wouldn't know I felt that way—they might just think I was missing those layouts!

what happened there?

ITALY

AFRICA

When we found these WWII era photos of my grandfather Francis at my cousin John's house, John said, "I always wondered if something happened there." Did my grandfather see something? Take part in something? Did something happen that made him not be the husband, the father, the friend he needed to be? I guess we will never know.

{ WHAT HAPPENED? }
by Laura Kurz

Leave questions unanswered.
Sometimes you just won't know what was happening in an old photo. Rather than hide it away, scrapbook it and simply voice your questions. Better to have it displayed so you can wonder and guess than have it tucked away in a box.

Using Your Own Handwriting

By Heidi Swapp

I have to admit—I love e-mail. I don't know about you, but I check for messages all day long. It's such an instantly gratifying way to communicate with friends and family.

However, in this day of instant communication, I am especially touched when I receive a handwritten note. And I adore when my kids take crayon to construction paper and write notes to me. (What mom doesn't?!) When Colton made me this card below, my heart melted—misspellings included.

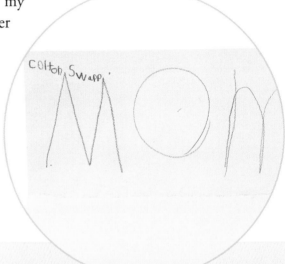

Handwriting Play

Ready to get started? I want you to play with your handwriting. Choose a word (like "happiness") and experiment with writing it in different sizes. Write with pencil. Write with pen. Write in cursive. And manuscript. Write in your messiest handwriting—and in your nicest. This is your starting place! You will love to look back at this page and discover just how much you've learned!

① _____

② _____
pen

③ _____
fast

④ _____
slow

⑤ _____
lowercase

⑥ _____
all caps

⑦ _____
soft

⑧ _____
hard

⑨ _____
big

⑩ _____
little

⑪ _____
cursive

⑫ _____
print

⑬ _____
messy

⑭ _____
neat

⑮ _____
fat

⑯ _____
skinny

Handwriting Treasure Hunt

Okay, let's take a look at your handwriting. Let's go on a treasure hunt around your house. Go and look in your journal, your day planner, your calendar, notes on your fridge, cancelled checks, to-do lists, scrapbook pages, and more (bet you didn't know that you wrote so much, huh?).

I've talked about my "Heidi" fonts. Now I want you to make a list of your handwriting fonts. I want you to see how your handwriting changes (or stays the same!).

Here is a list of MY handwriting fonts:

❶ _____

❷ _____

❸ _____

❹ _____

❺ _____

❻ _____

❼ _____

❽ _____

❾ _____

❿ _____

⓫ _____

⓬ _____

⓭ _____

⓮ _____

Last Chance to Complain

I keep hearing you say it: "I don't like my handwriting." Really, it's time for us to just get past it. Guess what? Everyone is critical of his or her handwriting. I want you to just get those critical thoughts out of the way for once and for all. So. Right now, I want you to go and make a list of everything you could ever possibly hate about your handwriting. Get it all out. Go ahead. It's all right. Let it go. Ahhhh, doesn't that feel better?

I don't like my handwriting because...

1

2

3

4

5

6

7

8

9

10

5 Essential Tools for Great Handwriting

❶ Zero-Centered Ruler

I love my zero-centered ruler. (It's a ruler with the zero in the center and numbers counting out in both directions.) I place it where I want my lettering to be and then make tick marks to represent each letter in the word. This ensures that my word is perfectly spaced. You'll be happily surprised at how consistent spacing will improve your handwriting!

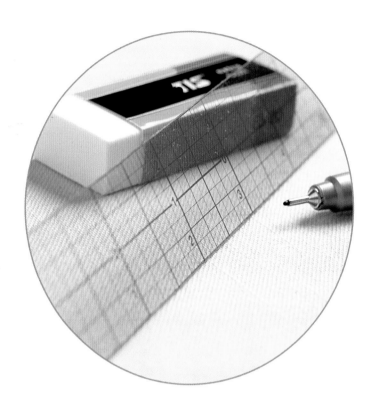

❷ .5mm Mechanical Pencil

Here's one of my fundamental rules of handwriting on your scrapbook page—always start with pencil.

For me the best kind of pencil is a quality .5mm mechanical pencil. Experiment with the type of pencil that fits in your hand. After all, comfort is important, too!

❸ Quality Eraser

Let's be honest—the microscopic eraser included on even the most expensive mechanical pencil will not get you very far in the scrapbooking world. You need a REAL eraser. (My preference is a white eraser like the one shown here.)

Now, people have differing opinions about which eraser is the best. Just promise me one thing: Don't buy a cheap pink eraser like the kind you used in elementary school. It will crumple your paper, leave smears and make a big mess on your page. You need an eraser that's easy to use and won't leave ugly marks on your page.

Get in the habit of reaching for a separate eraser. The best way to do this is to always write with a pencil with a worn-out eraser. Trust me, the habit will form quickly.

❹ Black Point Pens

When people ask me about my favorite scrapbooking supply, I always say that I love pens! To write on your scrapbook pages, you need a quality pen with a dense tip. I prefer a Zig Millennium or Sakura Micron pen (I don't recommend felt-tipped or ball point pens because they don't deliver a quality line.)

Start with one pen (a .5 point size) and purchase additional pens in the following "must-have" point sizes:

- .8-point
- .1-point
- .3-point
- .05-point

These point sizes work together to give the right look for any scrapbook occasion. Many people think that their .5-point will be OK in every situation. Nope. Depending on the size of your words and the amount of space you have, your handwriting looks so much better when you choose the correct point size.

Tip: Pens are inexpensive; about two dollars each. You'll need to replace your pens on a regular basis. Sometimes you don't realize the tip has lost its point until you start writing with a new pen!

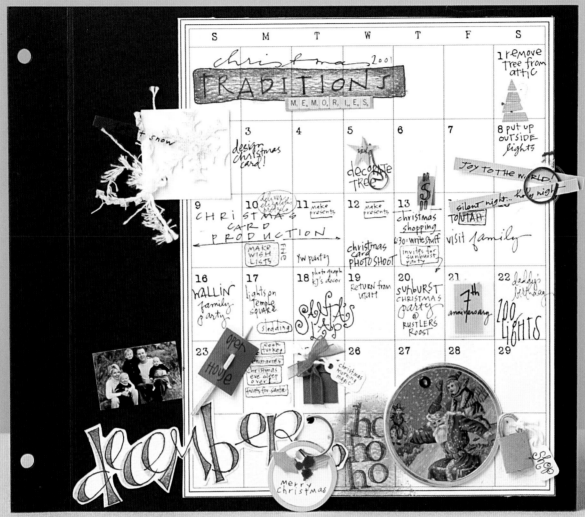

Christmas Calendar by Heidi Swapp. **Supplies:** Pens: EK Success; Other: Various found objects.

Give Me Just a Sentence or Two

I know, you're probably thinking something like "I don't know if I can write all my journaling by hand!" But it's OK. Remember when you first learned to swim? You didn't have to jump off the high dive on your first day (for your sake, I hope you didn't! Wink!). You don't have to make a big jump with your handwriting, either. How about this—you give me just a sentence or two, using one of these ideas:

• *Make it a combo!* Combine your handwriting with computer fonts and other forms of typography, including rubber stamps, stickers, printed word strips and more.

• *Start small.* Use your own handwriting on a cute little tag or inside a bookplate.

• *Experiment on other projects.* Try your new handwriting on other projects, such as calendar pages, greeting cards and notes to your child's teacher or soccer coach.

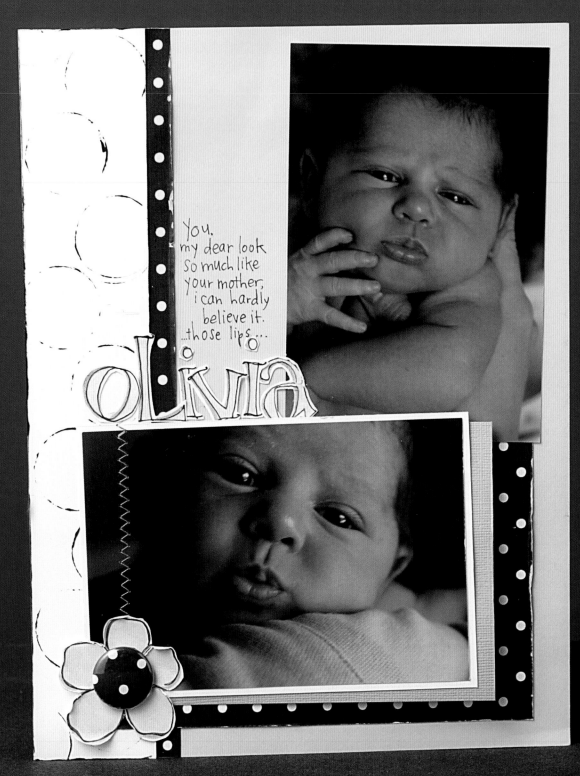

You,
my dear look
so much like
your mother,
i can hardly
believe it.
...those lips...

oLiVia

Olivia by Heidi Swapp. **Supplies:** Cardstock: Bazzill Basics Paper and Making Memories; Patterned paper: Chatterbox; Colored pencils: Sanford; Page pebbles: Making Memories; Pen: EK Success.

Letter Shape

Did you know that all letters have a basic shape? It's true. I first
noticed this when I saw a GAP store logo. The letters all have
a tall rectangular shape. When I saw the logo for Baby GAP,
I noticed how "baby" was written in square shape letters, and
spaced perfectly above the tall rectangular GAP.

I realized that legible handwriting could be based on writing
letters in patterns that mimic shapes! Letters come in three basic
shapes, which—squares, tall rectangles and wide rectangles.

- *Squares*—Letters that are as wide as they are tall. The letters
  for the word "Olivia" (on opposite page) are squares. (Note
  how that doesn't include the top of the "L".) Note: I cut out
  each letter so they had some dimension, then overlapped them.

Below, on this card, "Thank Heaven" is written in square shapes.

Thank Heaven for Little Girls mini album by Heidi Swapp.
Supplies: Cardstock: Making Memories; Ribbon: Berwick
Offray and May Arts; Stamps: Inkadinkado and Staples; Index
tabs: Avery; Ink: Clearsnap; Pen: EK Success.

• *Tall Rectangles*—Letters that are twice as tall as they are wide. On the layout below, I cut equally sized and shaped rectangles out of pink paper, then wrote the letters into my rectangular boxes to ensure that the letters would have the correct proportions.

Princess by Heidi Swapp. **Supplies:** Cardstock: Bazzill Basics Paper and Making Memories; Ribbon: Berwick Offray and May Arts; Brads: Adornit-Carolee's Creations; Rhinestones: Advantus; Photo corner: Making Memories; Charms: Embellish-It and Making Memories; Pens: EK Success and Sulky.

• *Wide Rectangles*—Letters that are twice as wide as they are tall. Notice how the width and height of the letters that spell out "What Limits?"on the layout below are wide rectangles.

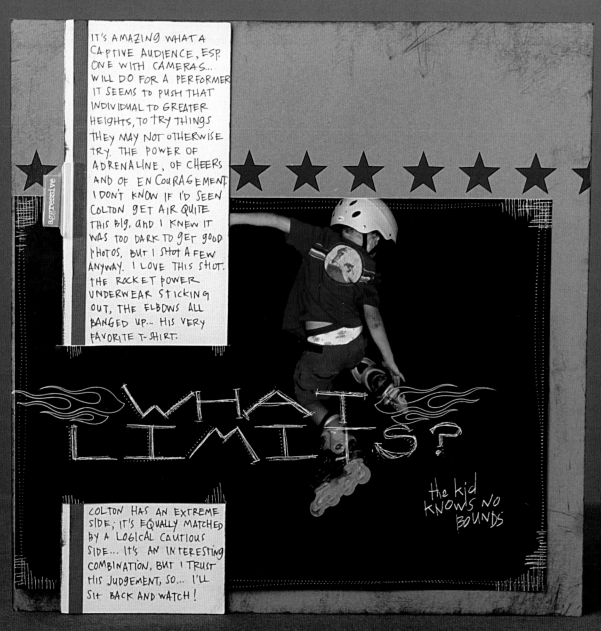

IT'S AMAZING WHAT A CAPTIVE AUDIENCE, ESP. ONE WITH CAMERAS... WILL DO FOR A PERFORMER IT SEEMS TO PUSH THAT INDIVIDUAL TO GREATER HEIGHTS, TO TRY THINGS THEY MAY NOT OTHERWISE TRY. THE POWER OF ADRENALINE, OF CHEERS AND OF ENCOURAGEMENT. I DON'T KNOW IF I'D SEEN COLTON GET AIR QUITE THIS BIG. AND I KNEW IT WAS TOO DARK TO GET GOOD PHOTOS, BUT I SHOT A FEW ANYWAY. I LOVE THIS SHOT. THE ROCKET POWER UNDERWEAR STICKING OUT, THE ELBOWS ALL BANGED UP... HIS VERY FAVORITE T-SHIRT.

WHAT LIMITS?

the kid KNOWS NO BOUNDS

COLTON HAS AN EXTREME SIDE; IT'S EQUALLY MATCHED BY A LOGICAL CAUTIOUS SIDE... It's AN INTERESTING COMBINATION. BUT I TRUST HIS JUDGEMENT, SO... I'LL SIT BACK AND WATCH!

What Limits by Heidi Swapp. **Supplies:** Index tabs, scenery, and tape: Advantus; Ink: Clearsnap; Pen: EK Success.

Letter Size

Another secret of legible handwriting is letter size. Believe me, your handwriting will look so much neater if your letters are a consistent size and shape. In fact, messy handwriting is usually messy because the letters are different shapes and sizes!

Practice an Assortment of Letters

Try all upper case, all lower case, all cursive and so on. As you practice, form your letters within hand-drawn boxes. In time, you'll feel confident about writing on a blank piece of paper.

Letter Spacing

Letter spacing is the third key to good handwriting. The space between each letter in a word should be about the same. It's true that some letters need more "personal space" than others (for example, the letter "W" takes up more room than the letter "I"), but it's important to allow the same amount of space between each letter. Next, it's time to learn four ways to space your letters for maximum legibility and visual impact.

Four Letter Spacing Strategies

There are many different ways to space your letters in a way that is consistent and attractive. Here, I share four ways to space your letters for maximum legibility and impact.

1. *Baseline-based spacing.* Baselines are the lines that "ground" your letters. Many baselines are solid, such as lines on a sheet of notebook paper or horizontal pencil marks to keep your letters on the straight and narrow! If you need help keeping your handwriting straight and evenly spaced, remember that you can always draw pencil lines to use as a guide for your journaling. (And, the great thing about pencils is that the marks can be erased!) Baselines can also be a line created by a page frame border, the top of another word or the top of a photo mat.

No More "Oops"

I always ask myself two questions before I pick up my pencil
and start journaling. The questions are:

1. *What do I want my journaling to say?*
2. *Where will I place my journaling on my page?*

I know you've seen those pages. You know the ones I mean—
the "oops" ones. The ones where the journaling is really messy.
The ones where the scrapbooker didn't think about what she
wanted to say ahead of time. Maybe her words trail off the
page. Or, maybe the words are all crammed together at the end.
You're simply not allowed to do that on your pages.

So, the first thing you need is a piece of scratch paper. Think
about what you want to say on your scrapbook page, but
ALWAYS write it on scratch paper first. Why? On scratch
paper, you can form complete thoughts. You can cross out
words to your heart's content! You can start over. You can
check the spelling of a word. And, you can figure out just how
much space you need on your page for journaling—all with
NO PRESSURE! No one will ever see it!

Love Your Handwriting, Right Now: Simple Tags

I know that writing on your scrapbook page can be scary at first. So, we're going to start by practicing with something small, like tags. Here, you'll find a page full of practice tags where you can practice your handwriting. Remember to try different point sizes with each tag to create a number of different looks!

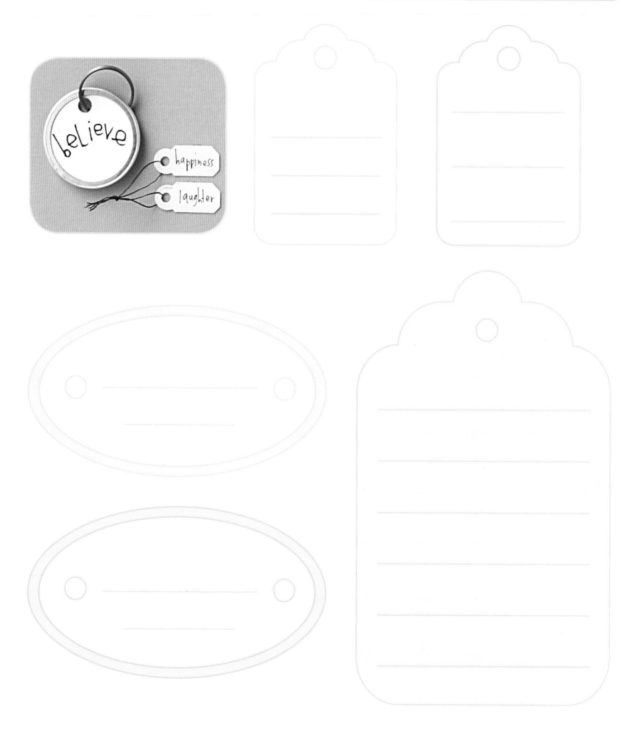

Mixing and Matching Fonts

Now that you're ready to write on your scrapbook pages, let me share one of my favorite things with you—mixing and matching handwriting with other types of lettering! Here, I combined handwriting, letter stamps, and computer fonts.

Baseball Buds by Heidi Swapp. **Supplies:** Label holder: Making Memories; Stamps: Advantus and Making Memories; Tape: Advantus; Pens: EK Success; Other: Cardstock.

I combined felt letters with a variety of handwriting styles and sizes!
Did you see how I cut out the bottom of the second letter "C" in
the word catch? I like to have fun with my letter, and now the word
"bites" looks like it's biting into the letter "C."

Fishing Charter by Heidi Swapp. **Supplies:** Cardstock: Making Memories; Iron-on letters: Advantus; Pens: EK Success.

New Ways to Write Old Words

When you learned to print in school, you were taught to divide your words in half just like the example I've shown below. However, I've discovered that it's also fun to divide my words into other shapes according to the Rule of Thirds.

Let's play with the lines of that basic handwriting paper. You can create all sorts of cool effects when you move your midline. Let me show you what I mean:

On these samples, I've played around with the midpoints of my graph paper, moving the center points of my letters up and down. You can try this technique with any letter.

Happiness 1: This is the typical way to write a word. Notice how the upper and lower portion of each letter is divided equally by the midpoint.

Happiness 2: This version of the word is an example that shows how I've moved the midpoint of each letter to the upper third of the letter height.

Happiness 3: This version of the word is an example that shows how I've moved the midpoint of each letter to the lower third of the letter height.

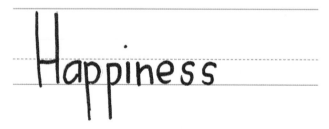

Now let me show you examples of how to use this lettering style in a creative way!

Now, look at the word "heights" on this layout. Here, I've moved the midline of the letters to the lower third of the letter height.

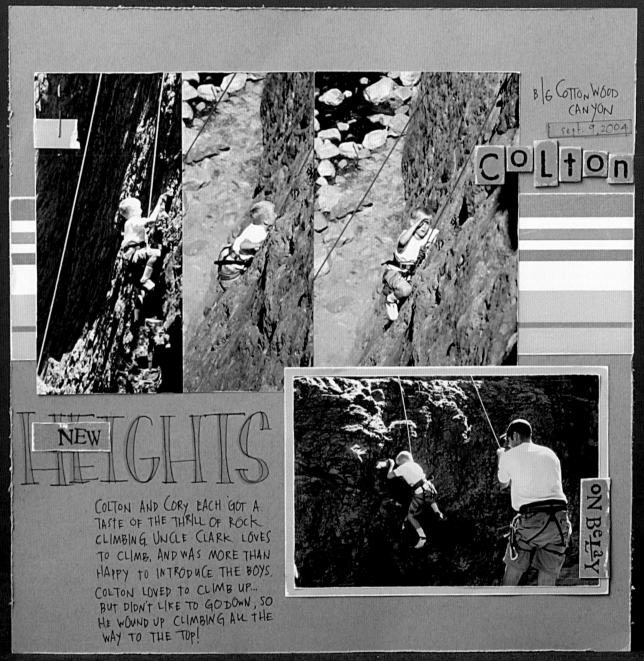

New Heights by Heidi Swapp. **Supplies:** Cardstock and rub-ons: Making Memories; Stamps: PSX Designs; Chipboard: Bazzill Basics Paper; Colored pencils: Sanford; Pens: EK Success.

most of our
OBSTACLES
would melt
away if instead
of cowering
before them,
we should make up
our minds to walk
BOLDLY
through them.

—— orison Swett Marden

"Rim to rim"

hiking the grand canyon... south rim to north.
2 miles; 11.5 hours. what an awesome experience!
stunningly beautiful. great company. and lots of
quiet time to allow my mind to drift, think and
create.

Rim to Rim by Heidi Swapp. **Supplies:** Cardstock: Making Memories; Photo corners: Kolo;
Colored pencils: Sanford; Pens: EK Success.

Students in my classes often ask me where they should add lines to the curves of their letters. This chart helps you learn where to place your lines.

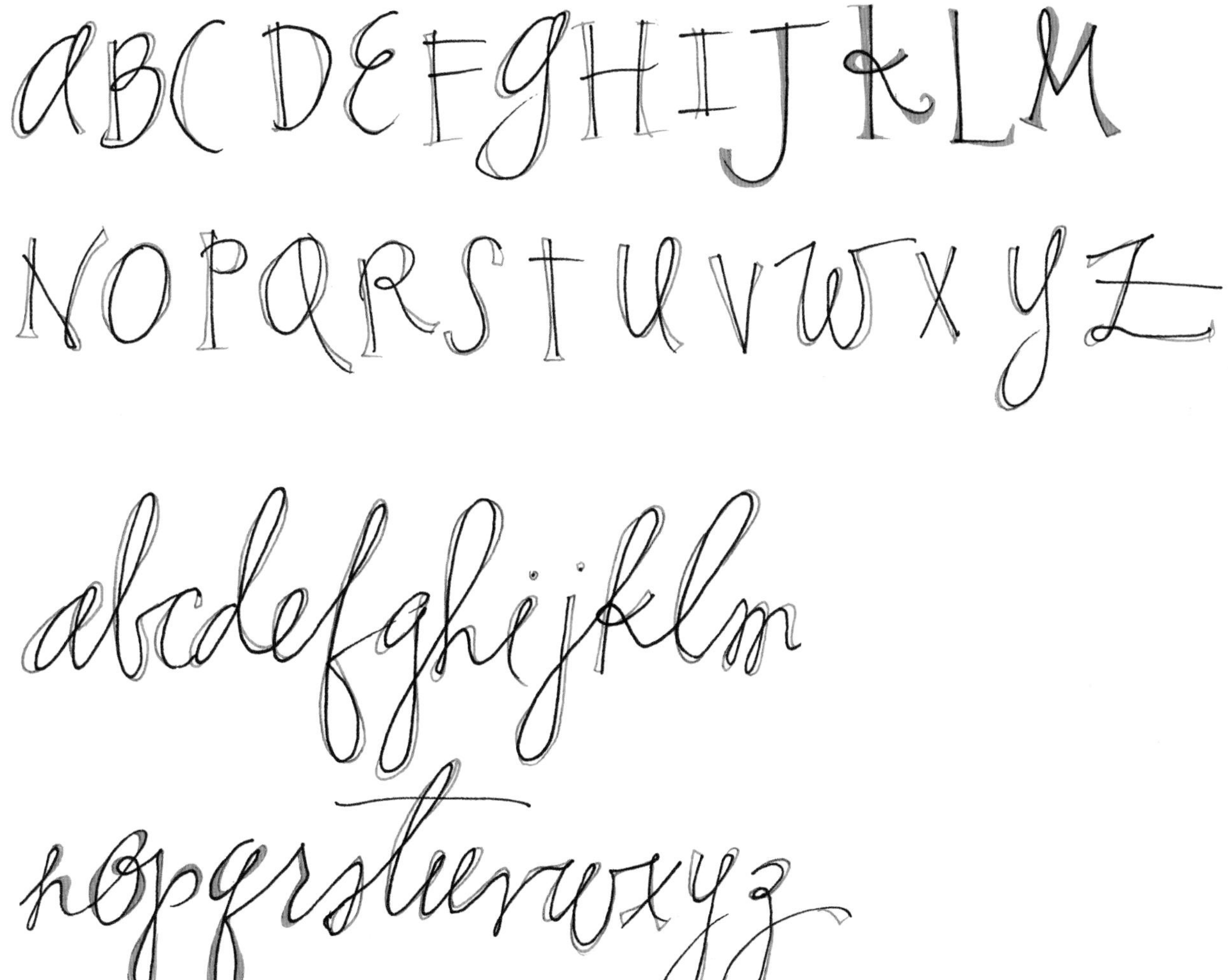

ABCDEFGHIJKLM

NOPQRSTUVWXYZ

abcdefghijklm

nopqrstuvwxyz

Try Your Own Voluptuous Letters

Sketch out a cursive alphabet and make the letters as voluptuous as I've done here!

Title Letters: Step-by-Step

I love shading and just having fun with my titles. Here are some easy examples you can create to add extra impact to the titles on your pages.

1. Pencil in the word on a straight baseline.
2. Draw a parallel line to the left vertical lines of the letter. Keep your spacing even.
3. Top off the ends or add serifs, making alterations as needed.

Variation: Try adding concave lines rather than parallel lines.

CHAPTER 2:

Quizzes, Questions & Quotes

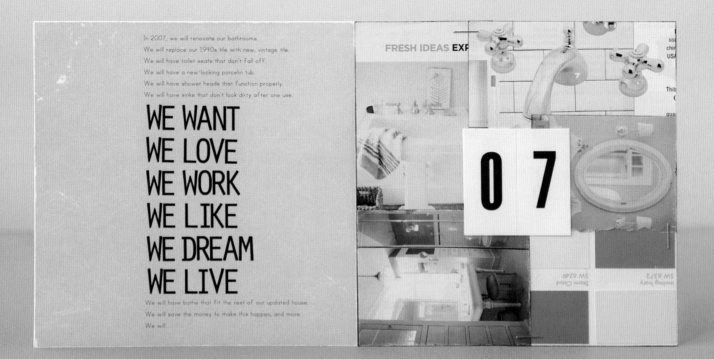

In 2007, we will renovate our bathrooms.
We will replace our 1940s tile with new, vintage tile.
We will have toilet seats that don't fall off.
We will have a new-looking porcelin tub.
We will have shower heads that function properly.
We will have sinks that don't look dirty after one use.

WE WANT
WE LOVE
WE WORK
WE LIKE
WE DREAM
WE LIVE

We will have baths that fit the rest of our updated house.
We will save the money to make this happen, and more.
We will.

FRESH IDEAS EXP

0 7

SOMETIMES YOU NEED A LITTLE HELP to get started with your journaling. Other times, you've got the basics down but need help showing the true emotion behind an event or set of photos. These quizzes, questions, and quotes will get your journaling juices flowing with creative and comprehensive ideas for scrapbooking about childhood to adulthood (and everything in between), people you love, places you've been, favorite activities and hobbies, plus the everyday details in between, including those you might often forget to include. Use these journaling inspirations to help you include the essentials and beyond for rich, detailed scrapbooks that truly encapsulate your life.

COMPLETE THAT PAGE!

10 Creative Ways to Journal about Your Baby

1. Download "baby timelines" from the Internet at sites such as *www.babyzone.com.* Simply fill in dates and times of first events.

2. Ask grandparents and other family members to send your baby short e-mails. Print the e-mails and include them as journaling on your pages.

3. Save congratulatory baby cards. Instead of showing the front of the card, photocopy the inside of the card to preserve handwritten wishes from friends.

4. Include a copy of your baby's birth announcement and birth certificate on a page.

5. Document your baby's doctor visits by saving appointment reminder cards.

6. Scan and print labels from your baby's first foods and add them to a scrapbook page. Jot down one or two sentences about how your baby reacted to each food.

7. Photocopy a page from a baby name book. Include the photocopied page on a layout about how you chose your child's name.

8. If you were granted three wishes for your baby, what would they be?

9. Ask your baby's siblings to draw pictures and/or write stories about your new baby.

10. Scan hang-tags from baby's clothing showing brands and sizes. Make a "tag timeline" that documents your baby's progression from newborn to 12-month clothing.

BRENDAN MICHAEL **by Nichol Magouirk > Supplies** *Patterned paper:* Art Warehouse, Creative Imaginations; *Metal stencil letters, wood numbers, safety pins, rub-on word, metal message and wood frame:* Li'l Davis Designs; *Large metal-rimmed tag, foam stamps and acrylic paint:* Making Memories; *Photo corners and letter "b":* EK Success; *Canvas, spray adhesive and transparency:* Creative Imaginations; *Computer fonts:* Times New Roman, Casablanca Antique and Stencil, downloaded from the Internet; *Baby name info:* Downloaded from the Internet; *Ribbon:* SEI.

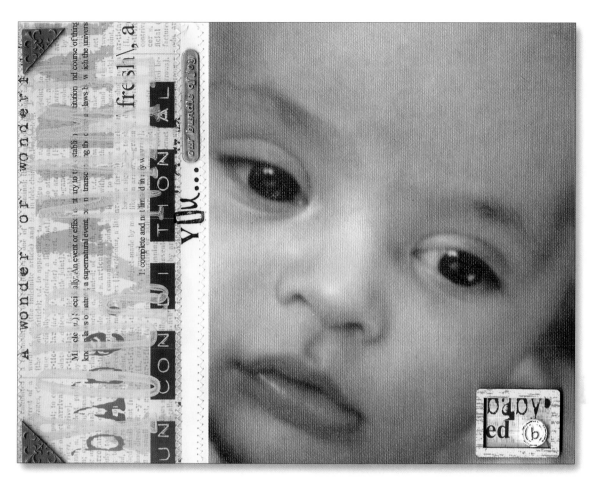

BRENDEN
MICHAEL

Daddy and I had already discussed using Michael as a boy's middle name when we found out we were having you. We wanted to carry on the name since daddy's middle name is Michael and Grandpa Magouirk's first name is Michael (even though he goes by his middle name, Brent). We had a difficult time agreeing on a first name for you though. I came up with the name Brenden one day and Daddy liked it too. When I suggested we spell it

BRENDEN

the 'Bren' for grandpa Brent and the 'den' for grandpa Dennis daddy loved it. And that's how we named you!

Brendan Irish Prince. Well known Irish playwright and wit Brendan Behan. M
Brendan Celtic Raven M
Brendan German Flame M
Brenden Irish Prince. Variant of Brendan. M
Brendon Irish Prince. Variant of Brendan. M

COMPLETE THAT PAGE!

10 Creative Ways to Journal about Your Child

1. Take photographs of signs of the places you visit. Signs often include titles (i.e. Monarch Park) and sometimes include interesting bits of information (established in 1966, etc.).

2. If you write notes to your child ("I love you" notes in her lunchbox, etc.), save them and include them on a scrapbook page.

3. Does your child like to draw? Encourage him to write about his picture (invented spelling and imperfect grammar are perfectly acceptable here!). Not only have you captured his handwriting, but you've also captured his unique way of thinking and communicating.

4. Toys often include developmental age range listings on the box. Scan and print the front of a toy box and use it as a journaling springboard about your child's current developmental stage.

5. Encourage elementary school–age children to write their own thoughts on scrapbook pages that you (or they) create.

6. Download a copy of a chore chart from sites such as *www.webmomz.com*. Fill it in to document your child's responsibilities.

7. Save copies of your child's school papers with positive comments. Scan positive comments into a background paper and print.

8. Did your child dog-ear a Christmas toy catalog? Scan pages that have his favorite toys circled and include them on a scrapbook page.

9. Kids are notorious for their literal and often funny interpretations of the world. Share your child's favorite cute sayings.

10. Ask traveling family members to send postcards addressed to your child. Include them on pages that chronicle the relationship between your child and this person.

GAME TALK **by Miley Johnson > Supplies** *Patterned papers:* Li'l Davis Designs (diamond shape), Treehouse Designs (red stripe); *Wood letters:* Li'l Davis Designs; *Computer fonts:* Dirty Ego and Avante Garde, downloaded from the Internet; *Bottle cap:* Manto Fev; *Cord:* Memory Lane Paper Company; *Other:* Brads, sunflower seeds and tag.

GAME TALK

Drew Style

Nebraska baseball...**ACCORDING TO DREW**

"those players are lucky because their moms signed them up for baseball."

"when I am growed up, I will be a baseball player, too. I already have a good glove"

"I have to practice my game face mom. You know I will play better if I have a good game face to scare the other team."

"how many more outs before we get to have another hot dog?"

SUMMER 2003

BIG RED

COMPLETE THAT PAGE!

10 Creative Ways to Journal about School

SCHEDULE **by Angie Cramer Supplies** *Computer fonts:* Times New Roman and Century Gothic, Microsoft Word; *Snaps:* Making Memories; *Other:* Colored paper clips.

① Make a photocopy of your child's school schedule as a quick way to journal about how he spends his days.

② Add school newsletters to your page layouts. The newsletters will give an idea of the school's philosophy as well as a "round-up" of important events going on at school.

③ Collect announcements and tickets associated with school carnivals and fairs, and include them on a scrapbook page.

④ Take a picture of your child on the first day of school. Record her hopes and fears for the upcoming school year.

⑤ Make copies of special awards and honors earned by your child. Certificates are a great way to document your child's school successes and interests.

⑥ Include a campus map on your layout. Circle classrooms and buildings where your child attended classes.

⑦ A photocopied college application can add insight into your child's (or your own) interests and personalities.

⑧ Graduation is for everyone—from preschool students to PhDs. Celebrate your (or your child's) achievements by including diplomas in your scrapbooks.

⑨ Ask your child for permission to include photocopied pages from her yearbook as journaling on your scrapbook pages.

⑩ Make a list of your favorite questions from this section (or make a list of your own). Ask your child the same questions every year as a way to document her scholastic growth.

SCHOOL DAYS **by Tracie Smith Supplies** *Patterned papers:* Daisy D's Paper Co. (red plaid and ivory plaid), Li'l Davis Designs ("Jump, Skip, Run, Smile" strip); *Epoxy letters, frames, label sticker, puzzle, wooden letters, band bottle cap and safety pin:* Li'l Davis Designs; *Buttons, vellum tag, ribbons and washer word:* Making Memories; *Woven labels:* me & my BIG ideas; *Rubber stamps:* PSX Design; *Stamping ink:* Stampin' Up!; *Pen:* Zig Millennium, EK Success; *Craft wire:* Artistic Wire Ltd.; *Embossing powder:* Ranger Industries; *Other:* Charm. **Ideas to note:** Tracie created pockets by stitching strips of denim onto cardstock. The fabric creates enough resistance so the tags won't fall through, and Tracie can add more at any time.

COMPLETE THAT PAGE!

10 Creative Ways to Journal about Your Teen

1. Make a photocopy of your teen's first job application. Include it on a scrapbook page that shares the story of his first job.

2. Working on a page about your teen's friendships? Scan high school I.D. cards from her and her friends and use them as journaling accents on a page.

3. Journaling about the prom? Save prom tickets, limo receipts and menus to help tell the story of your teen's prom experience.

4. Photocopy a page from your teen's calendar to use on a "day in the life" layout.

5. Download your teen's favorite songs onto a CD and include it on a scrapbook page.

6. Create your own "teen slang" dictionary page and include it on a layout.

7. With your teen's permission, tuck notes from her friends into a hidden journaling block on a layout.

8. Include a copy of your teen's first driver's license on a layout.

9. Photocopy your teen's school schedule and include it on a page.

10. Pull headlines from your teen's favorite magazine as a fun way to journal about your teen.

TEEN LINGO **By Mellette Berezoski > Supplies** *Patterned papers:* Anna Griffin (paisley), KI Memories (plaid), Making Memories (striped); *Antique brads, paper flower, metal letter tile and colored staples:* Making Memories; *Word pebble:* Wordz, Creative Imaginations; *Letter stickers and flower tag:* KI Memories; *Computer font:* Times New Roman, Microsoft Word; *Other:* Ribbon and floss.

PILLAR OF STRENGTH
by Mellette Berezoski

Supplies *Patterned papers:* Scrappin' Dreams, Creative Imaginations; *Vellum:* Bazzill Basics Paper; *Metal frame:* Scrapworks; *Bookplate:* Making Memories; *Flower medallion:* Sanook Paper Company; *Computer fonts:* Pegsanna and Fusi, downloaded from the Internet; *Other:* Ribbon.

1972
by Barbara Carroll

Supplies *Punches:* Family Treasures (flower), source unknown (square); *Button:* Making Memories; *Computer fonts:* Century Gothic and Monotype (journaling), downloaded from the Internet; 2Peas David Walker, downloaded from *twopeasinabucket.com*.

Mellette's opening sentence perfectly piques our interest while setting the stage.

We love how Mellette transitions her journaling from sharing the events of the day to describing her child's character.

Remember, important events happen when you don't have a camera. Let your memories dictate the pages you create, not just the photos.

COMPLETE THAT PAGE!

10 Creative Ways to Journal about Adulthood

1. Collect memos and e-mails from your job and use them on a scrapbook page as a way to journal about your job responsibilities.

2. List 10 things you can't live without. Write a sentence for each explaining why.

3. Ask your co-workers for business cards listing their titles. Create a scrapbook page that chronicles the people you spend your time with each day.

4. Photocopy your company's dress code. Include pictures of yourself dressed for work. Do you stick to the dress code, or do you modify it?

5. Look through your favorite magazines for interesting headlines that reflect your personality. Include these as journaling on an "all about me" page.

6. The other day, a friend's daughter asked her, "Is it hard work being a mommy?" Describe how you feel about being a parent.

7. Create a "top 10" list of your favorite songs. Are any of them songs you listened to as a teen?

8. If you could switch places with a celebrity for just one day, who would you switch with and why?

9. Create a timeline that shows your progress toward a goal, such as an exercise or financial goal.

10. Make a list of reasons why you like being an adult.

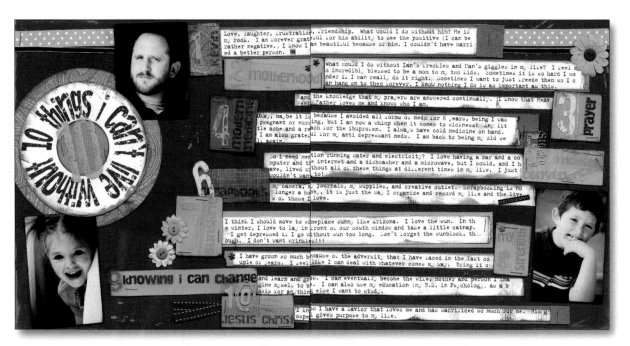

10 THINGS I CAN'T LIVE WITHOUT **by Shannon Wolz > Supplies** *Patterned papers:* Anna Griffin (green paisley), KI Memories (orange flower), source unknown (green bamboo); *Computer fonts:* Destroy, downloaded from the Internet; LB Typewriter, "Lisa's Favorite Fonts" CD, *Creating Keepsakes; Rubber stamps:* Ma Vinci's Reliquary (small numbers), Making Memories (large "10"); *Acrylic paint:* Delta Technical Coatings and Making Memories; *Buttons:* Junkitz, Bazzill Basics Paper; *Stamping ink:* Ranger Industries, Tsukineko; *Other:* Ribbon, transparency, chipboard, flowers, mini flower brads, wordstrips and colored staples.

Mom looks radiantly beautiful. Since last September, she has worked very hard to lose 45 pounds! We are all so proud of her. She looks great, feels even better and she is so energetic. Last week I couldn't believe the way she bounced up the stairs. That was something I had never seen her do before. I took these photos on the front lawn just before Mom and Dad set out for a party. They both looked really young and full of spirit. I bet they were the center of attention.

BEAUTIFUL **by Tracie Smith > Supplies** *Embossed paper:* K & Company; *Acrylic paint:* Anita's (green), Americana (gold); *Embroidery ribbon:* Bucilla; *Pressed flowers:* Nature's Pressed; *Safety pin:* Li'l Davis Designs; *Gold metal spine:* 7gypsies; *Pen:* Zig Millennium, EK Success; *Stamping ink:* VersaMark, Tsukineko; *Embossing powder:* Suze Weinberg; *Computer font:* CK Script, "The Best of Creative Lettering" CD Vol. 1, *Creating Keepsakes; Other:* Jewelry tag and canvas.

quiz: slice of life

This short and sweet quiz reveals the day-to-day you. Repeat annually for a personal year-end inventory, send to friends and use their answers to make a mini album, or give our Slice of Life quiz to each member of your family.

Friday, February 24, 2006

The last person I sent a card to:
Grandma and Grandpa Cordner in Yuma, AZ

What I ate for lunch today:
leftover barbecued beef sandwich

Something I just learned:
how to use Curves in Photoshop

My favorite song this year:
"Somewhere Only We Know" by Keene

The last book I read:
"The Solace of Leaving Early" by Haven Kimmel

What I'm wearing right now:
Paul Frank shirt, Joes Jeans, socks

The last phone call I made:
to Mom who wasn't feeling well today

Inside, I don't feel very different from when I was:
28—I'm only 29 now, but I feel very different from even just two years ago.

The last restaurant I ate at was:
El Matador in Bountiful, UT

My favorite TV show is:
Gilmore Girls

M E

me

Elisha Snow | Farmington, UT

From the music she loves to the last book she read, Elisha's answers to our quick and easy **Slice of Life** questions give us a glimpse into her day-to-day life.

materials patterned paper (American Crafts) • fabric tabs (Scrapworks) • ribbon (Textured Trios) • Elisia font • 8½ x 11 page

slice of life

1. The last person I sent a card to:
2. What I ate for lunch today:
3. Something I just learned:
4. My favorite song this year:
5. The last book I read:
6. What I'm wearing right now:
7. The last phone call I made:
8. Inside, I don't feel very different from when I was (how old?):
9. The last restaurant I ate at was:
10. My favorite TV show is:

friends forever

1. Which of your friends is most like you?
2. Which friend is most unlike you?
3. Which friend's party will you remember forever?
4. What long lost friend do you wonder about?
5. What's the funniest thing that's ever happened to you and a friend?
6. Do you still see any friends from childhood?
7. Do you have any close friends who live far away?
8. What is the age difference between your oldest and youngest friends?
9. Which friend has gotten you into the most trouble?
10. Which friend has kept you out of the most trouble?

looking back

1. What did you want to be when you grew up?
2. How did you help out around the house?
3. What were you most afraid of?
4. Who was your first crush?
5. What childhood story do family and friends still tease you about?
6. Which family vacation was your favorite?
7. What did you do in the summertime?
8. What did your childhood bedroom look like?
9. As a child, what was your greatest talent?
10. What was the nicest thing your parents ever did for you?

family either/or

1. Hamburger Helper or filet mignon?
2. Van or sedan?
3. Yellowstone Park or Disneyland?
4. McDonald's or Olive Garden?
5. Board games or video games?
6. Snow bunnies or water babies?
7. Early birds or night owls?
8. Road trip or air travel?
9. White or wheat?
10. On the team or in the bleachers?

quiz: hopes & dreams

How does real life compare to your hopes and dreams? Our Hopes & Dreams quiz asks you to place your life in perspective. Question 5 might also get you the birthday gift you've been dreaming of!

My current occupation is:
An art teacher
My dream job is:
I'm lucky to be living it!
If I could live anywhere in the world, it would be:
On a beach, where I could watch the sunset every single night.
The best birthday gift I could receive would be:
A little laundry elf.
If I had a million dollars, the first thing I'd buy would be:
A fabulous bottle of wine for my husband.
When I was a teenager, I thought that at my age I'd be:
Old and yucky. So glad I'm neither!
The goals I'm currently working on are:
Patience and balance. Always.
When I'm 80, I hope I am doing this:
Creating, playing, traveling, and smiling.
The person I'd like to be more like is:
My son, Riley. He's carefree, full of energy, and smart as a whip!

patience and balance

Stacey Sattler | Sylvania, OH

When Stacey first read this quiz, she imagined her answers would be wild and fanciful. But the more she thought about the questions, the more she realized she's "surprisingly content" with her life as it is.

materials patterned paper (BasicGrey, Paper Fever, Making Memories, Bo-Bunny, Anna Griffin, K&Company) • Courier New and 2Peas Essential fonts • *12 x 12 page*

hopes & dreams

1. My current occupation is:
2. My dream job is:
3. If I could live anywhere in the world, it would be:
4. If I could be someone famous, it would it be:
5. The best birthday gift I could receive would be:
6. If I had a million dollars, the first thing I'd buy would be:
7. When I was a teenager, I thought that at my age I'd be:
8. The goals I'm currently working on are:
9. When I am 80, I hope I am doing this:
10. The person I'd like to be more like is:

the happy couple

1. How long have you been married (engaged, together)?
2. How did the two of you meet?
3. Tell us about one of your significant other's lovable quirks:
4. What is your favorite thing to do together?
5. What is something you rarely agree on?
6. What's the most important thing you have in common?
7. What funny or pet names do you call each other?
8. What gift did he/she give you that meant the most?
9. What's the kindest thing he/she has ever done for you?
10. What's the most interesting thing about him/her?

best & worst

1. The age in life you've most enjoyed so far:
2. The age in life you hated most:
3. The best day of the week:
4. The worst day of the week:
5. Your finest cooking accomplishment:
6. Your worst cooking disaster:
7. The color that looks best on you:
8. The color that looks worst on you:
9. Your favorite movie of all time:
10. The worst movie ever made:

two by two

1. Two everyday things I couldn't live without:
2. Two of my favorite songs:
3. Two things I want to do before I die:
4. Two things I worry about:
5. Two stores I shop at:
6. Two things that scare me:
7. Two snacks I could eat every day:
8. Two people I'd be lost without:
9. Two nicknames I've been given:
10. Next two places I want to go on vacation:

quiz: what friends say

Ask your friends to tell you how it really is! Their answers will provide interesting insights and might persuade you to give an outfit or two to Goodwill!

real **✿** deal

a quiz about me, answered completely and without arm-twisting, by Tara

What do I do or say that makes you laugh?
You make me laugh constantly. you always go farther than anyone else I know with a joke and when you surprise me like that I cant help but crack up.

What do you believe comes easy to me?
People skills. You're a great talker. You're so good with people.

What do you believe I struggle with?
Feeling like you are enough.

If someone was meeting me at the airport, how would you describe me?
Tall and thin with super short black hair.

What piece of clothing should I wear more often?
A bra.

What outfit should I give to Goodwill?
Keep the orange sweatshirt. Give something of Dan's to the Goodwill.

What's the longest we've ever talked on the phone?
Two hours?

Would I ever jump out of an airplane?
No.

How do I let you know I care about you?
You take time for me. You take care of me. You make me laugh. You call me. You e-mail me. You send me goodies.

real deal
Cathy Zielske | St. Paul, MN

Cathy's friend Tara answered our **What Friends Say** quiz with delightful honesty and humor. A friend's perspective on our strengths and weaknesses is often an insightful addition to a self-discovery scrapbook.

materials patterned paper (My Mind's Eye) • chipboard letters (Heidi Swapp) • flower, brad (Making Memories) • Interstate font • *8½ x 11 page*

what friends say

1. What expression do I use—way too often?

2. What do I do or say that makes you laugh?

3. What do you believe comes easy to me?

4. What do you believe I struggle with?

5. If someone was meeting me at the airport, how would you describe me?

6. What piece of clothing should I wear more often?

7. What outfit should I give to Goodwill?

8. What's the longest we've ever talked on the phone?

9. Would I ever jump out of an airplane?

10. How do I let you know I care about you?

four for the record

1. Four jobs I have had in my life:

2. Four movies I could watch over and over:

3. Four places I have lived:

4. Four TV shows I love to watch:

5. Four places I have been on vacation:

6. Four websites I visit daily:

7. Four of my favorite foods:

8. Four places I would rather be right now:

9. Four people who have made a difference in my life:

10. Four things I'd like to learn to do:

fill in the blank

1. If I hadn't become a _____, I might have_____.

2. If I hadn't_____, I might never have met_____.

3. If I hadn't learned to_____, I would never have got to_____.

4. My_____is my most prized possession.

5. My ability to_____is one of my greatest skills.

6. If asked, my family will say my greatest accomplishment is_____.

7. I'm sorry that I will never see_____again.

8. Going to_____taught me that_____.

9. My life would be easier if I got my_____fixed.

10. I would be happier if I never saw another _____again.

it's a kid's world

1. If you could have one superpower what would it be?

2. What chore did you do last?

3. What was the last movie you saw at a theater?

4. What is your favorite song?

5. Do you get an allowance? How much?

6. How do you get to school?

7. What do you like to eat for lunch?

8. What's the nicest thing you've done lately for someone in your family?

9. What makes you mad?

10. Where would you like to go on vacation next year?

quiz: through the eyes of a child

If you want the scoop on the "real" you, interview your kids. They'd be happy to tell you what they really think.

1- What's the funniest thing I do?
   CAMBREE: TELL JOKES
   KADY: GIGGLE
   MARINNE: ROLL YOUR EYES AT ME.

2- What's my favorite TV show?
   CAMBREE: I DON'T KNOW
   KADY: THE PUPPY SHOW WITH THE WINNERS
   MARINNE: DESIGNER SHOWS

3- How tall am I?
   CAMBREE: THIS TALL (SHOWN WITH ARMS STRETCHED)
   KADY: BIG
   MARINNE: AROUND 6 FEET

4- What's my favorite thing to do?
   CAMBREE: SCRAPBOOK
   KADY: SCRAPBOOK
   MARINNE: SCRAPBOOK

5- What makes me sad?
   CAMBREE: WHEN I DIDN'T CLEAN MY ROOM
   KADY: SLIPPING ON ICE
   MARINNE: WHEN WE KEEP GETTING OUT OF BED BUT SHOULD BE SLEEPING

6- What makes me laugh?
   CAMBREE: JOKES I TELL
   KADY: JOKES
   MARINNE: WHEN I TICKLE YOU

7- How much time do I spend on the phone?
   CAMBREE: TWICE A DAY
   KADY: 5 MINUTES
   MARINNE: SOMETIMES A LOT

8- Am I a better driver than Dad?
   CAMBREE: YES
   KADY: YEP!
   MARINNE: KINDA

9- What do I do when you're at school each day?
   CAMBREE: (SHE DOESN'T GO TO SCHOOL YET)
   KADY: (SHE DOESN'T GO TO SCHOOL YET)
   MARINNE: SCRAPBOOK

10- What should I be famous for?
    CAMBREE: WORKING ON THE COMPUTER
    KADY: THE SCRAPBOOKING
    MARINNE: CRAZINESS

My Girls Questions About **me**

1- What's the funniest thing I do?
   I ACTUALLY DON'T THINK I'M VERY FUNNY.
   SOMETIMES I TELL CORNY JOKES

2- What's my favorite TV show?
   LOVE MONEY, AMAZING RACE AND ANY
   TYPE OF DESIGN SHOWS LIKE GET COLOR
   AND DIVINE DESIGN

3- How tall am I?
   5 FEET 10 INCHES

4- What's my favorite thing to do?
   THE GIRLS WERE PARTLY RIGHT, SCRAPBOOK
   HOWEVER, I REALLY LOVE TO BE WITH KENT.

5- What makes me sad?
   WHEN OTHER PEOPLE ARE SAD/SEEING MY
   CHILDREN OR OTHER CHILDREN HURT

6- What makes me laugh?
   KENT

7- How much time do I spend on the phone?
   NOT MUCH. I REALLY DON'T LIKE TALKING ON THE PHONE
   MY PHONE CALLS ARE USUALLY SHORT AND TO THE POINT

8- Am I a better driver than Dad?
   WE ARE EQUAL IN THE DRIVING DEPARTMENT

9- What do I do when you're at school each day?
   I DO MOM STUFF. HOUSEWORK, GROCERY SHOP, PAY BILLS
   AND SOMETIMES I SCRAPBOOK TOO

10- What should I be famous for?
    UMMM, MY CARDSTOCK COLLECTING ABILITIES

me

Amy Williams | Old Town, ME

After all three of her daughters answered our quiz questions, Amy decided to set the record straight by providing her version of the answers behind a clever, hinged journaling flap.

materials patterned paper, letter rub-ons (Karen Foster) • chipboard letters (Making Memories) • ribbon (Offray) • brad (Bazzill Basics) • hinges • Coluzzle cutting template (Provo Craft) • CK Stenography and CK Solid fonts • *12 x 12 page*

through the eyes of a child

1. What's the funniest thing I do?
2. What's my favorite TV show?
3. How tall am I?
4. What's my favorite thing to do?
5. What makes me sad?
6. What makes me laugh?
7. How much time do I spend on the phone?
8. Am I a better driver than Dad?
9. What do I do when you're at school each day?
10. What should I be famous for?

weird & wacky

1. What food would you like to eat every day, if your mom would let you?
2. What's your favorite joke?
3. If you could choose a different name, what would it be?
4. What would you like on your next birthday cake?
5. What's the first thing you show friends when they visit your house?
6. What's the scariest thing you've ever done?
7. Is your room messy or clean?
8. If you could only eat at one restaurant for the rest of your life, which one would you choose?
9. If you had a million dollars, what would you buy first?
10. If your parents let you have any pet you wanted, what would it be?

your favorite things

1. What's your favorite cereal?
2. What's your favorite TV show?
3. What do you like best about your pet?
4. What vegetables do you like best?
5. What toy would you never give away?
6. What do you take to bed at night?
7. What's your favorite game?
8. What's your favorite book?
9. What is your favorite candy bar?
10. What's the last thing of yours that mom displayed on the fridge?

getting to know you

1. What's your nickname and how did you get it?
2. What size shoes do you wear?
3. What's the best age to be and why?
4. How many kids do you want when you grow up?
5. Tell me about your best Halloween costume ever.
6. What thing do you and your brothers and/or sisters always fight about?
7. Who's your best friend?
8. What's under your bed?
9. What's your favorite holiday and why?
10. What's the best present you ever got?

quiz: childhood stories

Use these questions to journal what Mom, Dad, Grandma or Grandpa remember of their early family life. Remember you can use our **Childhood Stories** questions for your personal history too.

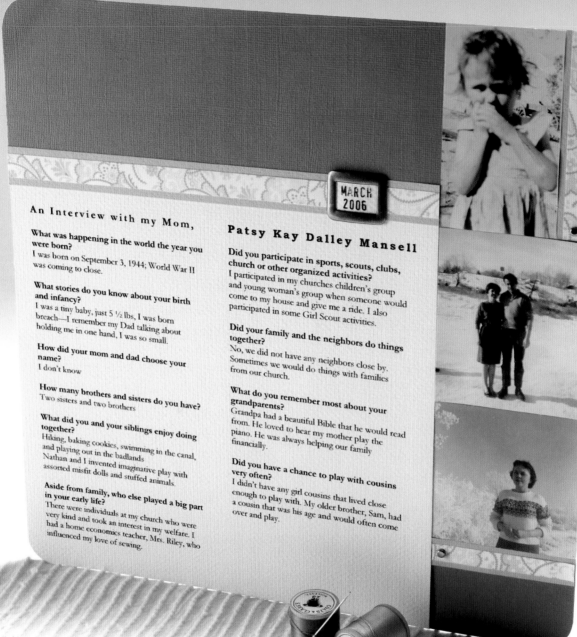

An Interview with my Mom, Patsy Kay Dalley Mansell

MARCH 2006

What was happening in the world the year you were born?
I was born on September 3, 1944; World War II was coming to close.

What stories do you know about your birth and infancy?
I was a tiny baby, just 5 ½ lbs, I was born breach—I remember my Dad talking about holding me in one hand, I was so small.

How did your mom and dad choose your name?
I don't know

How many brothers and sisters do you have?
Two sisters and two brothers

What did you and your siblings enjoy doing together?
Hiking, baking cookies, swimming in the canal, and playing out in the badlands Nathan and I invented imaginative play with assorted misfit dolls and stuffed animals.

Aside from family, who else played a big part in your early life?
There were individuals at my church who were very kind and took an interest in my welfare. I had a home economics teacher, Mrs. Riley, who influenced my love of sewing.

Did you participate in sports, scouts, clubs, church or other organized activities?
I participated in my churches children's group and young woman's group when someone would come to my house and give me a ride. I also participated in some Girl Scout activities.

Did your family and the neighbors do things together?
No, we did not have any neighbors close by. Sometimes we would do things with families from our church.

What do you remember most about your grandparents?
Grandpa had a beautiful Bible that he would read from. He loved to hear my mother play the piano. He was always helping our family financially.

Did you have a chance to play with cousins very often?
I didn't have any girl cousins that lived close enough to play with. My older brother, Sam, had a cousin that was his age and would often come over and play.

bits and pieces
Wendy Smedley | Centerville, UT

Would Wendy's children ever have known that their Grandma was a 5½-pound baby, or that she got her love of sewing from her home economics teacher, Mrs. Riley? Not if Wendy hadn't given her mother our **Childhood Stories** quiz.

materials patterned paper (Anna Griffin) • metal accents (Nunn Designs) • Book Antiqua font • *12 x 12 page*

childhood stories

1. What was happening in the world the year you were born?
2. What stories do you know about your birth and infancy?
3. How did your mom and dad choose your name?
4. How many brothers and sisters do you have?
5. What did you and your siblings enjoy doing together?
6. Aside from family, who else played a big part in your early life?
7. Did you participate in sports, scouts, clubs, church or other organized activities?
8. Did your family and the neighbors do things together?
9. What do you remember most about your grandparents?
10. Did you have a chance to play with cousins very often?

home & neighborhood

1. Where did you live growing up?
2. What did you like about growing up there?
3. What didn't you like?
4. How did growing up there shape you?
5. How old was your house, what was unique about it?
6. What did you love most about your home or hometown?
7. Did your family do things with neighbor families?
8. What places were within walking distance?
9. Where was your favorite place to go in your hometown?
10. What did the kids in your neighborhood do for fun?

your school years

1. What was the name of your elementary school, and what did it look like?
2. Who was your favorite schoolteacher?
3. What school subjects did you like the best?
4. What did you keep in your desk?
5. How did you get to school each day?
6. What games did you and your friends play at recess?
7. Did you eat school lunch or bring food from home?
8. Who was your best friend in elementary school?
9. Did you ever go back and visit the school?
10. What did you do during your summer vacations?

about your family

1. Who's the smartest person in your family?
2. What is your dad really good at?
3. What can you do better than dad?
4. How are you like mom?
5. How are you different from mom?
6. How old is mom?
7. How tall is dad?
8. What one thing is mom always saying to you?
9. What did you and dad do together that you'll always remember?
10. How do you know that mom and dad love you?

quiz: home & neighborhood

Our early lives at home shape who and what we become. Find out about your family's childhood homes and neighbors. Photos of hometowns, neighborhoods and local businesses may help with these questions.

Where did you live growing up?

134 Lexington Road

What did you like about growing up there?

Everyone knew each other.

What didn't you like? It was in the middle of nowhere! The closest shopping mall was a good thirty minutes away. Can you imagine?!

How did growing up there shape you?

It gave me a good sense of community and family values.

How old was your house and what was unique about it? It was built in 1976. It had five bedrooms, which was unique back then. With nine kids in the family, we needed at least five bedrooms!

What did you love most about your home or hometown? I loved that our house was nestled in a good neighborhood.

Did your family do things with neighbor families? There was always a summer block party each year in the cul-de-sac. So much fun.

What places were within walking distance? "Town" was about two and a half miles away. I'm not sure if that would be considered walking distance, but we certainly made the trek on the days we were bored!

Where was your favorite place to go in your hometown? Carvel for vanilla soft serve with rainbow sprinkles and the 5&10 for candy.

What did the kids in your neighborhood do for fun? In the winter we would go sledding for hours and hours. Any other time of the year, we would clock some serious mileage on our bikes.

take me home

Beth Proudfoot | Clinton, NJ

Beth journaled her own childhood with our **Home & Neighborhood** quiz. It was fun for her to stop and take time to remember her childhood, and it helped her better understand the values she holds dear today.

materials chipboard letters (Heidi Swapp) • chipboard flower (Memories Complete) • Times New Roman font • 8½ x 11 page

make a page based on our just for kids quiz

Ask the little ones in your life a handful of the questions below. Even though some of the answers will change from day to day (your daughter's best friend of the moment), others will probably stay the same for years (her fear of spiders). Either way, it will be fun to capture today's attitudes and preferences on a layout. Teresa quizzed both of her daughters at the same time, recording what they'd do with a million dollars,* what household rules they'd like to ditch, who they look the most like, and what they wish they'd been named.

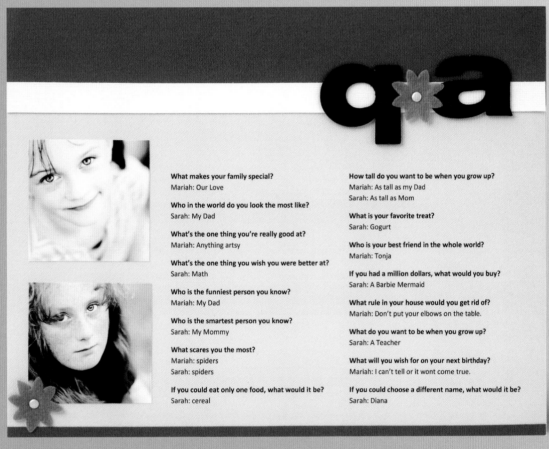

One thing's for sure, it would buy a lot of Barbie dolls.

What makes your family special?
Mariah: Our Love

Who in the world do you look the most like?
Sarah: My Dad

What's the one thing you're really good at?
Mariah: Anything artsy

What's the one thing you wish you were better at?
Sarah: Math

Who is the funniest person you know?
Mariah: My Dad

Who is the smartest person you know?
Sarah: My Mommy

What scares you the most?
Mariah: spiders
Sarah: spiders

If you could eat only one food, what would it be?
Sarah: cereal

How tall do you want to be when you grow up?
Mariah: As tall as my Dad
Sarah: As tall as Mom

What is your favorite treat?
Sarah: Gogurt

Who is your best friend in the whole world?
Mariah: Tonja

If you had a million dollars, what would you buy?
Sarah: A Barbie Mermaid

What rule in your house would you get rid of?
Mariah: Don't put your elbows on the table.

What do you want to be when you grow up?
Sarah: A Teacher

What will you wish for on your next birthday?
Mariah: I can't tell or it wont come true.

If you could choose a different name, what would it be?
Sarah: Diana

materials chipboard letters (Making Memories) • felt flowers (American Crafts) • brads (Creative Impressions) • acrylic paint • Calibri font • *11 x 8½ page by Teresa Olier, Sanford, NC*

just for kids quiz

1. What makes your family special?
2. Who in the world do you look the most like?
3. What's one thing you're really good at?
4. What's one thing you wish you were better at?
5. Who is the smartest person you know?
6. Who is the funniest person you know?
7. Who is your best friend in the whole world?
8. What will you wish for on your next birthday?
9. What's your favorite treat?
10. What's your favorite game to play?
11. What scares you the most?
12. What's the best present you've ever received?
13. How tall do you want to be when you grow up?
14. What job do you want to have when you grow up?
15. When will you be a grown-up?
16. If you could choose a different name, what would it be?
17. What rule in your house would you get rid of if you could?
18. If you had a million dollars, what would you buy first?
19. If you were a teacher, what subject would you teach?
20. If you could eat only one food for the rest of your life, what would it be?

make a page based on our
best & worst quiz

Follow Cathy's lead to share ten interesting facts about your life (and ten photos!) all on one layout. Read through the quiz questions below, and start freewriting your answers right on this magazine page, in your journal, or in a word-processing document. A single question might spark a page idea, or maybe you'll be inspired to answer all 20 questions on a layout. (If you manage that, we want to hear about it!

materials patterned paper (Autumn Leaves) • circle stamp (Catslife Press) • photo corners (Heidi Swapp) • Avenir font • *12 x 12 page by Cathy Zielske, St. Paul, MN*

best & worst quiz

1. My favorite smell of all time:

2. The worst smell ever:

3. My best physical feature:

4. My worst physical feature:

5. My finest accomplishment:

6. The worst trial I've overcome:

7. My best subject in school:

8. My worst subject in school:

9. The best place I've ever lived:

10. The worst place I've ever lived:

11. My most endearing personality trait:

12. My most annoying personality trait:

13. A time I felt invincible:

14. The closest I've come to death:

15. The best meal of my life:

16. The grossest thing I've ever eaten:

17. The season I look forward to most:

18. A month or season that I dread:

19. My favorite room in the house:

20. My least favorite room in the house:

TRACY WHITE'S

ideas for journaling about everyday life

ENTERTAINMENT

- What do you do for fun on the weekends?
- What is your family's favorite activity to enjoy together?
- Do you watch reality TV shows? Why or why not?
- What are your children's favorite cartoons?

- What TV shows do you enjoy the most?
- Why is scrapbooking important to you?
- How many hours a week do you spend scrapbooking?
- List your favorite scrapbooking supplies.

- How has your scrapbooking style changed over the years?
- Do you prefer to scrap-book alone or with a group of friends?
- Ever attended a scrapbook convention? Tell about your experience.

COMMUNICATION

- How do you communicate with your friends and family members?
- How many hours do you spend talking on the phone a week?
- How much was your cell phone bill last month? How many minutes do you typically use in a month?

- What's your "e-mail style"? Do you write short notes full of abbreviations or several paragraphs of information?
- Do you ever send items through "snail mail"?
- Do you have a central message board in your home? Do you write notes on scratch paper or on a bulletin board?

MONEY

- What does your financial picture look like right now?
- How has your financial picture changed over the past year?
- If you could change anything about your current financial situation, what would it be?
- Do you and your significant other agree about how to spend money?
- When you make a purchase, what do you use: Cash? Check? Debit card? Credit card?
- Do your children earn an allowance for doing their chores?
- How much cash is in your pocket today?
- How many times a month do you pay your bills?
- Do you pay your bills online or by check?
- Do you balance your checking account to the penny?
- What do you think about financial management software?

FASHION

- How do you dress for work?
- How do you dress for a casual weekend?
- Talk about an outfit that always gets you compliments.
- Share a story about your most comfortable outfit.
- Tell about your pajamas.
- Where do you like to shop for your clothes?

- What store represents your style?
- How many pairs of shoes are in your closet?
- Which is your favorite pair of shoes?
- Which shoes do you never wear? Why?
- Do you have an outfit hanging in your closet that you've never worn? Tell about it.

- Do you live in an apartment, a duplex, a house?

- Tell about the day you saw your home for the first time.

- Talk about the day you moved into your home.

- How do you make your living space into a "home"?

- How do you interpret popular quotes such as, "There's no place like home" and "Home is where the heart is"?

- What do you like best about your home?

- List changes you'd like to make to your home.

- Talk about a renovation or decorating project you undertook.

- Do you have a place for everything in your home?

- How do you keep your home clean?

- Where does your family like to gather in your home?

- How did you decide what colors to use in your home?

- What life events have you experienced within the walls of your current home?

- Consider making a timeline that shows different places you've lived.

- What memories do you have of your childhood home?

- Do you have a dream house? Describe it, inside and out.

- What treasures do you display inside your home? (A book collection? A music box collection?)

- Open a kitchen cupboard and look inside. What do the contents (and how they're arranged) say about the structure of your life today?

The 5 Senses

Here's a snapshot of my world as I write: My cat's sleeping next to me. Her little chest peacefully rises and falls—she's oblivious to the dozens of birds chirping in the big, old pine tree in my backyard—and her presence makes me feel calm. I can smell the faint acrid smell of Tilex clinging to the air—you see, I scrubbed my bathroom early this morning. (Gosh, there's nothing nicer than a clean house!) It's a glorious spring day and there's a slight breeze pushing the flag across the street. My mom just called to wish me luck on my upcoming business trip. It was good to hear from her and know that someone was thinking of me—I've been feeling a little lonely today.

Do I have a photo of this moment in my life? No, but it's a snapshot of my life nonetheless. If you don't know what to say on your next journaling entry, consider writing a snapshot of your life at that moment.

Write down the small sensory details of your environment. What's on your mind? How do you feel at this moment? What are the little details that make you feel comfortable or uncomfortable? (The chair I'm sitting on is pretty hard!)

Consider writing a snapshot of real life, of your life—it shares what you choose to surround yourself with and the things you value.

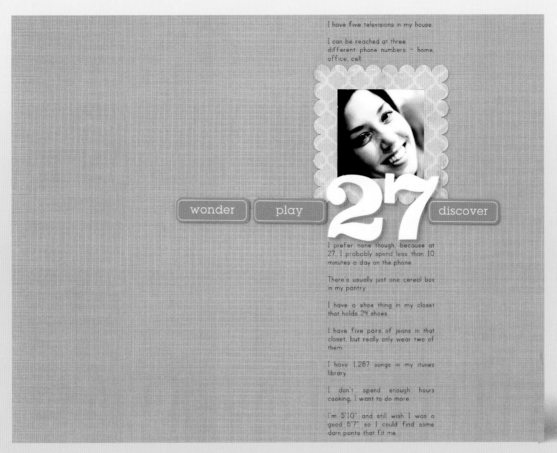

I have five televisions in my house.

I can be reached at three different phone numbers – home, office, cell.

wonder   play   27   discover

I prefer none though, because at 27, I probably spend less than 10 minutes a day on the phone.

There's usually just one cereal box in my pantry.

I have a shoe thing in my closet that holds 24 shoes.

I have five pairs of jeans in that closet, but really only wear two of them.

I have 1,287 songs in my itunes library.

I don't spend enough hours cooking, I want to do more.

I'm 5'10" and still wish I was a good 5'7" so I could find some darn pants that fit me.

materials foam number stickers (American Crafts) • word accents (Making Memories) • die-cut frame (Daisy D's) • Print Clearly font • 11 x 8½ page by Laura Kurz, Baltimore, MD

make a page based on our
by the numbers: NOW quiz

With 1,287 songs in her iTunes library, five televisions, and three phones, it's a wonder Laura has a moment's peace and quiet to complete a scrapbook page. But she manages to create very restful, minimalist layouts amidst all the chaos. This one shares ten fun facts about her life at age 27. You count only nine? The last one counts as two. Try our By the Numbers: Now Quiz, and find out how your numbers stack up.

by the numbers: NOW quiz

1. Number of things in my junk drawer:
2. Number of televisions in my home:
3. Number of telephone numbers I can be reached at:
4. Number of cereal boxes in my cupboard:
5. Number of hours per week I spend scrapbooking:
6. Number of hours per week I spend shopping:
7. Number of hours per week I spend cooking:
8. Number of hours per week I spend talking on the phone:
9. Number of pairs of shoes in my closet:
10. Number of pairs of jeans in my closet:
11. Number of CDs/books/DVDs I own (pick one):
12. Number of matching table settings I own:
13. Number of board games in my house:
14. Number of things stuck to my refrigerator:
15. Number of purses or handbags I own:
16. Number of pounds I weigh:
17. Number of pounds I wish I weighed (realistically):
18. Number of inches tall I am:
19. Number of inches tall I wish I were:
20. Amount of money I'd need to retire today:

Use a paper clip, a staple, and a sticky note on a layout, and write your journaling based on our By the Numbers: Now Quiz. Can you find all the elements of this combination prompt on Donna's layout? Okay, we'll help. Her five photos are attached with staples, as are the two yellow paper strips (cut from a sticky note). The paper clip (a huge one!) accents her title. For her journaling, Donna answered ten of her favorite questions from the quiz. Ten pairs of jeans, 57 things stuck to the fridge, 1 hour a week spent cooking—little numbers reveal a lot.

materials chipboard letters (American Crafts) • letter stickers (Heidi Swapp) • date stamp • notebook paper • sticky note • jumbo paper clip • staples • Courier New font • *12 x 12 page by Donna Downey, Huntersville, NC*

make a page based on our
by the numbers: THEN quiz

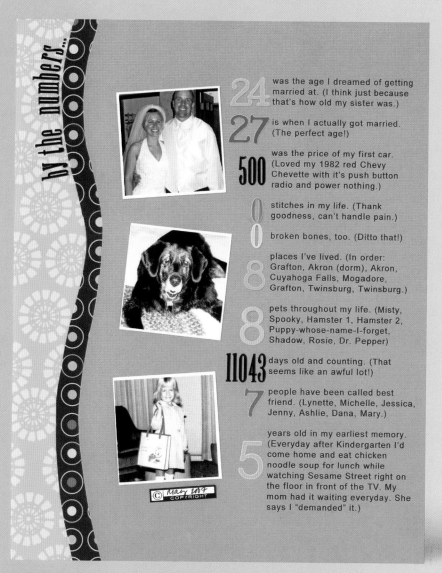

by the numbers...

24 was the age I dreamed of getting married at. (I think just because that's how old my sister was.)

27 is when I actually got married. (The perfect age!)

500 was the price of my first car. (Loved my 1982 red Chevy Chevette with it's push button radio and power nothing.)

0 stitches in my life. (Thank goodness, can't handle pain.)

0 broken bones, too. (Ditto that!)

8 places I've lived. (In order: Grafton, Akron (dorm), Akron, Cuyahoga Falls, Mogadore, Grafton, Twinsburg, Twinsburg.)

8 pets throughout my life. (Misty, Spooky, Hamster 1, Hamster 2, Puppy-whose-name-I-forget, Shadow, Rosie, Dr. Pepper)

11043 days old and counting. (That seems like an awful lot!)

7 people have been called best friend. (Lynette, Michelle, Jessica, Jenny, Ashlie, Dana, Mary.)

5 years old in my earliest memory. (Everyday after Kindergarten I'd come home and eat chicken noodle soup for lunch while watching Sesame Street right on the floor in front of the TV. My mom had it waiting everyday. She says I "demanded" it.)

Erin chose ten questions from our By the Numbers: Then Quiz and turned them into a charming layout that offers a glimpse into her life— past and present. It's probably the only way she'd ever have recorded these mundane but interesting facts about herself—like her earliest memory, the price of her first car, or the age she dreamed of getting married at.

&

To meet another scrapbooker who has never had stitches or broken a single bone (and who also can't handle pain), flip to page 143.

materials patterned paper (Autumn Leaves) • letter and number stickers (Doodlebug Design, Li'l Davis Designs, Making Memories, Scrapworks) • label sticker (7gypsies) • Arial font • 8½ x 11 page by Erin Sweeney, Twinsburg, OH

by the numbers: THEN quiz

1. Number of days old I am right now:
2. The age I was when I first walked:
3. The age I was in my earliest memory:
4. The age I was when I was first kissed:
5. The age I was when I moved out of my parents' house:
6. The age I was when I finally felt like an adult:
7. The age I dreamed of getting married at:
8. The age I actually got married at:
9. The age I'd go back to if I could:
10. The price of my first car:

11. The price of my first home:
12. Number of vehicles I've owned in my lifetime:
13. How much I made hourly at my first job:
14. Number of stitches I've had in my life:
15. Number of bones I've broken:
16. Number of countries I've visited:
17. Number of places I've lived:
18. Number of pets I've owned:
19. Number of ex-boyfriends in my past:
20. Number of people I've called my "best friend":

Tracy White's
ideas for journaling about relationships

DATING

- Do you remember your first date? What was it like?

- How old were you when you started dating?

- Think back: What's the best date you ever had?

- What qualities are most important to you in a date?

- What's your description of the ideal date?

- What's the sweetest thing a date ever did for you?

- What's the craziest date you ever had?

- Share a story about a romantic date. What were the components?

- Ever had a blind date? Was it fun? Awkward? Great? Horrible?

- What have you learned from different people you've dated?

- Was there someone who "slipped" away?

- Do you have any dating regrets?

- Talk about a time you broke up with someone and felt happy about it.

- Talk about a time you broke up with someone and felt miserable about it.

- Do you miss anyone you used to date? Why?

- Have any former dating relationships turned into strong friendships? Tell more.

- What lines have you heard from potential dates?

- Think about a creative way someone asked you out on a date.

- Talk about a time you had a crush on a date.

- Share a story about a time when you fell in love. How did you know it was real?

FAMILY

- How does your family spend quality time together?

- How do you handle disagreements between you and your significant other?

- How do you handle fighting between your children?

- Tell about a time when your family had "the best time ever."

- Take a snapshot in time and describe a moment

- when your children were in harmony.

- Talk about a time when your family had a conflict. How was it resolved?

- How do you feel when you're away from your family on a business trip or vacation?

- How do you show your family you love them?

- How does your family show you that they love you?

- When you're upset, how does your family comfort you?

- What kind of family rules do you have?

- Do you have a big extended family? How do you divide your time among various family members?

- Do your children spend time with their cousins and aunts and uncles?

MARRIAGE

- How did you know you were going to marry your spouse?

- Share your engagement story.

- What's the story behind your engagement ring and wedding band?

- How did you choose your wedding date?

- How long were you engaged?

- What did you learn about your spouse during your engagement?

- How did you choose where to be married?

- Talk about planning your wedding.

- What bridal magazines and books did you read as you planned your wedding?

- Where did you spend your honeymoon?

- Record the joys and challenges of being married (try a month-by-month or year-by-year perspective).

- As a married couple, how has your relationship changed?

- How have you divided up financial and home-based responsibilities?

- Do you have a "mission statement" as a couple?

- Is marriage exactly the way you thought it would be?

- What are the best things about your marriage?

- What do you love the most about your spouse?

- How did you celebrate your first anniversary? Your third? Your twenty-fifth?

- What traditions have you established as a married couple?

- How do you keep your marriage happy?

- Did you ever regret getting married?

- How do you work out problems in your marriage?

- Talk about a gift you've received as a couple. How does it symbolize your marriage?

PARENTING

- What are your parenting philosophies?

- Talk about your relationship with your parents. How has it changed from the time when you were a young child?

- What books and magazines have influenced the way you parent your children?

- Your child throws a temper tantrum at the grocery store. How do you handle it?

- List the blessings you've found in being a parent.

- List the challenges you've found in being a parent.

- How did your parents raise you?

- Do you raise your children with the same rules and philosophies as your parents used?

- Talk about a time your child was sick. How did you care for her?

PETS

- Did you choose your pet, or did your pet choose you?

- How do you interact with your pet?

- How does your pet interact with you?

- How does your pet make your life that much happier?

- List the ways you care for your pet.

BREAKING UP

- Ending a relationship is never easy, but you may find it therapeutic to write about how your relationship ended.

- What lessons have you learned from a break-up or divorce?

- It's not always easy to scrapbook the hard times. Give yourself time to process the information and then write about it when you feel the time is right.

- Talk about a "good" break-up, where you left a romantic relationship as friends.

- Who consoled you when you broke up?

- How did you get through each day as you worked your way through a break-up?

- Who was there for you when you needed someone to talk to about your former partner?

- What was the first thing you did when you reached your destination?

- Make a checklist of the places you visited while on your trip.

- What was your favorite place to visit?

- What was your least favorite place to visit?

- Did the places you visited meet up with your expectations?

- How did each member of your family react to the different places you visited?

- Tell about your lodging. Was it what you expected?

- Was your destination desolate or crowded with people?

- How did you feel the first time you saw the beach or mountains?

- Talk about a memory of playing in the sand and building a sand castle.

- Share a memory of boating, sailing or jet-skiing.

- Close your eyes. Remember the sights, the smells and the sounds of being on vacation. Journal the memories in your scrapbook.

- What's the most spectacular view you've ever seen?

- Describe a colorful sunset.

- What was the most beautiful thing you saw while on your vacation?

- Talk about a picnic you had on vacation.

- Tell about a time when you gathered with family around a campfire.

- Share a memory associated with setting up a campsite.

- Have you ever encountered any wild animals while camping? What did you do?

- Ever slept in a tent? What was the experience like for you?

- What foods do you like to cook on a camp stove or over a fire?

- What kind of special meals did you enjoy while on vacation?

- Take a photograph of your destination in the morning, at noon and in the evening. Journal about how your perspective changes with the day.

- What was the weather like while on your vacation? How did it influence your enjoyment of your vacation?

- Do you enjoy tours or prefer setting out on your own?

- Talk about a tour you took while on vacation.

- Share a story about your tour guide and/or other people on your tour.

- Talk about how your children behaved on a tour.

- Are there any legends or myths associated with your destination?

- Did you go to an amusement park? Ask everyone in your family to list their favorite rides.

Know Your Audience

Here's how I explain my job when I meet people at a scrapbook convention:
"I have the coolest job in the world, I'm the editor of CK."

But here's how I explain my job to people I meet in the business world: "I'm the editor of a magazine called *Creating Keepsakes.* We focus on creatively preserving memories in scrapbooks."

Isn't it funny how we phrase things differently depending on who we're talking to? Notice in the above example, how my enthusiasm and personal connection changed when I was talking to someone who didn't know what scrapbooking was.

FREEDOM **by Patricia Anderson > Supplies** *Patterned papers:* Rusty Pickle (blue) and 7gypsies (script); *Tag:* Rusty Pickle; *Letter stamps and brads:* Making Memories; *Acrylic paint:* Plaid Enterprises; *T-pin:* EK Success; *Computer font:* CK Chemistry, "Fresh Fonts" CD, *Creating Keepsakes; Other:* Twill and ribbon.

I don't know about you, but sometimes when I meet new people, I get a little shy, and sometimes I don't know what to say. But the more I get to know them, the easier it is to talk about things. The same is true with writing. If we don't know who we're writing to, sometimes we use stilted words—sometimes we fail to show our enthusiasm and connection.

Who are you writing to in your scrapbooks? Think about it. Are you writing to your child at his or her present age? To your child sometime in the future? To a stranger? To yourself? To a friend? The next time you journal, take a moment to think about who you're writing to. It's a sure way to feel more comfortable and help you write more easily.

Tracy White's

ideas for journaling on heritage pages

HERITAGE REFLECTIONS

My ancestors were both Swiss and English. The Swiss part of me feels so connected with my mom and grandfather. I have such good memories of my grandfather, a man who I remember as being sweet, gentle and tender-hearted. When I think about my heritage, I remember the traditions and values that have been passed down through my family. How about you?

- What are your overall feelings about your family's heritage?

- How would you describe your heritage?

- How was your heritage reflected in the way you were raised?

- What symbols characterize your heritage?

- Do you feel like you are a part of your heritage?

- How do you connect with your heritage?

- What do you remember about your grandparents' house?

- What scents are evocative of time spent with your grandparents?

- Do you feel as if you are part of your family tree? Why or why not?

- What values are important to your family?

- Identify the values that have been handed down from generation to generation in your family.

- What family heirlooms have been passed through generations in your family?

- If you could have one memento of a favorite grandmother or grandfather, what would it be? What's the significance?

- Why is it important to you to scrapbook heritage photographs?

- What have you learned about yourself as you've scrapbooked heritage photographs?

- What questions have you asked and answered while scrapbooking heritage photographs? What mysteries still intrigue you?

- Which ancestors do you feel you've bonded with (even if you've never met them)?

- If you could go back in time, which ancestors would

you like to join for dinner? Why?

- As you do your heritage research, keep track of your research and phone calls. This is documentation you can use as journaling information on your pages.

- Do you consider any family members to be heroes? Why?

- What stories are passed down through your family time and time again? Why do you think those particular stories have become part of your family folklore?

- Do you have any family mysteries?

- Tell about the cemetery where your family members are buried.

- Look for items such as high chairs that may have been passed down through several generations. Journal about how the items have been used by different family members.

- How are family members posed in your pictures? What do the poses suggest about their relationships? What do the poses suggest about how society today has changed?

- Ask three generations of family members to answer the same question, such as: "What did you like to do after school?" Or "Who was your best friend in high school?"

- Look for "old-fashioned" items that are no longer in popular use (record players, typewriters). Write about the items, how they were used and how they've been replaced.

- Imagine how your ancestors would react to today's current technology.

- Create a photo-journalism collage that combines pictures and words of yesterday and today.

- What types of toys are the children playing with in heritage photographs? Contrast that to what's popular now.

- From your photographs, can you get an idea of what life was like during the time period of your ancestors? Piece together a day-to-day schedule of the lives they lived. How is this different from your life today?

- Compare hairstyles in old photographs to current looks today.

- Document the homes and cities where your parents lived growing up. Consider including blueprints or home plans if available.

- Interview your parents and grandparents on significant anniversaries (25th, 50th) and ask them to recall their hopes and dreams on their wedding day. Did their lives go as planned?

HERITAGE PHOTOGRAPH REFLECTIONS

We don't always have a lot of information about the people in our photographs. Sometimes we're lucky just to have a name and a date. Yet, you can still journal about heritage photographs. Here are several jumpstarts to help:

- What captivates you about a certain photograph?

- Do you have a photograph taken in your current hometown? How have things changed since the year the picture was taken (farmland, new buildings and so on).

- Think about the subjects of the photograph. How do you think they felt the day the picture was taken?

- Have you ever met the person in the picture? How about one of her children?

- What personality traits would you associate with this person based on the photograph?

- Show photographs to other family members. Ask for their recollections.

- Do you know where the photograph was taken? Consider adding information about the location.

- Don't be afraid to write things such as, "I'm not sure who this person is, but she looks like my grandmother."

- Look for details on outfits. Write about what it was like to live in an era of a certain kind of dress.

- What kind of expression is the subject of your photograph wearing? What do you think it was like to be photographed during a time when people didn't smile for the camera?

- Look for historical details in photographs, such as 48 stars on a flag or older models of cars that still exist today.

Grandparents

Questions by Lisa Bearnson

- Tell me about a challenge you had in your life and how you made it through.
- When did your family get a TV set? What were some of your favorite shows?
- What were some of the most fun or wild things that you and your friends did? Did you have a curfew?
- Looking back, what are the things people tend to make a big deal about but aren't really that important after all?

Questions by Emily Magleby

- What is your favorite memory of Mom or Dad when she or he was little?
- Tell me about when you fell in love with Grandma or Grandpa.
- Which appliance or electronic device were you most excited about getting?
- If you could live your life over, what would you do differently?

Questions by Fred Brewer

- What was your greatest accomplishment before age 18?
- What did you feel when you saw your first child for the first time?
- What's the biggest difference between your era growing up and my generation that you still don't understand?

Parents

Questions by Jessica Sprague

- As you look back, do you have any favorite years? Is there a time in your life that you'd like to live over again?
- Are there any photos of you as a child? As a teenager? Where are they stored?
- Are there any family heirlooms that have been passed from one generation to another?
- What traditions (holidays, religious ceremonies, etc.) did you have in your home while growing up?
- What historical events stick out in your mind that you've lived through?
- What do you love most about your life right now?

Questions by Becky Higgins

- When you were dating and first married, what kind of long-term goals did you have as a couple, and which of those goals have been met?
- During the child-rearing years, what were some of the "simplest pleasures" that helped both of you deal best with such a busy life?
- As a child, what did you do with your spare time? What were your favorite pastimes?
- In your teenage years, do you remember some of the trends (such as clothing) that you followed?
- After all these years of marriage, what are some of your favorite bits of advice for a happy marriage?

Questions by Jennifer McGuire

- What were your favorite family vacations as a child?
- What do you remember about the day I was born?
- What do you remember about your wedding day?
- What are your favorite photos from your childhood?
- What characteristics about me remind you of you when you were younger? How are we similar?

Aunts/Uncles

Questions by Emily Falconbridge

- What naughty thing did my mother or father do as a child?
- Do you see any similarities between me as a child and my parent as a child?
- What makes you the best aunt or uncle ever?

Questions by Ingunn Markiewicz

- What were my parents like when they were young and dating?
- Did you have any special family traditions while you were growing up?
- What was it like growing up as the youngest/middle/oldest child in your family?
- What was life like for a young person in the '50s, '60s and '70s?

Questions by Tiffany Tillman

- What was your impression of my father or mother as a child?
- What were your fondest memories of your parents?
- What did you believe you would do as an adult?

Siblings

Questions by Maggie Holmes

- What do you know now that you wish you would have known years ago?
- What is the greatest lesson you learned from Mom and Dad?
- In what ways are you the same as Mom or Dad?
- What do you miss from our childhood days?

Questions by Jill Hornby

- What is one of your best memories growing up?
- What did you love most about our hometown?
- What are three predictions you have for the next year? (These can be personal, family, political . . . anything.)

Questions by C.D. Muckosky

- Which traditions from your youth are you trying to carry on for your own family?
- Who has had a big impact on the way that you live your life and why?
- What makes you, you?

Nieces/Nephews

Questions by Amanda Probst

- What are your favorite stories about your grandparents?
- What were your favorite treats that your grandparents gave (or sneaked to) you?
- What kinds of games or other pastimes do you enjoy with your cousins?
- Do you like your "position" in the family order? What are the benefits and drawbacks?

Questions by Allison Davis

- What qualities do you like most about your parents?
- Where do you see yourself in 10 years?
- What was the best or worst job you ever had?

Questions by Kelly Purkey

- What is your favorite thing to do after school?
- Who is your best friend and why do you like him or her?
- What is your favorite thing about your mom and dad?
- What was your favorite outfit to wear when you were young?

quiz: they're the greatest

Family members play different roles in your life. Use our They're the Greatest quiz to scrapbook which family member you lean on in times of trouble, which one makes you laugh and which one you are most like.

Surrounded by Family

1. If you were lonely, who would you call? Mom
2. Who in your family do you really admire? Bob He balances work, family and faith in a seemingly effortless way.
3. Who is the most interesting family member? Matthew His interest in so many things is contagious.
4. What is one of your mom's greatest strengths? Oh, she has so many! I would have to say her way of getting through really tough times. She perseveres, never complains and always has a positive attitude.
5. What one quality of your dad's would you like to have? I think I have a lot of his qualities but the one that missed me was his determination. When he decided to do something, it got done.
6. Who is the funniest person in your family? All the men in my family, on both sides have a great sense of humor. They crack me up all the time.
7. Who is the best cook in your family? Bill with Kate a close second. When Bill cooks Mexican or Kate cooks pasta, it is heavenly!
8. Which family member would you turn to first if you were in trouble? I am happy to say that there isn't a family member that I could not turn to in times of trouble. Both sides are filled with caring people who would help.
9. Who wrote or phoned last? Mom
10. Who in your family are you most like? That is a hard one. Physically, I look a lot like my dad although I am hoping that some of those genes that contribute to my mother's youthful appearance have been handed down to me. Personality wise, I think I am a mixture of both my mother and father.

surrounded by family

Barbara Carroll | Tucson, AZ

Barbara's answers to our quiz questions spoke of a large and supportive family that she could call on anytime. The obvious photo choice was this snapshot of the extended family. Barbara journaled in two font colors to distinguish her answers from her questions.

materials large brads (Bazzill Basics) • Univers Light Condensed font • *12 x 12 page*

they're the greatest

1. What did you want to be when you grew up?

2. How did you help out around the house?

3. What were you most afraid of?

4. Who was your first crush?

5. What childhood story do family and friends still tease you about?

6. Which family vacation was your favorite?

7. What did you do in the summertime?

8. What did your childhood bedroom look like?

9. As a child, what was your greatest talent?

10. What was the nicest thing your parents ever did for you?

word association

1. Ocean

2. Sneakers

3. Picnic

4. Playground

5. Trampoline

6. Dessert

7. Camera

8. Telephone

9. Flat tire

10. School bell

he said, she said

1. What attracted you to your partner?

2. What does she or he do that makes you laugh?

3. Where was your first date?

4. What has your mate said about you that surprised or flattered you?

5. Was it love at first sight or a friendship that blossomed?

6. How do you settle your differences?

7. Do you agree about the temperature in the house?

8. Are there places you'd now like to revisit with your partner?

9. Who in his/her family adds the most to your relationship?

10. What holiday requires the most compromise?

quiz: he said, she said

Copy this quiz twice. Give your partner one copy and keep the other for
yourself. Answer your questions in private. No cheating or collaborating now!
The He Said, She Said quiz will reveal how you both see the world.

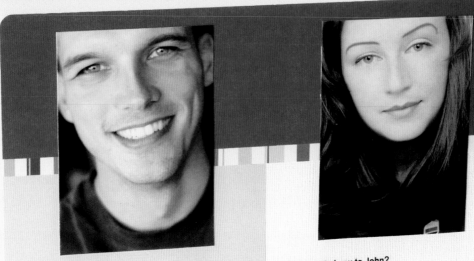

What attracted you to Teresa?
Her eyes, smile, and attitude.

What does she do to make you laugh?
She's a clown. I'm constantly laughing about something she
says or does.

Where was your first date?
Sports Dome.

What has she said that surprised or flattered you?
She always tells me that I'm flawless. Perfect in every way.

Was it love at first sight or a friendship that blossomed?
Both. We became friends immediately and were married a
week later.

How do you settle your differences?
Argue and make faces at each other until we give up.

Do you agree about the temperature in the house?
Almost never!

Are there places you'd now like to revisit with her?
The Eternal Flame in Honolulu.

Who in her family adds the most in your relationship?
Her parents.

What holiday requires the most compromise?
None.

What attracted you to John?
His eyes. Then he smiled so both.

What does he do to make you laugh?
Everything. He's like having my own personal Jim Carey.

Where was your first date?
The Sports Dome.

What has he said that surprised or flattered you?
He's always bragging about me. His co-workers know me
before I even meet them.

Was it love at first sight or a friendship that blossomed?
Love at first sight. Now he's my best friend.

How do you settle your differences?
Yell and get on with life.

Do you agree about the temperature in the house?
I think that's the only thing we will never agree on.

Are there places you'd now like to revisit with him?
The Eternal Flame to renew our vows.

Who in his family adds the most in your relationship?
His grandparents.

What holiday requires the most compromise?
None.

seven years later

Teresa Olier | Colorado Springs, CO

Teresa always knew she and her husband were alike, but until she did
this quiz and read his answers, she didn't realize just how much. Her
title helps us see how these similarities have held steadfast over time.

materials patterned paper, acrylic accent (KI Memories) • Arial Narrow and Square 721 Ex
BT fonts • *8½ x 11 page*

MY HERO

Why: To aspire toward exceptional qualities, to celebrate those people who motivate or inspire you.

Who is your hero? How are you your own hero? Why do we need heroes in our lives?

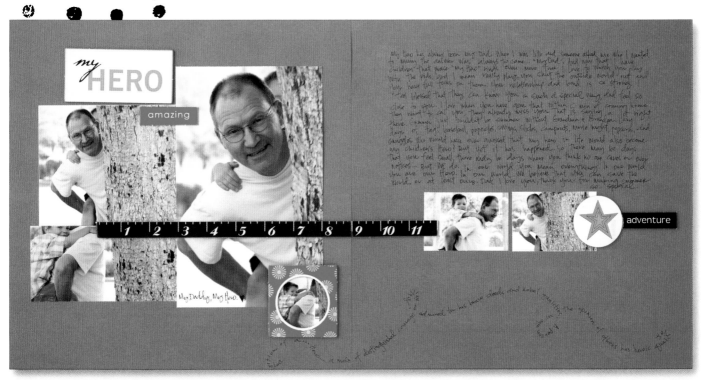

journal your gratitude
MY HERO by Jamie Harper

My Hero by Jamie Harper. **Supplies:** Cardstock: Bazzill Basics Paper; Patterned paper and chipboard: Scenic Route.

"A HERO is no braver than an ordinary man, but he is BRAVER five MINUTES longer." —RALPH WALDO EMERSON

12 JOURNALING IDEAS ABOUT HOME

1. Describe your smallest home.

2. Describe your largest home.

3. Write about the home you loved best and the reasons why.

4. What does "there's no place like home" mean to you?

5. When you walk into your home, how do you feel?

6. What items in your home make it feel like yours?

7. If you could change anything about your home, what would it be?

8. Do you believe "home is where the heart is"?

9. What's your favorite room in your home?

10. Describe your childhood home, your parents' home, your grandparents' home.

11. If you were going to redecorate your home, where would you shop for new furnishings?

12. What little touches make your house a home?

WORDS TO LIVE BY

Why: To be a role model, to appreciate the people who have influenced you.

What words do you live by? How do your actions show what you value? Scrapbook about a person you admire who lives what he or she believes.

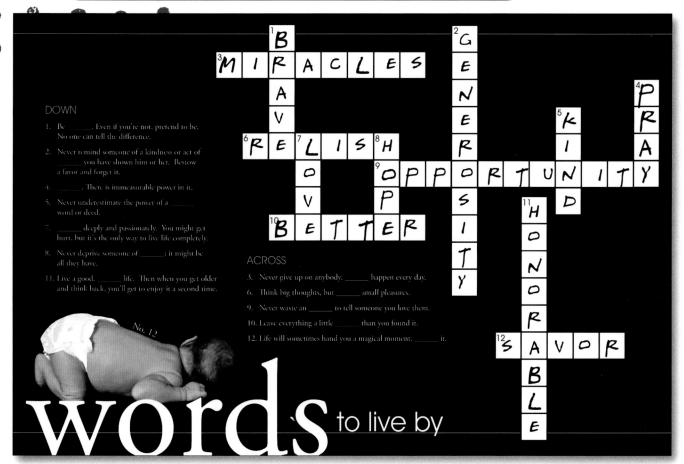

DOWN

1. Be _____. Even if you're not, pretend to be. No one can tell the difference.

2. Never remind someone of a kindness or act of _____ you have shown him or her. Bestow a favor and forget it.

4. _____. There is immeasurable power in it.

5. Never underestimate the power of a _____ word or deed.

7. _____ deeply and passionately. You might get hurt, but it's the only way to live life completely.

8. Never deprive someone of _____; it might be all they have.

11. Live a good, _____ life. Then when you get older and think back, you'll get to enjoy it a second time.

No. 12

ACROSS

3. Never give up on anybody. _____ happen every day.

6. Think big thoughts, but _____ small pleasures.

9. Never waste an _____ to tell someone you love them.

10. Leave everything a little _____ than you found it.

12. Life will sometimes hand you a magical moment. _____ it.

words to live by

list defining words
WORDS by Deena Wuest

Words to Live By by Deena Wuest. **Supplies:** Software: Adobe; Digital crossword puzzle: Anna Aspnes; Fonts: Avant Garde, Garamond Pro, and Gregor Miller's Friends.

"It's NICE to be important, BUT it's more IMPORTANT to be nice." —ANONYMOUS

BELIEVE

Why: To give people perspective on your actions,
to reflect on your beliefs.

What do you believe? How has your faith influenced your life?
How have your family's beliefs been passed along to you?

celebrate childhood innocence
WHY THE WORLD NEEDS SUPERMAN by Jamie Harper

Why the World Needs Superman by Jamie Harper.
Supplies: Cardstock: Bazzill Basics Paper; Patterned
paper: Chatterbox; Chipboard: Me & My Big Ideas; Stickers:
Scrapworks; Font: Times New Roman.

"Sometimes I've BELIEVED as MANY
as six IMPOSSIBLE things before breakfast."

—LEWIS CARROLL, ALICE IN WONDERLAND

PASSIONS

Why: To define yourself outside of your traditional roles, to remind yourself of what makes you happy.

What are you passionate about? What are your family members passionate about? How did you discover your passions, and how have they played out in your life?

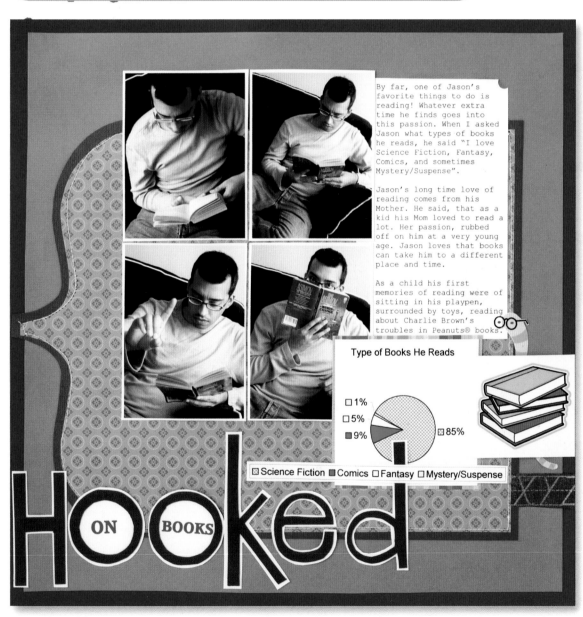

By far, one of Jason's favorite things to do is reading! Whatever extra time he finds goes into this passion. When I asked Jason what types of books he reads, he said "I love Science Fiction, Fantasy, Comics, and sometimes Mystery/Suspense".

Jason's long time love of reading comes from his Mother. He said, that as a kid his Mom loved to read a lot. Her passion, rubbed off on him at a very young age. Jason loves that books can take him to a different place and time.

As a child his first memories of reading were of sitting in his playpen, surrounded by toys, reading about Charlie Brown's troubles in Peanuts® books.

Type of Books He Reads

- ☐ 1%
- ☐ 5%
- ☒ 9%
- ☒ 85%

☒ Science Fiction ☒ Comics ☐ Fantasy ☐ Mystery/Suspense

graph a hobby
HOOKED ON BOOKS by Heidi Sonboul

Hooked on Books by Heidi Sonboul. **Supplies:** Cardstock: Bazzill Basics Paper; Patterned paper: Adornit-Carolee's Creations and Scenic Route; Other: Clip art.

CHANGE

Why: To remind yourself that you can accept changes, to gain confidence to tackle new things.

How do you handle change in your life? How have you handled transitions like moving, changing schools, entering a new relationship, getting married, starting a new job?

record landmark experiences
1999 by Mou Saha

1999 by Mou Saha. **Supplies:** Patterned paper: Frances Meyer and Rusty Pickle; Stamps 7gypsies, K&Company, and Stampendous!; Ink: Tsukineko; Tabs: Making Memories; Crown: 7gypsies; Buttons: Rusty Pickle and Wal-Mart; Embroidery floss: DMC; Pen: American Crafts.

"We did not CHANGE as we grew older; WE just became More CLEARLY ourselves."

—LYNN HALL

IT'S A MISTAKE

Why: To learn from mistakes, to offer reassurance that we're all human.

Write about a mistake you've made, big or small. What did you learn from it? What would you like others to learn from it?

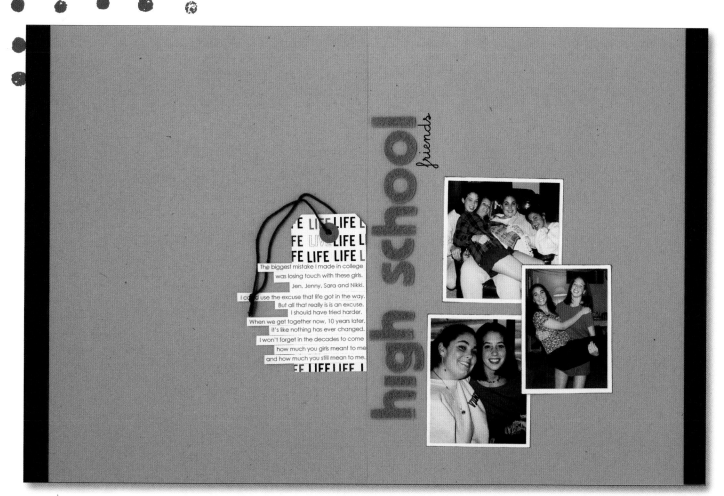

The biggest mistake I made in college was losing touch with these girls. Jen, Jenny, Sara and Nikki. I could use the excuse that life got in the way. But all that really is is an excuse. I should have tried harder. When we get together now, 10 years later, it's like nothing has ever changed. I won't forget in the decades to come how much you girls meant to me and how much you still mean to me.

find the positive
HIGH SCHOOL FRIENDS by Laura Kurz

High School Friends by Laura Kurz. **Supplies:** Cardstock: Bazzill Basics Paper; Stickers and rub-ons; American Crafts; Tag: Old Navy; Font: Century Gothic.

"Mistakes are the PORTALS of discovery."

—JAMES JOYCE

quiz: best & worst

The things you love coupled with those you hate show the range of who you are. Use our Best & Worst questions (see page 95) to take a playful look at yourself, or send this quiz to family and friends.

the color that looks best on you:

white...a brand new crisp white button down dress shirt, but white isn't a color. so i am going to say pink.

the age in life you've most enjoyed so far:

the most carefree, wild and fun i have had was between the ages of 21-23. however, i think the most amazing and enjoyable moments of my life have been in the last 5 years. motherhood has offered me a far greater apreciation for life than i could ever have known.

the color that looks worst on you:

i have been told that yellow and green tones don't always compliment my skin tone, but i wear them anyway!

the worst day of the week:

monday

the age in life you hated most:

it would have to be between the ages of 11-13. i still remember vividly how out of place i felt in my own skin. i compared myself with everyone else around me and i never thought i measured up...although, the glasses, braces and training bra probably didn't help matters.

Your favorite movie of all time:

Gladiator...but i can't pick just one so, Pretty Woman, League of Their Own, Meet Joe Black and Shawshank Redemption.

Your finest cooking accomplishment:

i'm still waiting for that to happen, but i have learned how to make a mighty fine old fashioned oatmeal.

your worst cooking disaster:

cooking a turkey...every blasted time i have tried!

the worst movie ever made:

Pulp Fiction...i know it is a cult classic, but it is just painful for me to watch. i just don't get it?

The best day of the week:

wednesday...because it falls in the middle of the week and i have usually crossed 2 or 3 things off of my to do list by then.

best and worst

factoids

best and worst factoids
Donna Downey | Huntersville, NC

Donna managed to keep her page open and airy, despite answering all of our **Best & Worst** questions. Separate blocks for each question enabled her to turn her journaling into contemporary-looking design elements.

materials bookplate (BasicGrey) • Studio font alphabet dies (QuicKutz) • stamping ink • Tahoma and Desyrel fonts • *12 x 12 page*

conversation

Elizabeth Dillow | Colorado Springs, CO

Elizabeth's striking page is made from a single quiz question she asked her young daughter. A handwritten thank-you note and photo dates along the sides of the black-and-white photos make the layout even more personal.

materials patterned paper (KI Memories) • Baskerville font • 8½ x 11 page

us according to sarah

Teresa Olier | Colorado Springs, CO

Teresa's daughter Sarah is at the stage when she knows exactly how old her mother is, but thinks her mother's first name is Mom. Teresa was able to capture this moment in Sarah's development with our **About Your Family** quiz.

materials rub-on letters (Autumn Leaves) • Swiss911 XCM BT and Arial Narrow fonts • 11 x 8½ page

quiz: two by two

If you are journaling on smaller size pages, use this fun and easy quiz (see page 95)—it can be as simple as two one-word answers to each question.

Just Two?

- Two everyday things I couldn't live without:
  My camera
  My computer
- Two of my favorite songs:
  My Life · The Beatles
  Crazy Love – Van Morrison
- Two things I want to do before I die:
  Get over my fear of flying.
  Travel
- Two things I worry about:
  Matthew
  Kate
- Two stores I shop at:
  Target
  Making Memories Unforgettable
- Two things that scare me:
  Flying
  Heights
- Two snacks I could eat every day:
  Guacamole
  Popcorn
- Two people I'd be lost without:
  My husband
  My children (I know, I cheated!)
- Two nicknames I've been given:
  Bobo
  Moosh
- Next two places I want to go on vacation:
  Yellowstone
  Utah

just two?
Barbara Carroll | Tucson, AZ

Barbara embellished her layout with a green number on a black background. She inserted a text box into a word-processing document and selected black for the fill. She typed a white number '2' into the text box. She printed onto green cardstock allowing her white '2' to show through as green.

materials paper flowers (Prima) • brads (Karen Foster) • Berkeley LT and Univers Condensed fonts • 8½ x 11 page

favorite clean
Stacy Julian | Liberty Lake, WA

Our **Two by Two** quiz encouraged Stacy to scrapbook a delightful, handwritten page for an existing My Favorite Things album. In keeping with her "clean" theme, Stacy used bright, "citrus-scent" colors.

materials patterned paper (Paper Fever) • ribbon (Strano Designs) • flowers (Prima) • ric rac • brads • *8 x 8 page*

This is my computer. This photo of my computer was taken by my camera. My computer and my camera have become my most important possessions. Yes, my car and my cell phone are nice and useful, but nothing I own right now brings me as much joy or provides me with a connection to the things I love to do than my camera and my computer. My computer connects me to the larger world, the world outside my 6000 square feet of real estate. I share my crafts with others through the computer. I have made friends online whom I never would have met otherwise – people from around the world. When I started scrapping three years ago, I already had a knack for picture taking. I was the quintessential life tourist. And after more than ten years as an appraiser, not having a camera somewhere on my person, well, I felt naked. As my passion for scrapping grew, so did my passion for photography, so much so that I now take photographs professionally. And being that it's a digital camera, my computer is an essential piece of equipment for my business. So, my two favorite things are now permanently linked together. My camputer. My compera. My favorites.

favorites
Tina Cockburn | San Diego, CA

Tina's solution for handling larger amounts of journaling is to keep a really short line length and to use a narrow font. Short line lengths and WIDE fonts result in fewer words per column and lots of hyphenation.

materials letter stickers (American Crafts) • stitching rub-ons (Doodlebug Designs) • corner punch (EK Success) • Dymo label maker • staples • stamping ink • Vogel font • *8½ x 11 page*

quiz: word association

Here's the ultimate in fun, funky and fast quizzes (see page 119). Just write a short paragraph about what comes to mind when you think about the following words:

 ocean

The smell of salt in the air. Rocky shorelines. Just a bit too chilly to swim. Ferry rides to Mukilteo. Fresh crab. My dad's boat. The San Juan Islands. The ocean reminds me that I am currently land-locked. It reminds me of home.

 school bell

Makes me jump. Still startles me after all these years. It's time. To start. To sit up. To be smart. To make friends. To not make enemies. To try and exist with a just a trace of dignity. It's time to put in your time until you get to be the real you.

picnic

Hot. Bugs. Itching to be eating inside instead. I'm not an outdoorsy type of girl. I make no apologies for that. I like to think I make up for it in other areas, but I'm presently at a loss to say exactly what those areas are.

camera

The vehicle to capture slices of my life. A tool of incredible power and creativity. A passion as early as I can recall. A magic machine. The thing that reminds me how things were so I won't soon forget.

 word association

 dessert

No thank you. I'll have more of my entrée. Especially the part with the potatoes. Desserts are last on my list of things to enjoy. I like the meal part way too much. Desserts keep you sitting in one place longer than you should be sitting there.

flat tire

I am helpless. I am crying and alone and I curse myself for not remembering how my Dad made me go through the process of changing a tire so that when the time came, I would know how to do it. Sorry Dad. I'll pay attention next time.

 sneakers

My first pair of Nike Cortes. So proud. So cool. They were white with a red stripe. They were the first pair of shoes I had that truly fit my skinny feet. It felt like I was walking on puffy clouds I swear. I ran faster in those shoes.

word association

Cathy Zielske | St. Paul, MN

Cathy's carefree layout captures slices of her life in short, random, **Word Association** paragraphs. Vivid descriptions make photos on this hand-painted layout unnecessary.

materials stamps, acrylic paint, brads (Making Memories) • Myriad font • *12 x 12 page*

the *art* of predictions

I Predict by Amanda Probst. **Supplies** Cardstock: Prism Papers; Stamps: FontWerks; Ink: Stampin' Up!; Pens: Precision Pens, American Crafts; Marvy Uchida; Fonts: CK Fast Food, downloaded from www.scrapnfonts. com; Century Gothic and Impact, Microsoft Word.

Some areas to make predictions about:

- Family members
- Household plans or activities
- Relationships (this was a favorite growing up—predicting things like whether cousin K would still be with boyfriend M by the end of the year)
- Finances (just for kicks, guess how much cash you'll have in your wallet on December 31)
- Community
- Global events
- Self (will you really stick to those goals you set?)
- Scrapbooking (how many layouts will you complete?)
- Children
- Technology

LAST JANUARY, I had leftover photos I didn't use on layouts, along with some pictures that were still in my "to do" pile. I recently decided to use them for a "review" layout based on a favorite childhood tradition: predictions. On New Year's Day, we made predictions for the coming year, then the next year we read what we had written. It was hilarious!

I hadn't made predictions in ages—until this layout. I used four photos for predictions in four areas of my life: family, marriage, children and household. This is a simple layout, but it covers pretty accurately the stories of my month. ck

BY AMANDA PROBST

scraplift an old layout, and reflect your current perspective

Find a layout you love from your past; then borrow the topic and the design scheme, and make it all over again. But this time, share current pictures and today's perspective. And, what the heck, why not use the same title, too? Cathy's layouts prove that, while the little details may change, personalities are forever. And thank goodness for that!

quotable coley

"Why do I have to do all this work?" —said whenever he is taking a bath, while pretending to scrub the sides of the tub.

"Catch it to me, Mom!"—said whenever he wants you to throw him the ball.

"I think I'll eat it now!"—said while eating, quoting a line from Sponge Bob Square Pants.

q u i r k y   c o l e y

teeth clacking
Coley always clacks his teeth together, usually while he's waiting for something important to happen.

obsession with sieve
Coley constantly pretends he is the St. Paul Sieve, and no matter where we are, he asks anyone who will listen: "Do you know Sieve?"

song repitition
Coley will latch on to a song and sing it over and over and over again. Currently in rotation: We are family, by Sister Sledge.

visits to the closet
Coley goes into the closet to answer nature's call. At least he keeps his diaper on!

three years old

materials epoxy accents (Making Memories) · plastic watch crystal · circle punch · Anandale Mono font · 8½ x 11 page by *Cathy Zielske, St. Paul, MN*

quotable coley

"Yeah...sure...what the heck!"
—one from Cole's repertoire of personal catch phrases.

"What, what, whattie what?"
—yet another one of Cole's super memorable catch phrases.

"Tough crowd."
—said after he told a joke while we were driving in the car, and no one laughed.

"Mom, you need some new material!"
—said to Mom, after he decided my tall stories about Leggy McClure just weren't all that funny.

quirky coley

lego builder extraordinaire
From making every Star Wars space ship known to man, to creating the Lego Beatles, Cole's interest and command of Lego bricks is unconscious.

eco-friendly
After watching *An Inconvenient Truth*, he became very interested in the environment, and can now do a mean Al Gore interpretation.

musical obsessions
Still loves Queen and the Beatles.

the MacBook Pro
A.k.a. Cole's second home. From Club Penguin to watching endless (approved) YouTube clips, Cole has to be pried away from the laptop. But he really does find great clips.

7

materials patterned paper (Mustard Moon) · foam stickers (American Crafts) · stamping ink · Avenir font · 8½ x 11 page

Cathy's favorite fun things
Cathy Zielske, Creative Director

B L O G G I N G

"Just thinking about this movie makes me laugh. It's the most oft-quoted film in the Zielske household. Even Coleman will occasionally say, 'But this one goes to 11!' "

"I may be weird, but for me, writing is fun. I love keeping a blog, just for the chance to take a mental break and write about whatever is on my mind at the moment."

"While the person in the seat next to me stares blankly at a measly serving of airline peanuts, I'm enjoying my third episode of *Friday Night Lights*. That, my friend, is fun!"

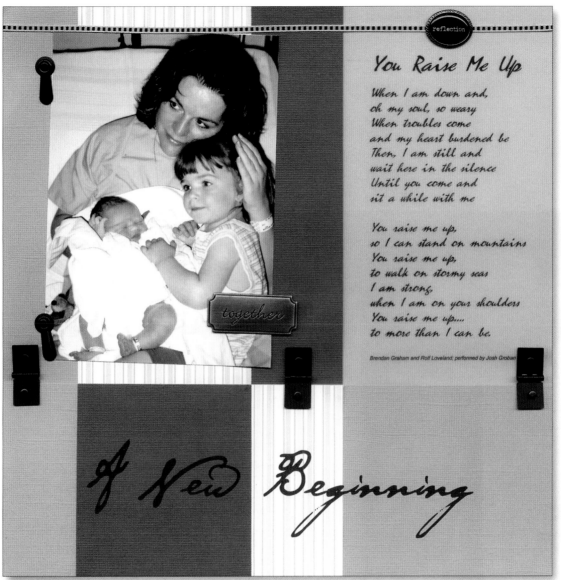

reflection

You Raise Me Up

When I am down and,
oh my soul, so weary
When troubles come
and my heart burdened be
Then, I am still and
wait here in the silence
Until you come and
sit a while with me

You raise me up,
so I can stand on mountains
You raise me up,
to walk on stormy seas
I am strong,
when I am on your shoulders
You raise me up....
to more than I can be.

Brendan Graham and Rolf Loveland; performed by Josh Groban

A New Beginning

A NEW BEGINNING **by Kathleen Kruk > Supplies** *Patterned paper:* Anna Griffin; *Vellum:* Paper Adventures; *Textured cardstock:* Bazzill Basics Paper; *"Together" plaque, "Reflection" bubble word and oval frame:* Li'l Davis Designs; *Ribbon and black hinges:* Making Memories; *Brads:* OT's Embellishments; *Photo corners:* 7gypsies; *Computer fonts:* Hannibal Lecter and Mariah, downloaded from the Internet; Arial, Microsoft Word; *Song lyrics:* "You Raise Me Up" by Brendan Graham and Rolf Loveland, performed by Josh Groban.

Next time you're stuck on "journaling," think about sharing the story with a group of friends over lunch. What would you say?

Another idea? Take those pages that have no journaling on them (you know the ones I'm talking about) to a friend's house. "Talk" through the pages with her to get a feel for what's most important to you as share your pictures with her. Soon you'll know exactly what words to add to your pages.

COMPLETE THAT PAGE!

10 Creative Ways to Journal about Birthdays

DEAR ABBY by Erin Lincoln > Supplies *Patterned papers:* Rusty Pickle (stamps), me & my BIG ideas (red), Frances Meyer (blue); *Letter stickers:* Chatterbox; *Snaps and tags:* Making Memories; *Computer font:* CK Cosmopolitan, "Creative Clips & Fonts for Special Occasions" CD, *Creating Keepsakes; Safety pins and red bookplate:* Li'l Davis Designs.

① Go to *www.famousbirthdays.com* and print a list of famous people born on your birthday. Do you share any characteristics with them?

② Do a search online for news headlines on the day you (or a family member) was born.

③ Make a photocopy of your birth certificate and include it on a scrapbook page.

④ Create a timeline of your favorite birthday celebrations by including pictures and journaling about various birthday celebrations on a layout.

⑤ What astrological sign is associated with your birthday? Which characteristics match your personality? Which ones don't?

⑥ Ever been given a surprise birthday party? Get the party-planning details from friends and family members and tell "the story behind the party" on a layout.

⑦ Include a copy of your child's birthday wish list on a scrapbook page.

⑧ Check archives of your hometown newspaper for birth announcements from year's past to include on your pages.

⑨ Chronicle your child's growth by capturing her inked hand and footprints each year.

⑩ Save handwritten birthday cards. Photocopy handwritten messages from friends and family members to include on a scrapbook page.

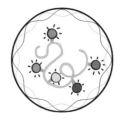

COMPLETE THAT PAGE!

10 Creative Ways to Journal about the Holidays

1. Have your older child draw a map showing his plan for trick-or-treating through your neighborhood. Have him add as many details as possible (street names, neighbors' houses, etc.).

2. Look for a Halloween book at the library. Read the story and then think about how you can turn your child's Halloween into a similar story on a scrapbook page.

3. Check out the Thanksgiving Day projects your child completes at school. Is there an art project or a worksheet that documents how your child feels about your family? Consider including it as journaling on a scrapbook page.

4. Collect Thanksgiving-themed die cuts. Pass one out to each guest at your Thanksgiving dinner and ask them to record their favorite thing about Thanksgiving.

5. Guest books are often associated with weddings. However, it can be delightful to have a guest book open at each party and/or family event you host. After the event, make photocopies of the guest pages and include them on your layouts.

6. The holiday season is busy! Many of us likely keep a calendar or day planner during this time to keep things straight. Consider making a photocopy of your planner or calendar page. It'll document just how busy you were during the holidays!

7. If you have preschool or elementary school students, save their seasonal artwork and workbook pages to include as journaling on your layouts.

8. Document love and friendship by including Valentine's Day cards in a pocket on a scrapbook page.

9. The holidays are often associated with parties. Include a party invitation on a scrapbook page to document a party you gave or attended.

10. Do you celebrate uncommon holidays? Go online and search for web sites that document various holidays. Jot down fun facts associated with the creation of these holidays.

THE STORY BEHIND THE EASTER BUNNY **by Kyra Harris** > **Supplies** *Vellum:* Bazzill Basics Paper; *Computer fonts:* Tweed and AvantGarde, downloaded from the Internet; *Chalk:* Craf-T Products.

the story behind the easter bunny

When we were little girls, Mom used to say that if we prayed to the angels all of our wishes would be granted. I think in the beginning, she proved that her words were true by showing if we asked for a treat we would get it and in a child's mind, that meant only one thing - candy. I remember playing in the back playroom of our house on Larkspur, interlacing my fingers and saying outloud, "Dear Angels, we've been good. Please bring us some licorice." Amazingly enough, our "prayers" were answered when Mom would deliver our treats when we weren't looking. Well, that was when I was a kid and my little sister was only a few years old. Many years later, when we had moved to our home on Rose Lane, Shana was still praying to the angels for treats. I was in junior high and I had outgrown such things. But Shana still did until one day in April 1988. The angels were generous that day and left Shana some malted chocolate balls as a special treat. At the time, she thought nothing of it but little did she know that those malted candies would alter her young life. A few days later, we would celebrate Easter with our family. That usually meant going over to Aunt Olga and Uncle Peter's house in the early afternoon for an early dinner with Mom's side of the family. However, to a young child Easter officially began in the early morning by finding the basket that the Easter Bunny left for you. On that particular day, we were all happy with our piles of sugar and then it happened. Shana must have noticed something that she had never noticed before. Mom was eating a handful of Whoppers with her morning coffee and something clicked inside her eight-year-old

When we were little girls, Mom used to say that if we prayed to the angels all of our wishes would be granted. I think in the beginning, she proved that her words were true by showing if we asked for a treat we would get it and in a child's mind, that meant only one thing - candy. I remember playing in the back playroom of our house on Larkspur, interlacing my fingers and saying outloud, "Dear Angels, we've been good. Please bring us some licorice." Amazingly enough, our "prayers" were answered when Mom would deliver our treats when we weren't looking. Well, that was when I was a kid and my little sister was only a few years old. Many years later, when we had moved to our home on Rose Lane, Shana was still praying to the angels for treats. I was in junior high and I had outgrown such things. But Shana still did until one day in April 1988. The angels were generous that day and left Shana some malted chocolate balls as a special treat. At the time, she thought nothing of it but little did she know that those malted candies would alter her young life. A few days later, we would celebrate Easter with our family. That usually meant going over to Aunt Olga and Uncle Peter's house in the early afternoon for an early dinner with Mom's side of the family. However, to a young child Easter officially began in the early morning by finding the basket that the Easter Bunny left for you. On that particular day, we were all happy with our piles of sugar and then it happened. Shana must have noticed something that she had never noticed before. Mom was eating a handful of Whoppers with her morning coffee and something clicked inside her eight-year-old

mind. Mom was eating Whoppers that looked an awful lot like the malted balls that had appeared only a few days earlier. You could see the wheels turning as her petite body cautiously walked up to Mom and peered up with her large, deep blue eyes and asked a question. "Mom, are you the Easter Bunny?" Mom remembers looking back at her younger daughter and asked a question. "Mom, are you the Easter Bunny?" Mom remembers Well, what do **you** think?" Shana woefully nodded her head and proceeded to ask another question. "Mom, are you the Tooth Fairy?" Again, Mom's response was, "Well, what do **you** think?" Shana knew that answer too but she continued her line of questioning. Needing to know the full truth, Shana asked an unsettling question that probably shook up her entire belief system. "Mom, are you Santa, too?" Mom couldn't take anymore and finally nodded, hoping not to crush the hopes and dreams of her young daughter. Mom remembers that Shana's eyes began to well up but no tears ever fell. She had learned that our mother played the roles of childhood icons and that was enough to deal with on that spring day. When I think back and reminisce, I'd like to think that Mom does continue to play the role of guardian angel for both of her daughters, even if we don't believe she will deliver candy to us. She has delivered so many things over the years...so much more than the combined efforts of the Easter Bunny, the Tooth Fairy and Santa Claus.

Photograph of Shana taken in April 1983 or 1984. Journaling written by Kyra in May 2003.

January
Journaling Prompts

January 1:
New Year's Day

How do you celebrate the new year?

January 6:
Epiphany/Three Kings Day

As a child, we tried to leave our tree up until Epiphany. What's your process for taking down your tree?

January 11:
Amelia Earhart Day

How has being a woman affected your life?

January 17:
Benjamin Franklin's Birthday

Are you thrifty or a spender?

January 18:
A. A. Milne's Birthday

Which Winnie the Pooh character do you have the most in common with?

Third Monday of January:
Martin Luther King, Jr. Day

Do you have a dream? What is it?

February
Journaling Prompts

February 2:
Groundhog Day

Do you want six more weeks of winter? Why or why not?

February 14:
Valentine's Day

Who holds the key to your heart?

February 24:
National Tortilla Chip Day

What's your favorite snack?

Third Monday of February:
Presidents' Day

Write about the most honest person you know.

February:
Mardi Gras

How do you celebrate your life?

March
Journaling Prompts

March 2:
Dr. Seuss's Birthday/ Read Across America Day

What's your favorite Dr. Seuss book?

March 11:
Johnny Appleseed Day

Write about someone who has made a difference in your life.

March 17:
St. Patrick's Day

How do you celebrate St. Patrick's Day?

March:
National Nutrition Month

What's your favorite healthy food?

March:
National Women's History Month

If you were writing your own history, what would it say?

March 20:
First Day of Spring

What represents spring to you?

April
Journaling Prompts

April 1:
April Fools' Day

Do you play practical jokes on people?

What are some of your favorites?

April 2:
International Children's Book Day

Who is your favorite fairy-tale character and why?

April 15:
Income Taxes Due

Do you wait until the last minute, or do you file your taxes in January?

April 22:
Earth Day

How does the theme of "reduce, reuse, recycle" play out in your life?

April:
Spring Break

How do you celebrate spring break?

How did you celebrate it in the past?

April:
Easter

What are your family Easter traditions?

May
Journaling Prompts

May 1:
May Day

Do you have any May Day traditions?

May 5:
Cinco de Mayo

How do you celebrate your own heritage?

Second Sunday in May:
Mother's Day

If you have kids, write about the best parts of motherhood.

If you don't have kids, interview your mom.

First Saturday in May:
National Scrapbook Day

What do you love best about scrapbooking?

First Week of May:
National Teacher's Week

Write about the teachers in your life, who influenced you the most?

Last Monday in May
Memorial Day

How do you celebrate Memorial Day?

June
Journaling Prompts

June 14:
Flag Day

If you designed your own family flag, what would you include on it and why?

Third Sunday in June:
Father's Day

Write about something amazing you learned from your father.

June 20:
First Day of Summer

What do you like best about summer?

Third Saturday of June:
National Hollerin' Day

This North Carolina holiday celebrates the art of "hollerin'" as a way to communicate over distances without a phone.

How would you communicate if there were no phones?

End of June:
Last Day of School

How do you feel when school's out for the summer?

End of June:
Graduation

Write about a graduation ceremony that impacted your life.

July
Journaling Prompts

July 1 or 2:
Canada Day

Interview your Canadian friends about what this holiday means to them.

July 2:
World UFO Day

I don't know that this is a "real" holiday, but it's kind of fun. If you made up your own holiday, what would it be?

July 4:
Independence Day

How do you celebrate the Fourth of July?

July 14:
Bastille Day
(French National Holiday)

How has your life been influenced by French culture?

Last Sunday of July:
Parents' Day

How did your parents (as a unit) affect your life?

July:
Family Reunions

How does your family stay connected?

August
Journaling Prompts

First Sunday of August:
Friendship Day

Jot down the reasons why you love your friends.

August 13:
International Left-hander's Day

Celebrate the left-handed people in your life.

August 19:
National Aviation Day

Journal about your first flight on an airplane.

August 26:
National Women's Equality Day

What would your life be like if women didn't have the right to vote?

August:
Family Vacations

What are your travel traditions now? What were they like as a child?

August:
Summer Sports

What sports do you and your family enjoy in the summer?

September
Journaling Prompts

September 1:
Labor Day

How do you celebrate Labor Day?

First Sunday of September:
Grandparents' Day

Journal about your relationship with your grandparents.

September 11:
Patriot Day

Where were you on 9/11 and how has it affected your life?

September 17:
Constitution Day

If you were going to write your own constitution, what would it say?

September 22:
First Day of Fall

What symbolizes fall for you?

September:
Back to School

Describe your favorite classes and most influential teachers.

October
Journaling Prompts

October 9:
Leif Eriksson Day

Write about something you've discovered in your life.

Second Monday in October:
Columbus Day

What's something you'd like to explore?

October 16:
National Dictionary Day

Use the definition of a word in your journaling today.

October 16:
National Boss Day

What's the best thing you've learned from a boss?

Fourth Sunday in October:
Mother-in-Law's Day

Journal about your relationship with your mother-in-law.

October 31:
Halloween

What's your best childhood memory of Halloween?

November
Journaling Prompts

November 3:
National Sandwich Day

What's your favorite sandwich?

November 7:
National Magazine Day

What magazines do you love to read and why?

First Tuesday of November:
Election Day

Write about your voting experiences.

Fourth Thursday of November:
Thanksgiving

How does your family celebrate Thanksgiving?

November 11:
Veterans' Day

Write about a friend or family member who served in the military.

November 30:
Stay at Home Because You're Well Day

How would you spend a "free" day at home?

December
Journaling Prompts

December 4:
National Cookie Day

What's your favorite cookie and why?

December 21:
First Day of Winter

What are your best winter memories?

December 24:
Christmas Eve

Write about your family's Christmas Eve traditions.

December 25:
Christmas

What's on your holiday wish list?

December 31:
New Year's Eve

Describe how you ring in the new year.

December:
National Stress-Free Family Holiday Month

How do you stay relaxed so you can enjoy the holidays?

materials patterned paper (SEI) • letter stickers (Chatterbox) • metal flower (Making Memories) • sticker tabs (*Lucky* magazine) • brad • *11 x 8¹/₂ page by Jessica Fulkerson, Los Angeles, CA*

make a "predictions" page

Scrapbook your predictions for where you'll be a year from now—in your career, your relationships, your personal growth, even your geographic location. On this layout, Jessica used page flags from *Lucky* magazine to answer each question she has about her future. It's a great way to put a few hopes, dreams, and concrete goals on paper. Then next year make another layout about whether or not your prophecies came true.

"Happiness depends upon ourselves."
—*Aristotle*

Visit futureme.org *to send yourself an e-mail postdated to arrive one year in the future.*

journal about your unique physical characteristics

Our physical quirks can be just as interesting as our personality quirks. Scrapbook yours, using the checklist below to get you started. Incidentally, Angie wants to emphasize that the blurb about her "almost perfectly straight teeth" is not meant to be egotistical; it is merely there to balance out the slightly gross things she revealed about herself—including the fact that, when she blows her nose, she sometimes gets snot in her eyes. But isn't her heart-shaped mole cute?

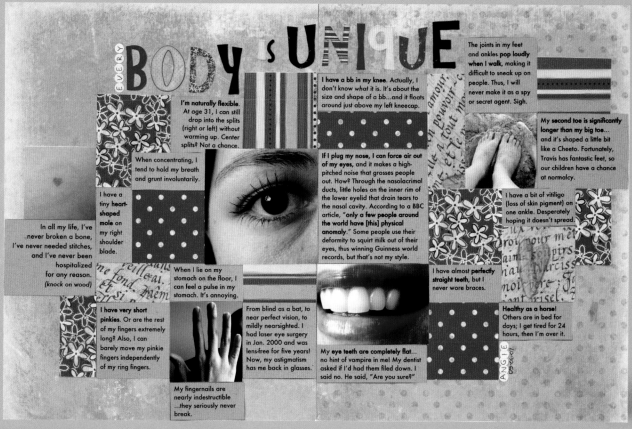

materials patterned paper (Bo-Bunny) • letter stickers (Sweetwater, Bo-Bunny) • 8½ x 11 spread by Angie Lucas, Sandy, UT

unique physical characteristics questionnaire

Toes: ☐ long ☐ short ☐ average ☐ other_____

Fingers: ☐ long ☐ short ☐ average ☐ other_____

Eyes: ☐ close together ☐ far apart ☐ almond-shaped ☐ saucer-shaped

Ears: ☐ attached lobes ☐ detached lobes ☐ piercings (#_____)

Legs: ☐ unusually long ☐ unusually short ☐ bowlegged ☐ knobby-kneed

Arms: ☐ gangly ☐ muscular ☐ freckled ☐ hairy

Torso: ☐ long torso ☐ short torso ☐ thick middle ☐ six-pack abs ☐ no comment

Belly button: ☐ innie ☐ outie ☐ often visible ☐ never visible

List features you're most often complimented on:

List features you've never been complimented on:

List body parts you used to have but don't have now:

List body parts you have acquired or enhanced:

If you've ever heard a sentence like this, fill in the blanks:
"That's the _[adjective]_ -est _[body part]_ I've ever seen!"

start your journaling with the phrase "ladies and gentlemen"

The options for completing this phrase are truly endless. "Ladies and Gentlemen: Start your engines." "Ladies and Gentlemen: Please take your seats. The concert is about to begin." "Ladies and Gentlemen! It's time for the amazing! The unbelievable! The inflammable! Weirdo the Wonder Clown!" (Not all of them are scrapbook-worthy.) Kim used the phrase to kick off an air-travel analogy. "Ladies and Gentlemen" are the first words plane passengers hear when they're about to reach their final destination. And Kim definitely feels like she's about to arrive in a foreign land.

Stuffed animals in the dishwasher

Love a food one day, hate it the next

Up, down, up, down

NO NO NO

Big kid envy

Hitting Daddy's TV with a plastic golf club

Fiercely independent

Fake laugh and fake cry

10/22/06

13 MONTHS

Ladies and Gentleman,
Please return your chairs and trays to their full, upright position. You may want to buckle your seatbelts, as it looks like we could be in for a bumpy ride. I think we've just arrived in

toddLERViLLE

materials patterned paper (Fancy Pants Designs, My Mind's Eye, Scenic Route Paper Co.) • chipboard letters (Heidi Swapp) • labels (Dymo) • stamping ink • Square 721, Bell MT, and Mouser fonts • *12 x 12 page by Kim Turpin, Victoria, BC, Canada*

make a layout about a color

Crayola crayons have such delicious color names: macaroni and cheese, pig pink, fuzzy wuzzy brown, and mauvelous, to name a few. Look through your Crayola box for colors that remind you of someone or something, and make a layout about it! (Using the actual crayon on the page is optional.) For Stacy, sky blue conjured up images of her high-flying son Trey.

materials crayon (Crayola) • brads • machine stitching • ribbon • 8½ x 11 page by Stacy Julian, Liberty Lake, WA

PLAY ALONG

Write the name of the person each crayon makes you think of:

Fun Facts: Binney & Smith, Inc., introduced the first Crayola crayons in 1903 with just 8 colors in a box: black, blue, brown, green, orange, red, violet, and yellow. In 1949, 40 more colors were added. Since then colors have been added and subtracted from the palette six additional times. The most recent change was in 2003, when Crayola users voted to retire 4 shades (blizzard blue, magic mint, mulberry, and teal blue) and voted in 4 brand new colors (inchworm, jazzberry jam, mango tango, and wild blue yonder) in honor of the company's 100th anniversary.

materials Maple Lane shadow box (EK Success) • patterned paper (Wübë) • chipboard letters (Making Memories) • letter stamps (Provo Craft) • ribbon (Offray) • stamping ink • brads • CK Newsprint font • *project by Amy Williams, Camden, ME*

use song lyrics for your journaling

Now make sure they're meaningful song lyrics. Don't just take the easy way out and let U2, Frank Sinatra, or Sarah McLachlan express all the sentiments in your scrapbooks. But when a song is deeply inspirational to you, it can be a great way to express what's in your heart. Amy borrowed these lyrics from "Dream Big" by Ryan Shupe and the RubberBand and turned them into a beautiful and hopeful décor piece for her daughter Marinne's bedroom.

Simple staffers share lyrics they thought they knew

What Angie Lucas thought: "Hush, hush. We go downtown. It's so scary!"

Actual lyrics sung by 'Til Tuesday: "Hush, hush. Keep it down now. Voices carry."

What Cathy Zielske thought: "I got no love, no love you, Korea."

Actual lyrics sung by Van Halen: "I got no love, no love you'd call real."

What Jennafer Martin thought: "Donuts make my brown eyes blue."

Actual lyrics sung by Crystal Gayle: "Don't it make my brown eyes blue."

What Rachel Gainer thought: "This is where I grew up. I went to prison; then I fixed it up."

Actual lyrics sung by Nickelback: "This is where I grew up. I think the present owner fixed it up."

For more fun with misheard lyrics, go to kissthisguy. com.

Ah, Mad Libs! Those gloriously funny elementary-school pastimes in which a story is presented with important words missing and children are asked to fill in the blanks. To try this exercise on your own, write your journaling, then erase a handful of words, and ask a child or a close friend to supply the missing words. Keep in mind that, depending on age and gender, children tend to pick adjectives like "smelly" and "weird" and nouns like "booger" and "fart." Knowing this, Marnie turned to a grown-up friend who knows her son Nigel very well. Marnie says the resulting journaling is much more colorful and descriptive than she'd have written on her own. And it's mostly true.

"The adjective is the banana peel of the parts of speech."
—Clifton Paul Fadiman

Once upon a time there was an **outstanding** boy named Nigel. He was a very **active** boy who liked to do many **adventurous** things.

Inside, Nigel liked to use his **clever** imagination, creating **interesting** scenes with his toys. He would build castles for the **daring** pirates to attack in the thick of the night as they **sailed** by sea in their black sail pirate ship. Or Nigel would recreate scenes from his favorite movie, **Harry Potter** using his many lego ships and his **many** action figures. If tired, Nigel liked to read **fun** books which taught him of **exciting** places and **magical** people.

Outside, Nigel liked to ride his **fast** and **shiny** bike. He could pedal **quick** and was allowed to ride to the **park** by himself. Nigel also liked to play with his **best** friends who lived on his street. Basketball, tennis, hockey—they played it all.

Before bed, Nigel liked to watch a **little** tv and then once in his pjs, he would **kiss** his **mom**, swish his **blanket**, read his **book** and say his prayers. What a sweet, **kind**, **loveable**, and **good** boy he was.

materials patterned paper, border sticker (My Mind's Eye) • chipboard letter (BasicGrey) • photo turns (Making Memories) • brads (Junkitz) • stamping ink • Garamouche font • 8½ x 11 page by Marnie Flores, New Albany, OH

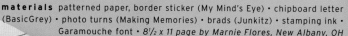

5lb bag of **flour** spread across the kitchen.

3 bottles of your **sister's** nail polish painted on the walls.

1 bottle of **syrup** poured directly on to the dining room table.

24 raw **eggs** smashed all over the living room.

2 quarts of **milk** poured straight into the carpet.

it is a good thing

you are

cute

materials patterned paper (BasicGrey) • paper frills (Doodlebug Design) • buttons • dimensional adhesive • Arial and CAC Pinafore fonts • *12 x 12 page by Marie Lottermoser, Bellevue, WA*

use numbers to describe someone's personality

How do I peg thy personality? Let me count the ways. In Marie's case, this means accounting for all the mischief her little boy has caused in the last four years. Thank goodness this list isn't the work of a single afternoon! Marie can laugh about these little "accidents" now that a bit of time has passed and she's all finished scrubbing the raw eggs out of her living room carpet. She created this layout so that, when her little angel has a son of his own, he'll remember what he was really like.

> "Today you are You, that is truer than true. There is no one alive who is Youer than You."
> —*Dr. Seuss in* Happy Birthday to You

make a layout about your child's (or your) personality quirks

materials patterned paper, letter stickers (Scenic Route Paper Co.) • chipboard number • stamping ink
• 12 x 12 page by Tia Bennett, Puyallup, WA

What exactly is a quirk? Well, according to *dictionary.com*, it's "a peculiarity of action, behavior, or personality; mannerism." Quirks set us apart, making us just a little bit different from everybody else in a (hopefully) good way. Some of us have more quirks than others. Pick one or many, and record them on a layout, as Tia did with her son Baylor's unique way of announcing his age.

Simple staffers share some of their quirks

Angie Lucas unintentionally adopts other people's accents while talking to them (think waiters at Italian restaurants, Australian tourists, and British coworkers).

After putting away the dishes, **Rachel Gainer** must open every cupboard to make sure everything is straight and in its place.

Cathy Zielske doesn't like rainwater to touch her hands. She blames it on growing up in the Pacific Northwest, where her hands were always damp.

Except for dinner, **Stacy Julian** eats all her meals standing up.

Elisha Snow can't stand for her collarbones to be touched, and because of that, she can't bring herself to get a massage.

Wendy Smedley has a hard time completing one thought before moving on to the next one, whether she's thinking out loud, having a conversation, or writing an...

"Maggie: "But I'm weird."
Peggy: "No, you're quirky. Quirky and weird are two different things."
—*Julia Roberts as Maggie and Joan Cusack as Peggy in* **The Runaway Bride**

quiz: four for the record

It's easier to get a glimpse of the breadth of who you are if you journal about several things in one category. Try these for starters (see our quiz on page 97):

Random Little Facts

1. **Four jobs I have had in my life:**
   Subway sandwich maker | Administrative Assistant | Assistant Curator | Momma and Wife

2. **Four movies I could watch over and over:**
   Almost Famous | School of Rock | Crouching Tiger, Hidden Dragon | Star Wars trilogy

3. **Four places I have lived:**
   Hacienda Heights, CA | Angwin, CA | Loma Linda, CA | South Lancaster, MA

4. **Four TV shows I love to watch:**
   Survivor | The Amazing Race | Lost | The Office

5. **Four places I have been on vacation:**
   Alaska | Korea | Hawaii | Cape Cod

6. **Four websites I visit daily:**
   Dogpile | BabyCenter | Two Peas in a Bucket | Simple Scrapbooks

7. **Four of my favorite foods:**
   Anything Chinese | Mexican | Japanese | or that I don't have to cook personally

8. **Four places I would rather be right now:**
   On vacation | Sleeping | Back in California | Hawaii

9. **Four people who have made a difference in my life:** My mother | My sister | Jack | Matthew

10. **Four things I'd like to learn to do:**
    Ride a snowboard | Fly without fear | Pack lightly | Play the acoustic guitar

random little facts
Margaret Scarbrough | South Lancaster, MA

For easy-on-the-eyes journaling, Margaret used a warm, dark grey text instead of the usual black. She also separated her four answers with simple forward slashes.

materials letter stickers (Scrapworks) • corner rounder (Creative Memories) • Arial font • 8½ x 11 page

make a layout about things you hate

Hate, in general, is not a good thing. And normally it wouldn't belong in a scrapbooking magazine that's all about having fun. But when you direct your hatred toward an object or a task, then it's perfectly okay. In fact, it's usually pretty funny. So go ahead, make a list of the things that drive you batty; then find photos (or not), and make a layout.

> "Oh, you hate your job? Why didn't you say so? There's a support group for that. It's called EVERYBODY, and they meet at the bar."
> —*Drew Carey*

my *hate* to-do list

Everyone has them. Those pet peeves and annoyances of life. I am no exception. Let's start with the telephone. I don't like it. I know it's a handy invention. It helps coordinate activities, pass on info and order pizza. Talking on it just to talk on it though drives me nuts. Send me an e-mail or talk to me face to face and I'm much happier.

Now, the next thing I don't like is flying. I have a thing about crowded places and also about heights. Put them together and well, you might be able to tell why I don't like planes very much. I can deal with it though, I just bring a book and pretend that I'm at the beach. Problem solved (unless of course turbulence occurs, then my illusion is shattered.)

Annoyance number three has to do with sick children. Well, not actually sick kids per se. It's deciding on whether they're healthy enough for school. I mean if they have a fever or they're vomiting it's black and white. It's those borderine cold decisions that are the difficult ones to make.

The next annyonance is vegetables. They've plagued me since childhood. I mean I know they're good for me and I'm supposed to be adult about it but I just don't like them very much. If they came up with a chocolate version, that would work for me.

Of course, an annoyance list couldn't be complete without household duties. The two biggest ones for me are cooking and matching socks. The cooking thing probably has to do with the picky eaters at my house. (They get it honestly, see the vegetable post above; but it still doesn't make it fun.)

That's it. Nothing earth shattering, just annoying.

materials Photoshop (Adobe Systems) • papers, ribbon by Leora Sanford; photo frames by Katie Pertiet; arrow brush by Jackie Eckles; flourish brush by Anna Aspnes (designerdigitals.com) • SP Wonderful Wendy and Times New Roman fonts • 8½ x 11 page by Terri Davenport, Toledo, OH

create a mini-album about your family's secret language

Elisha set out to create an album about her family's inside jokes, but along the way, it became clear that almost all of the Christopher family's signature expressions came from one person: dad. So Elisha collected them all into a mini-album and paired them with amusing pictures of her dad. Think about your own family. What quotes or expressions come up often in conversation? What did you roll your eyes at when you were a teen? What secret meanings does your family have for common words? Start your own collection!

our ~~family's~~ dad's
SECRET LANGUAGE

This book initially started out as "The Christopher Family Language" album, but quickly evolved into its current title. Why? Because after I had gathered quotes and sayings that our family uses over and over, I realized that 99.9% of them came from dad. Who knows where dad got his zany sense of humor from, or why he says the things he does. But it's things like this that make him truly unique and adored by us all.

um, aloha!

During our very first trip to Hawaii the popular phrase amongst the kids was, "um, hello!" So after hearing us say it to each other non-stop during our stay, dad felt it appropriate to change the phrase to "um, aloha!" Even after we got back it kinda stuck around. It in essence means "get a clue!"

hug a dad

We don't know how or why this phrase came to be, but it's a dyslexic way of saying, "give your dad a hug." Dad would often times come downstairs, see us in the kitchen, and immediately hug each one of us tightly and say, "give your hug a dad," or "have you given your hug a dad today?"

pass the bananas

A sure sign of dad's old(er) age. One night at the dinner table he couldn't for the life of him come up with the word for "napkin." So he asked someone to pass the bananas. We all stared at him blankly until he was finally able to come up with the right word. The term stuck around.

how much?

This is one of dad's stranger phrases. "How much?" is simply his way of asking, "what?" Like if you say, "Dad I'm going out," and he didn't hear you (or wasn't paying attention) he says, "how much?" We gave up a long time ago trying to figure out where this odd question came from.

what it is?

When you call dad on the phone this is what he asks you (for some strange reason). This question makes absolutely no sense, but we all know that when he asks, he means, "what's going on?" or "what's up?" You may often find a "dude" added to the end: "what it is, dude?"

hair on your chest

When we were young, dad would solely use this phrase on the boys: "if you eat those peas it'll put hair on your chest." But as we all got older it became extremely funny to him to say it to the girls as well. The girls never thought it was that funny—we were actually rather repulsed by it.

drink your own bathwater

If dad is ever disgusted by something that we do or eat, he'll always use the expression, "anyone that would [eat carrots] would drink their own bathwater." He's been saying this for as long as we can remember. While it mostly just applies to food items, it doesn't always have to.

materials 6 x 6 album (Heidi Swapp) • patterned paper, ribbon (SEI) • chipboard letters (Pressed Petals) • rub-on letters (American Crafts) • acrylic paint (Making Memories) • brads • Lane-Upper and Arial fonts • *project by Elisha Snow, Farmington, UT*

"I have to play this every night before I go to bed, and I can't put it down until I've gotten at least 300 points in one game."

Elisha's favorite fun things

Elisha Snow, Assistant Editor

" 'First it's candy; then it's gum!' My mom introduced me to this; it was a favorite of hers as a child."

"I still collect Barbies. My favorite is my '60s hippie Barbie. Check out the outfit and those glasses."

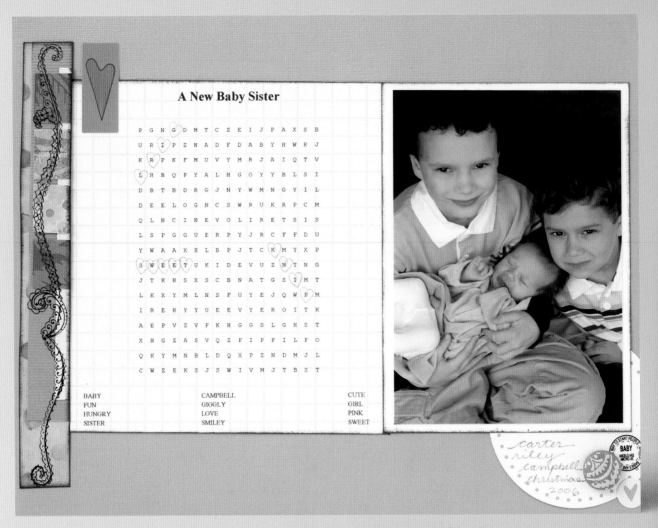

A New Baby Sister

```
P G N G D M T C Z E I J P A X S B
U R I P Z N A D F D A B Y H W K J
K R P K F M U V Y M R J A I Q T V
L H B Q P Y A L H G O Y Y B L S I
D B T B D R G J N Y W M N G Y I L
D E E L O G N C S W R U K R P C M
Q L N C I N E V O L I R E T S I S
L S P G G U E R P Y J R C F F D U
Y W A A X H L B P J T C M Y X P X
S W E E T U K I D E V U Z N T N G
J T K H S X S C B N A T G S I M T
L K X Y M L N S F U Y E J Q W P M
I R E H Y Y U E E V Y E R O I T K
A E P V Z V F K H G G S L G H S T
X H G Z A S V Q Z F I P F I L F O
Q K Y M N B L D Q X P Z N D M J L
C W Z E K S J S W I V M J T B S T
```

BABY	CAMPBELL	CUTE
FUN	GIGGLY	GIRL
HUNGRY	LOVE	PINK
SISTER	SMILEY	SWEET

materials patterned paper (BasicGrey, K&Company, Scenic Route Paper Co.) • journaling spot (Heidi Swapp) • heart stickers (Heidi Grace Designs) • rub-ons (BasicGrey) • fabric brad (K&Company) • heart stamp (Doodlebug Design) • 11 x 8 1/2 page by Stacey Sattler, Sylvania, OH

visit *puzzle-maker.com* to create a word search about your family

Tired of laboring over your journaling? Here's an easy solution. List all the words you can think of about a particular person or topic; then visit *puzzle-maker.com* to turn your list into a word search! No grammar or sentence structure necessary. (And the computer does all the hard work for you.) Stacey asked her boys to help her come up with words that describe their new baby sister; then she typed them into the magic word-search-making machine and printed it out on grid paper. The boys had fun participating, and now that the page is done, they love searching for the words.

scrapbook about what's in your fridge or pantry

Why take pictures of the items in your cupboards? Because it's funny, and it's surprising to realize how familiar brand-name faces are to you. Chances are, even without being able to see the product names, you could identify every person or creature on Celeste's page. And one day these familiar faces may change. New product mascots emerge; old ones retire or are updated. Look in your cupboards for a chance to preserve a small cross section of pop culture for yourself or your posterity.

The other day, I noticed lots of smiling faces looking back at me in the cupboard. I thought to myself..."gee look at all my kitchen friends." It's amazing how many of them "live" in my kitchen. You might think it's silly, but they are quite happy and comforting aren't they?

materials patterned paper (American Crafts, Mustard Moon) • foam letter stickers (American Crafts) • District Thin font • 8½ x 11 page by Celeste Smith, West Hartford, CT

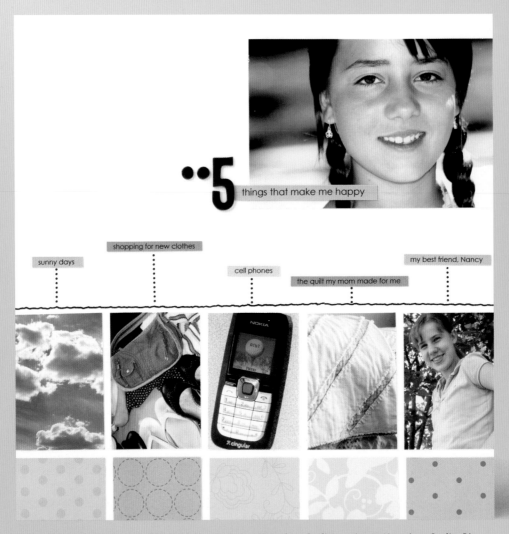

5 things that make me happy

sunny days

shopping for new clothes

cell phones

the quilt my mom made for me

my best friend, Nancy

materials patterned paper (SEI) • chipboard number (American Crafts) • rub-ons (American Crafts, Die Cuts With a View) • Century Gothic font • *12 x 12 page by Kim Morgan, Pleasant Grove, UT*

have your child photograph five "happy things" for a page

Kim handed the camera to Hannah, nearly 13, and encouraged her to take pictures of her five favorites. Is it any surprise that clothes, cell phones, and friends made the list? This is a great way to find out what's going on in your preteen's life.

scrapbook eight pictures of things you love for no reason

Walk around your house with a camera, and look for things that make **you smile** or even laugh out loud. (It's best to do this when you're alone.) Snap pictures of eight favorite objects—flower pots, sunglasses, books, and trinkets—and add them to a layout. When these items are no longer a part of your life, because they're out of style or no longer useful, you'll love having this layout to remind you of things that once mattered to you, for whatever reason.

materials patterned paper, border sticker (My Mind's Eye) • chipboard letters, rub-on letters, chipboard flower (American Crafts) • plastic heart (Heidi Grace Designs) • brad • 8½ x 11 page by Rachel Gainer, Saratoga Springs, UT

Rachel's favorite fun things
Rachel Gainer, Associate Editor

"My husband and I love strategy games, and Ticket to Ride is one of our favorites. I never win, but I keep trying. Complaining about losing is half the fun!"

"At home, I have a metal bulletin board that's just covered in Magnetic Poetry. I'm constantly rearranging the words into phrases that make me smile."

"I'm a bookworm. When I'm alone, my favorite thing to do is read. *The Secret Life of Bees* was a poignant and uplifting story. I couldn't put it down!"

list all of your child's nicknames on a layout

It certainly helps if your child is actually named Nick—
it's much more punny that way—but even if your kids are named Breanna (aka "Bugaboo") and Thomas (aka "The Tank"), take the time to record their pet names on a layout. It won't be long before they outgrow these childish monikers and insist on teen-approved nicknames only.

materials patterned paper (Scenic Route Paper Co.) • Diesel die-cut font (QuicKutz) • chipboard accent (Fancy Pants Designs) • brads • 8½ x 11 page by Karen Glenn, Orem, UT

CHAPTER 3:
Form & Function

YOU'D NEVER USE THE SAME LAYOUT design for every page in a scrapbook, so why would you configure your journaling the same way every time? Learn how you can add variety to the way you shape your journaling by expanding on the traditional paragraph format. By using lists, timelines, calendars, conversations, and Q&A style journaling, you can record your feelings, experiences, and day-to-day life in fun and unique ways that capture even more of your personality. These formats not only add variety and interest to your layouts, they'll help you include even more detail and information to enrich and expand your scrapbooks.

LIST JOURNALING

SOMETIMES JOURNALING CAN FEEL LIKE A CHORE, SO I USE TIME-SAVING SHORTCUTS TO
share meaningful stories in my scrapbooks. If you sometimes struggle with journaling, here
are a few tricks for getting your words on paper.

What We Did in 2006

I love creating summary albums and pages to record stories and events quickly, while I still remember the details. This little album was perfect for housing a month-by-month summary of our year. All I had to do was write a bulleted list of highlights for each month and then browse through the picture folders on my computer, which are organized chronologically, and choose one to represent each month.

Quick Tip: If you're like me, you sometimes feel the need to record every detail. But if you don't have the time or the desire to write deep, reflective journaling, make a mini-album! Because it's so small, it'll force you to get to the point fast.

My Little Sister

I absolutely love using list-style journaling. I don't consider myself a phenomenal writer, so I often use this journaling method to avoid even having to think about punctuation and grammar. A list of facts or a collection of descriptive words can do the trick just as well as any carefully crafted paragraph could. And it's so easy!

fun
a blonde at heart
young
sweet and kind
a great aunt
easy going
strong & athletic
carefree
short like me
my sister
my friend

my little sister

ashley
nineteen years old

Use LISTS

UTILIZING A LIST CAN help you highlight a fun activity and what was going on or being said at that precise time. On her layout, Cindy Tobey highlights how her daughter tried on hat after hat in a souvenir shop. The 14 photos and playful comments help illustrate the fun.

To journal with flair like Cindy did:

· Introduce the activity, what it entailed, and who was involved.

· Number your photos and corresponding comments for easy reference.

· Simplify busy pages by cropping photos and controlling color.

15 Hats *by Cindy Tobey.* **Supplies:** *Patterned paper:* Adornit–Carolee's Creations, American Crafts, Crate Paper, Fancy Pants Designs, and Scenic Route; *Stickers:* Making Memories and Me and My Big Ideas; *Rub-ons:* Hambly Screen Prints; *Ribbon:* Cosmo Cricket; *Chipboard:* American Crafts and BasicGrey; *Brads:* BoBunny Press and Sassafras; *Paint:* Making Memories; *Punches:* EK Success and Fiskars Americas; *Fonts:* CK Kelly and DejaVu Sans Condensed; *Adhesive:* Glue Dots International, Scrapbook Adhesives by 3L, and Tombow.

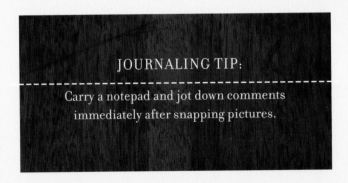

JOURNALING TIP:

Carry a notepad and jot down comments
immediately after snapping pictures.

1. Your teacher said you were the most compassionate toddler she has ever worked with.
2. You made Tami smile at the bagel place today.
3. You thought of the best gift to give to Kay.
4. You gave me lots of hugs and said "I love you" lots.
5. You said God's book is your favorite book.

5 ways you brightened my day

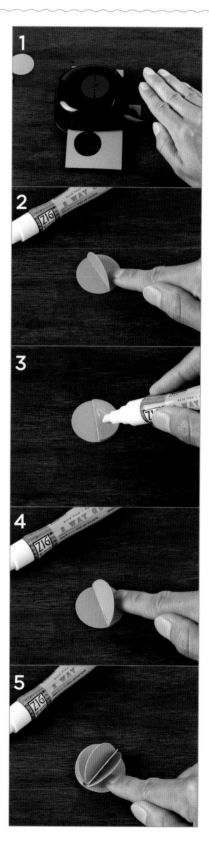

5 Ways You Brightened My Day by Jennifer McGuire. **Supplies:** *Patterned paper:* Making Memories and Stampin' Up!; *Clipboard:* Stampin' Up!; *Paint:* Ranger Industries; *Stickers:* Doodlebug Design; *Rhinestones:* Hero Arts; *Font:* American Typewriter; *Other:* Adhesive.

How to Create Your Own 3-D Ball Accent

1 Punch eight identical circles. Apply adhesive to one circle.

2 Fold another circle in half, and adhere one half to first circle.

3 Fold circle over, and apply adhesive to second half.

4 Fold third circle in half; apply adhesives to both halves. Adhere to first two circles.

5 Repeat with all other circles, creating a 3-D ball. Adhere final circle to first circle.

LOVE BY THE NUMBERS

by Erin Lincoln

Paint a by-the-numbers portrait of your loved ones' personalities. Erin filled this six-up album with random photos and images left over from other projects to give a surprisingly rich look at each family member. Number stickers correspond to brief but thoughtful captions. Just a few words are enough to sum up each trait.

FAST TIP

Give your project added style without added stress. Create one eye-catching design element (such as the colorful title blocks Erin used here) and repeat that design on each page or spread. Variation in color and pattern keeps the look fresh.

Supplies: *Patterned paper:* Cosmo Cricket, Imaginisce, and Making Memories; *Stamps:* Autumn Leaves, Hero Arts, and Impress Rubber Stamps; *Buttons and ink:* Papertrey Ink; *Pen:* Sakura; *Die cuts:* QuicKutz; *Punch:* EK Success; *Other:* Adhesive.

1. Family time. 2. Beer. 3. Inflatable kayak.
4. Frederick, MD. 5. Coffee. 6. Tinkering in his shop.
7. Traveling. 8. Being an excellent father. 9. Poker.
10. Playing Frisbee with the guys. 11. Cigars. 12.
EMPL. 13. Relaxing. 14. BBQing. 15. Building planes.
16. Being a total and complete ham.

matt

what he loves
by the
numbers

1. Being adorable. 2. Bubbles. 3. Coloring. 4. His
family. 5. Helping Mama unload the dishwasher.
6. Goofing around with Daddy. 7. Climbing on
everything in sight. 8. Curious George. 9. Wearing
hats. 10. His two blankies. 11. Macaroni and Cheese
lunch with Mama 12. His Bellybutton. 13. Train set
at Nana and Grandad's 14. Being with Daddy. 15. Ice
cream. 16. Sliding 17. Cozy Coupe rides
18. Play-Doh.

hank

what he loves
by the
numbers

*Capture the details of your day-to-day
life in a list, like Erin did, and let your
photos do the storytelling.*

DISTRESS CHIPBOARD FOR A MINI ALBUM

Rough up the edges of your chipboard mini albums with a craft knife for a weathered look. This is a fantastic technique to turn to when you're creating a mini album for a guy—nothing too girly here! Finish it off with a layer of paint and buttons. You can protect your chipboard by adding an extra, clear acrylic cover to your mini album. And, for an extra dose of fun, replace several of the chipboard pages with acrylic too.

Bonus Ideas:

- Stamp on your acrylic pages, just as you would a transparency, with opaque solvent ink.
- Use a chipboard ring instead of a simple circle for your first chipboard page. Then adhere the title to the center of your acrylic cover. It'll look as though the title is floating in the middle of the ring.

You Make Me Smile by Jennifer McGuire. **Supplies:** *Chipboard and acrylic album:* Tinkering Ink; *Ink and inking tool:* Ranger Industries; *Stamps:* Hero Arts; *Ink:* Tsukineko; *Rub-ons:* Stampin' Up!; *Button brads:* Imaginisce; *Other:* Beaded chain, cardstock, and ribbon.

Bonus Idea: Use different chipboard shapes for album pages that will catch your viewer's attention.

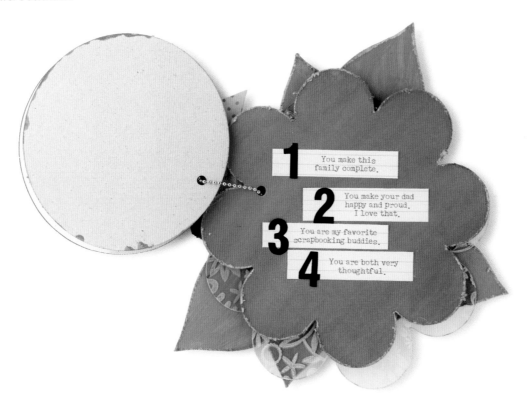

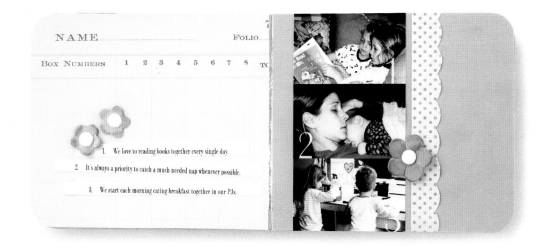

NAME _____ FOLIO

BOX NUMBERS   1   2   3   4   5   6   7   8   TO

1.   We love to reading books together every single day.

2.   It's always a priority to catch a much needed nap whenever possible.

3.   We start each morning eating breakfast together in our PJs.

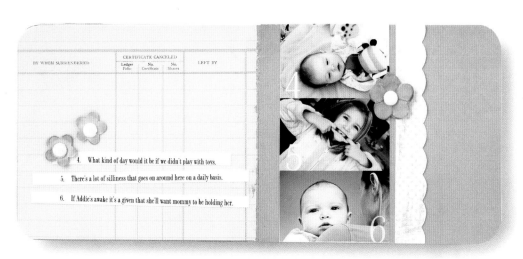

| BY WHOM SURRENDERED | CERTIFICATE CANCELED | | | LEFT BY |
| | Ledger Folio | No. Certificate | No. Shares | |

4.   What kind of day would it be if we didn't play with toys.

5.   There's a lot of silliness that goes on around here on a daily basis.

6.   If Addie's awake it's a given that she'll want mommy to be holding her.

| | CERTIFICATE CANCELED | | | | CERTIFICATE ISSUED | | | |
| Date | Journal Folio | Certificate Number | Number of Shares | Pro-tion | Date | Journal Folio | Certificate Number | Number of Shares | Pro-tion |

7.   It's always fun to play with play doh.

8.   After supper its bathtime.

9.   Every afternoon Emily is off to kindergarten.

Print journaling on one page. In a single document, Rebecca typed up one short sentence to go with each of her photos—no fancy formatting required! Just cut the strips apart and go.

FRESH TIP

how to have 🌢 fun on a
rainy day

Step 1: go to Fired Up and pick out your ceramic piece. Love on it and cuddle it for a few minutes. **Step 2**: pick out your paint colors. They do not need to bear any resemblance to the real colors of the animal you have chosen to paint. **Step 3**: Try to find the smallest paintbrush in the brush jar, as big brushes just won't work for you. **Step 4**: Make funny "concentration" faces as you decide where to start. **Step 5**: Paint your background color (note: this step is only necessary if you are older than 4 and have an actual plan of how your piece will turn out). **Step 6**: Make more funny faces as you paint. **Step 7**: Get paint in your hair, which will later have to be scrubbed out. **Step 8**: Make a super-cute face while adding your 6th pastel color to your shark. **Step 9**: Use a wet Q-tip to erase the color you accidentally painted on your rabbit's eyeball. Try not to get too upset. **Step 10**: Proudly show off your finished product.

How to Have Fun on a Rainy Day *by Brigid Gonzalez.* **Supplies** *Software:* Adobe Photoshop CS3; *Fonts:* Kalinga and Times New Roman.

Winterland *by Wendy Sue Anderson.* **Supplies** *Cardstock:* American Crafts; *Patterned paper:* Cosmo Cricket (ledger) and October Afternoon (pink); *Ribbon:* Making Memories; *Ink:* Clearsnap; *Paper snowflakes and scallop tag:* Making Memories; *Letter stickers, brads and pen:* American Crafts; *Adhesive:* Glue Dots International and Tombow; *Other:* Thread.

Hoeppner Home *by Megan Hoeppner.* **Supplies** *Cardstock:* American Crafts, Core'dinations, Die Cuts With a View and Stampin' Up!; *Patterned paper:* Bella Blvd and October Afternoon; *Flocking:* Doodlebug Design; *Ribbon:* American Crafts; *Letter stickers:* October Afternoon; *Stickers:* Bella Blvd; *Square punch:* Fiskars Americas; *Pen:* Marvy Uchida; *Adhesive:* Scrapbook Adhesives by 3L.

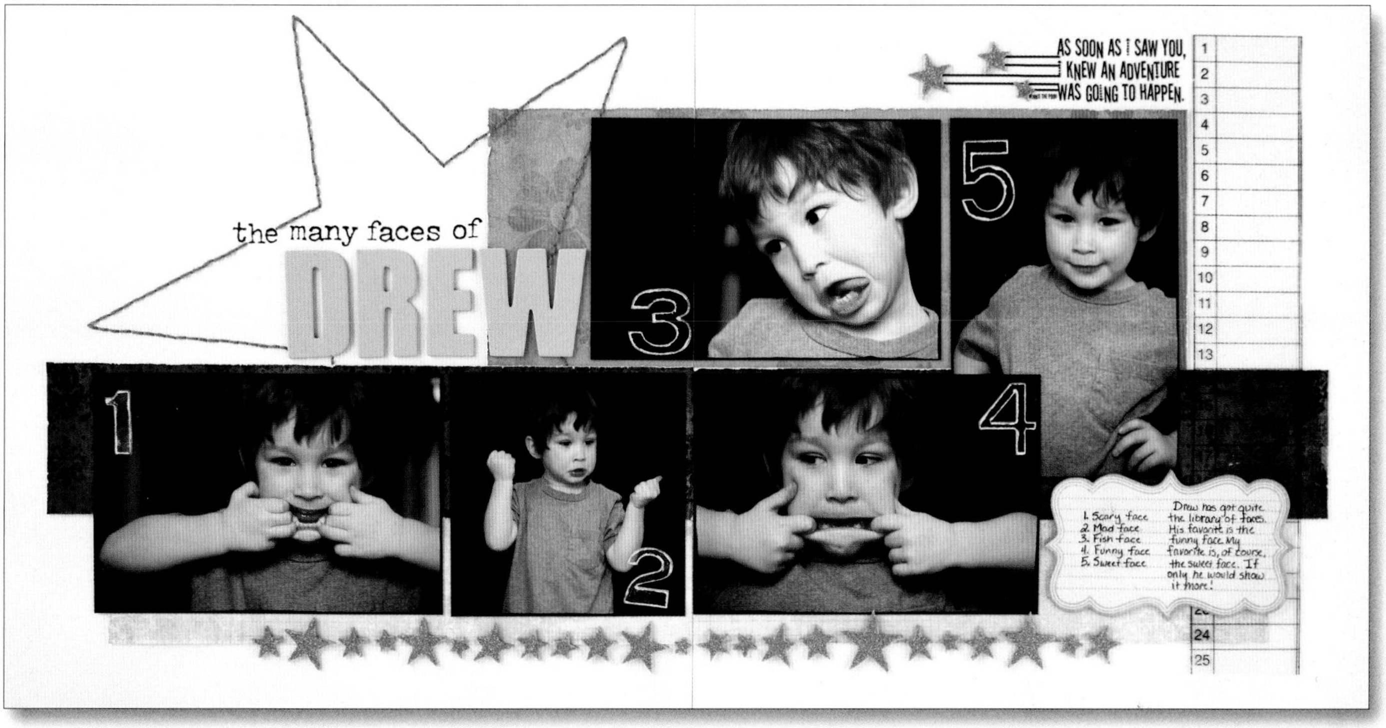

AS SOON AS I SAW YOU, I KNEW AN ADVENTURE WAS GOING TO HAPPEN.

the many faces of DREW

1. Scary face
2. Mad face
3. Fish face
4. Funny face
5. Sweet face

Drew has got quite the library of faces. His favorite is the funny face. My favorite is, of course, the sweet face. If only he would show it more!

The Many Faces of Drew *by Allison Davis.* **Supplies** *Cardstock:* Bazzill Basics Paper; *Patterned paper, transparency, rub-ons, acrylic numbers and chipboard:* Fancy Pants Designs; *Ink:* ColorBox Fluid Chalk, Clearsnap; *Paint:* Making Memories; *Glitter:* Doodlebug Design; *Embroidery floss:* DMC; *Pen:* Zig Memory, EK Success.

the Knuckler

the "knuckler" has been a favorite way to create outbursts of laughter in the mcguire children for years.

1 step 1: warn small boy of the knuckler that is about to occur.

2 step 2: show small boy knuckler.

3 step 3: knuckler is placed under small boy's chin and tickles around.

4 step 4: small boy laughs hysterically, begging dad to do it again.

The Knuckler by Jennifer McGuire. *Photos by Lisa Russo Photography.* **Supplies** *Punches:* EK Success; *Cardstock:* Bazzill Basics Paper; *Patterned paper:* Studio Calico; *Stamps and ink:* Hero Arts; *Glitter glue:* Stickles, Ranger Industries; *Letter stickers:* Making Memories; *Adhesive:* 3D-Dots, EK Success; Dot 'n' Roller, Kokuyo; *Other:* Thread.

LEGO

ONE Brandon and Daddy would sit for hours making up Star Wars fighter ships. Here we have two "X-wing fighters!"

TWO Now, Brandon makes them on his own! This is a gunner ship. A clone trooper is driving and Anikan is shooting at the bad guys! And it's called a T-wing fighter.

THREE This one is a space police ship driven by a droid. The person laying down in the back is an alien robber being taken to jail.

FOUR Here we have an M-wing fighter (name made up by Brandon because it looks like an "M.") It's also being driven by a droid and has a rocket under the ship.

FIVE This one is so cool. It's another space police ship made out of a fire chief's truck. This one is driven by a clone trooper!

SIX This is called the Voyager III. It is a bad guy ship that is driven by a storm trooper and shoots guns from the front and the back.

CREATIONS

YOUR HARD WORK PAID OFF—YOU'VE MASTERED YOUR FAVORITE HOBBY! SHOWCASE YOUR MOST SPECTACULAR CREATIONS.

Lego Creations by *Julie DeGuia*. **Supplies** *Software:* Adobe Photoshop CS2; *Paper:* Art Warehouse, Candles and Cakes Solids Paper Pack by Danelle Johnson (blue strips) and Mon Petit Ballon Bleu Solids Paper Pack by Katie Pertiet (white); *Stamps:* Numbers by Katie Pertiet; *Elements:* Between the Lines Borders by Katie Pertiet and Staple Its! by Pattie Knox; *Fonts:* Bernard MT Condensed and Skia.

{ LEAD THE WAY }
WITH NUMBERS

SPELL out numbers to introduce descriptions.

INCLUDE a boxed number by each photo to help connect related items.

TEN
PLAYFUL TITLE IDEAS

1. #1 FAN
2. [INSERT WORD] MANIA
3. CATCH OF THE DAY
4. GUILTY AS CHARGED
5. I SEE A PATTERN HERE
6. MADE WITH LOVE
7. V-I-C-T-O-R-Y
8. WELCOME ABOARD
9. YES, I'M HOOKED!
10. LET THE GAMES BEGIN ck

FLIP stickers over and add metal leafing to back for shapes that shine.

10 things
i love
about you

1. your kindness
2. your laugh
3. your patience
4. your heart
5. your smile
6. your taste in music
7. your smarts ☺
8. your humor
9. your generosity
10. you are a great 14-yr-old!

10 Things *by Jennifer McGuire.* **Supplies:** *Stickers:* Doodlebug Design; *Stamp:* Stamping Bella; *Ribbon:* American Crafts; *Punch:* We R Memory Keepers; *Ink:* Hero Arts; *Adhesive:* Tombow; *Other:* Metal leafing.

❶ Flip sticker over.

❷ Press lots of metal leafing over sticky part.

❸ Brush off extra leafing.

Define the Details

Do you love layouts that use lots of photos to showcase the little details in life, but find that too many detail photos can leave a layout feeling unfocused? Use wallet-size photos to surround and support your focal point photo, just as Aly Dosdall did on her layout about her sons starting a new school year. Each wallet-size photo focuses on a different detail, giving a visual record of the changes the boys experienced as they embarked on the new school year. But the smaller size of the detail photos keeps the focus on the boys.

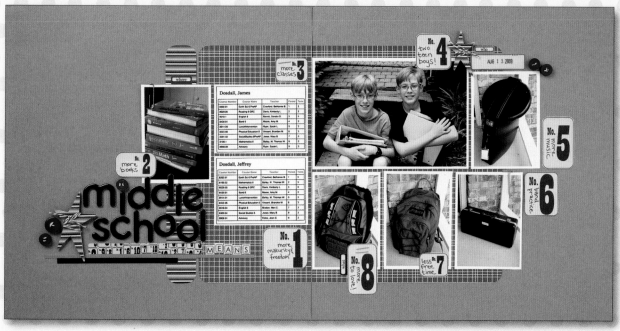

Middle School Means *by Aly Dosdall.* **Supplies:** *Cardstock and patterned paper:* Jillibean Soup; *Stickers:* American Crafts and Jillibean Soup; *Chipboard:* Scenic Route; *Baker's twine:* Kraft Outlet; *Buttons:* Creative Imaginations; *Stamp:* Shiny Stamp; *Pen:* EK Success; *Other:* Adhesive, paper clips, and staples.

I'm Sensing *by Joannie McBride.* **Supplies:** *Cardstock:* Core'dinations; *Patterned paper:* Imaginisce; *Punches:* Marvy Uchida; *Stickers and pen:* American Crafts; *Adhesive:* Scrapbook Adhesives by 3L and Therm O Web; *Other:* Tags and staples.

Capture everything you're sensing

Besides the who, what, when, where, and why of a story, try detailing the things you sensed during an event. What did you see? What did you hear? What did you smell? What did you touch? What did you taste? Joannie McBride used this technique to capture all of the activities her son experienced on a day at a local farm.

Capturing this type of detail will help your relive the event for years to come, bringing to mind things you may otherwise forget. After all, one of the biggest payoffs of scrapbooking is reliving all of the great times you've had. Try capturing this type of detail for your next big event and see if it doesn't make a difference in the type of story you capture.

THE NUMBERS TREND TAKES A FUNCTIONAL ELEMENT and sets it loose—showcasing numerals in artistic ways to accent clothing, home accessories, wall art, and more. Try this look on your scrapbook layouts, using numbers decoratively and functionally as accents or design elements that represent various facts and figures related to the topic of your page. Consider using significant numbers as a layout theme, such as your age, or the number of kids you have, or for lists such as, "Top 10 reasons," "100 things I love," or "1 thing about me for each year of my life."

Ten Things I Love About You *by Shelley Aldrich.* **Supplies:** *Cardstock:* EK Success; *Rub-ons:* My Mind's Eye; *Ink:* Clearsnap; *Colored pencils:* Newell Rubbermaid; *Pens:* EK Success and Pantone; *Adhesive:* Therm O Web; *Other:* Measuring tape. **ck**

photo taken
Sept 1, 2007

life lis

Make a list
LIFE LISTS by Amanda Probst

Life Lists by Amanda Probst. **Supplies:** Cardstock: Prism Papers; Patterned paper, ribbon, and tabs: Luxe Designs; Brads: 7gypsies; Pen and stickers: American Crafts; Fonts: Century Gothic, Impact, and Rockwell.

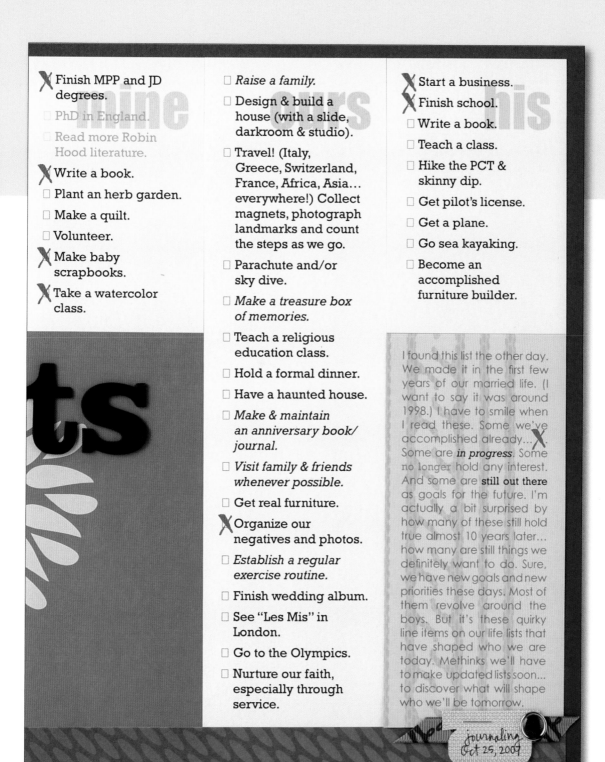

mine

- ☒ Finish MPP and JD degrees.
- ☐ PhD in England.
- ☐ Read more Robin Hood literature.
- ☒ Write a book.
- ☐ Plant an herb garden.
- ☐ Make a quilt.
- ☐ Volunteer.
- ☒ Make baby scrapbooks.
- ☒ Take a watercolor class.

ours

- ☐ *Raise a family.*
- ☐ Design & build a house (with a slide, darkroom & studio).
- ☐ Travel! (Italy, Greece, Switzerland, France, Africa, Asia… everywhere!) Collect magnets, photograph landmarks and count the steps as we go.
- ☐ Parachute and/or sky dive.
- ☐ *Make a treasure box of memories.*
- ☐ Teach a religious education class.
- ☐ Hold a formal dinner.
- ☐ Have a haunted house.
- ☐ *Make & maintain an anniversary book/ journal.*
- ☐ *Visit family & friends whenever possible.*
- ☐ Get real furniture.
- ☒ Organize our negatives and photos.
- ☐ *Establish a regular exercise routine.*
- ☐ Finish wedding album.
- ☐ See "Les Mis" in London.
- ☐ Go to the Olympics.
- ☐ Nurture our faith, especially through service.

his

- ☒ Start a business.
- ☒ Finish school.
- ☐ Write a book.
- ☐ Teach a class.
- ☐ Hike the PCT & skinny dip.
- ☐ Get pilot's license.
- ☐ Get a plane.
- ☐ Go sea kayaking.
- ☐ Become an accomplished furniture builder.

I found this list the other day. We made it in the first few years of our married life. (I want to say it was around 1998.) I have to smile when I read these. Some we've accomplished already…☒. Some are **in progress**. Some no longer hold any interest. And some are **still out there** as goals for the future. I'm actually a bit surprised by how many of these still hold true almost 10 years later… how many are still things we definitely want to do. Sure, we have new goals and new priorities these days. Most of them revolve around the boys. But it's these quirky line items on our life lists that have shaped who we are today. Methinks we'll have to make updated lists soon… to discover what will shape who we'll be tomorrow.

journaling
Oct 25, 2007

"Happy people plan ACTIONS, they don't plan RESULTS." —DENNIS WHOLEY

LAUGHTER IS ALSO A GREAT STRESS RELIEVER. *Like most women, Mary juggles hundreds of little tasks each day, and sometimes the frenetic pace leaves her feeling dispirited and overwhelmed. After Mary shared these feelings with her husband, he jokingly suggested that she hire an assistant. His comment inspired Mary to create this comical page about two possible candidates: her husband and her pug. "Creating this layout helped me record my frustration without sounding bitter," she says. "It made dealing with the situation a lot easier."*

> "A day without laughter is a day wasted."
>
> CHARLIE CHAPLIN

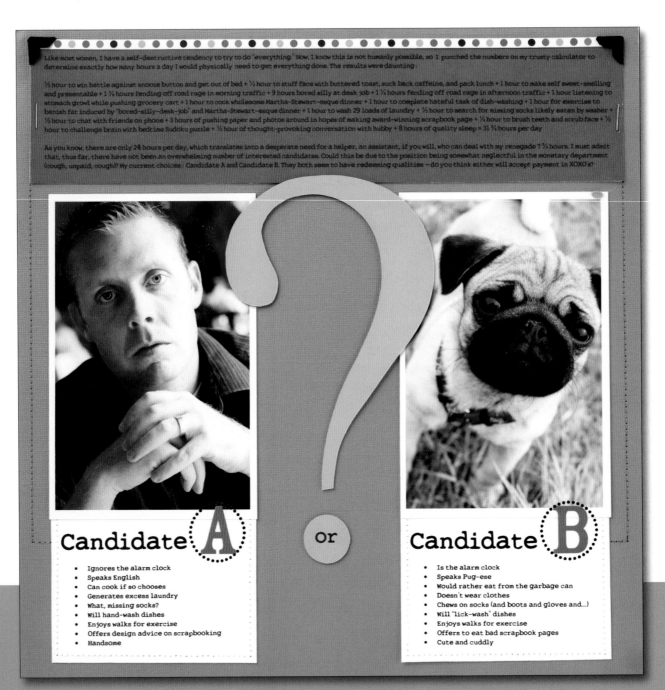

materials patterned paper, letter stickers, dotted circle rub-ons (American Crafts) • photo corners (Canson) • staples • machine stitching • AL Messenger font • *12 x 12 page by Mary MacAskill, Calgary, AB, Canada*

Timelines can convey a sequence and help you recall specifics later. On her 17-photo layout, Mandy Douglass organized her Hawaii itinerary into an easy-to-follow timeline.

Aloha by Mandy Douglass. **Supplies:** *Cardstock and brads:* American Crafts; *Patterned paper:* Pebbles and SEI; *Stickers:* American Crafts and SEI; *Font:* Chalet Comprime; *Adhesive:* Scrapbook Adhesives by 3L; *Other:* Hole punch and paper piercer.

by Jen Jockisch

Summers are packed with memories in the making, from water park visits to family vacations. By using pages photocopied from a calendar for her layout's background, Jen found a place to take note of every special day. There's plenty of room for her free-spirited creativity, too—wallet-size photos and accents are arranged playfully across the pages, going "outside the lines" with stylish flair.

FRESH TIP

Break free of binder rings by using a sparkly strand of beads to bind your album.

Supplies: *Album and punches:* EK Success; *Patterned paper:* 7gypsies, American Crafts, Cosmo Cricket, Die Cuts with a View, Pebbles, and Sassafras; *Ribbon:* American Crafts, Fancy Pants Designs, Maya Road, and Prima; *Chipboard:* American Crafts and Crate Paper; *Stickers:* Jenni Bowlin Studio, Pink Paislee, and Sassafras; *Rub-ons:* Crate Paper; *Rhinestones:* BoBunny Press; *Buttons:* American Crafts, Fancy Pants Designs, Jenni Bowlin Studio, and Sassafras; *Pebbles:* Prima; *Ink:* Clearsnap; *Tickets:* Jenni Bowlin Studio and SEI; *Felt and pen:* American Crafts; *Other:* Adhesive and bead strand.

Save the glue for paper and plastic embellishments. A stapler can make attaching ribbon effortless.

FAST TIP

ARE YOU READY FOR SOME FOOTBALL?

by Katrina Simeck

Include touchable accents in an otherwise no-nonsense digital design to increase an album's friendliness factor—a must for a sports-themed album. Katrina added a chipboard and vinyl sticker to her title page and scattered die-cut pieces throughout, mounting them with dimensional adhesive for added pop.

Supplies: *Photo book:* Mypictales.com; *Chipboard die cuts:* BasicGrey; *Letter stickers:* American Crafts; *Punches:* Fiskars Americas; *Other:* Brads and ribbon. **Digital Supplies:** *Patterned paper:* Gina Cabrera; *Frames:* Katie Pertiet; *Font:* Avant Garde BK.

Elisha
then

was destined
to be a
mother

was always
a girly-girl

tried her hand
at almost every
sport

Elisha
now

loves being
a mother

is still a
girly-girl

can't play sports
and doesn't like
to watch them

Taylor
then

had the
funniest
personality

loved being on
skateboards
and motorcycles

always had his
hair combed and
shirt tucked in

Taylor
now

is the silent,
hilarious type

still loves
skateboards and
motorcycles

lives in t-shirts
and jeans

Witney
then

was an
incredible
dancer

was always
a girly-girl

was a social
butterfly

Witney
now

still loves
to dance

is still a
girly-girl

still has so
many friends

FRESH TIP

When working with older photos from many different time periods, convert them all to black and white to achieve a cool, uniform look. This step will also make choosing background colors much simpler.

FAST TIP

When gathering information from family members for a project of this type, keep everyone on track by sticking to three main points per person.

ALL THROUGH THE YEAR

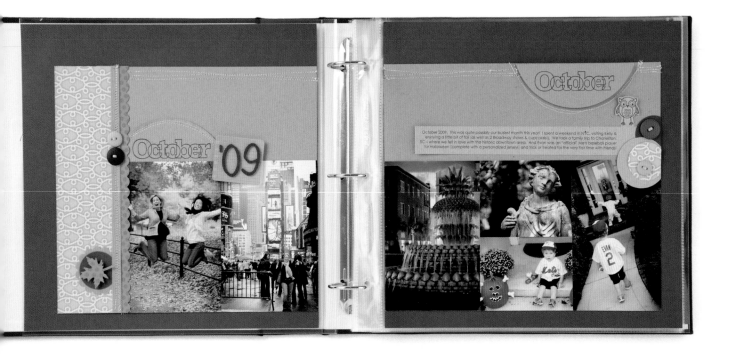

by Susan Weinroth

Oh, what a busy year! Susan rounded up her family's highlights of 2009 in an album with a single spread dedicated to each month. By sticking to a simple, sophisticated design, she ensured that her project will transcend trends—this album will look just as fresh in ten years as it does today. (Another plus? Cutting down the time required to lay out each page to just minutes!)

FRESH TIP

When using many multi-colored photos, like Susan did here, choose a couple of colors that stand out—like orange and yellow—and pair them with basics like brown and kraft. This way, you won't overwhelm your photos!

Supplies: *Cardstock:* American Crafts and Bazzill Basics Paper; *Patterned paper:* American Crafts, October Afternoon, and Studio Calico; *Stickers:* American Crafts and Studio Calico; *Stamps:* Hero Arts and Studio Calico; *Ink:* Tsukineko; *Buttons and brads:* American Crafts; *Adhesive, circle cutter, and punches:* Fiskars Americas; *Font:* Century Gothic; *Other:* Embroidery floss and thread.

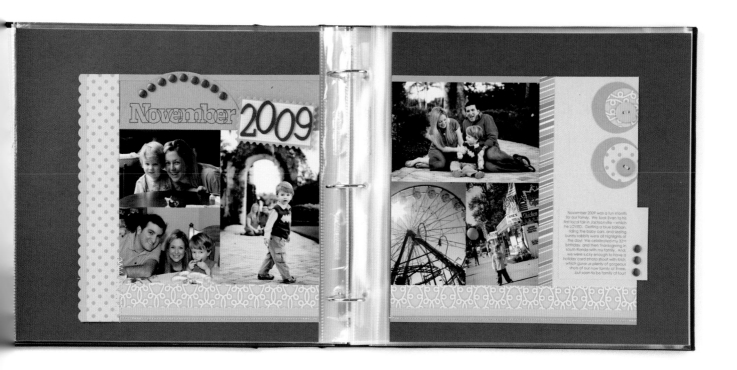

Once you've found or designed a sketch to help you lay out your album, feel free to rotate or flip it to add variety to succeeding pages. Remember, too, that a sketch is a guideline, not a straitjacket. Accents that cross the boundaries give pages a sense of vitality.

10 YEARS

LIVED IN PROVO OFF OF 1ST NORTH AND 4TH EAST

BRIAN GRADUATES FROM BYU

BRIAN WORKS FOR STEWARTS LAWN CARE

I WORK FOR NU SKIN AS A TOUR GUIDE

BRIAN GETS A JOB WITH E&Y IN CALIFORNIA

WENT TO DISNEYLAND TO CELEBRATE OUR ANNIVERSARY

by Jackie Stringham

Commemorate a special birthday or anniversary with an album featuring one spread dedicated to each year. The 9" x 9" album Jackie used for her project allowed her to create a balanced design at lightning speed. She used four 4" x 4" squares for each page, matting them on white cardstock with equal margins for a tidy look. This approach let her cut all her paper and cardstock pieces at the same time, speeding up the process even more.

Supplies: *Cardstock and stitching template:* Bazzill Basics Paper; *Flowers:* Bazzill Basics Paper and Making Memories; *Embroidery floss:* DMC.

WELCOME BABY TREVOR!

OUR YEAR LONG DISNEY ADVENTURE

OUR FIRST REAL CHRISTMAS TREE

BRIAN PASSES THE CPA EXAM

WE MOVE FROM LAKE FOREST TO UTAH

LIVE IN MISSY AND JARED'S BASEMENT

00-GO-RYDER
MOVING SERVICE
www.yellowtruck.com

5

4TH YEAR IN WEST JORDAN

VACATIONING WITH FRIENDS IN LAKE TAHOE

BECOMING VICE PRESIDENT

KATIE AND TREVOR LEARNING TO READ

WINNING HALL OF FAME

GEO CACHING WITH FAMILY

9

Make this design your own by substituting your favorite patterned paper in for one of the cardstock colors, or consider switching the numbers out for letters and use photos that correspond with each letter.

FRESH TIP

Everyday Album B

March 2009 *by Wendy Sue Anderson.* **Supplies** *Cardstock:* American Crafts; *Patterned paper:* Cosmo Cricket and Making Memories; *Ribbon:* American Crafts and Cosmo Cricket; *Chipboard:* American Crafts (letters) and Cosmo Cricket (van); *Rub-ons and pen:* American Crafts; *Buttons:* Making Memories; *Corner rounder punch:* EK Success; *Foam squares:* 3L; *Other:* Adhesive and thread.

Shopping List:

- 6 sheets of white cardstock
- 1 sheet of brown polka dot patterned paper
- 1 sheet of striped patterned paper
- 1 sheet of grid patterned paper
- 1 sheet of circle patterned paper
- Chipboard letters and accents
- 1 sheet of rub-on accents
- Corner rounder punch
- Ribbon scraps
- Pen
- Adhesive
- Buttons
- Thread and string
- Album

INSTRUCTIONS:

1. Arrange photos and adhere to page.

2. Adhere strips of patterned paper, title and ribbon.

3. Add journaling.

4. Finish your look with stitching and embellishments.

BONUS TIP: Use un-cropped 4" x 6" photos to save even more time!

Variation #1

To create her "April 2009" layout, Wendy Sue Anderson used one less photo and accented her layout with a few more embellishments.

BONUS TIP: Use scraps of ribbon to create a fun accent for journaling spots.

Variation #2

Wendy Sue created her album based on highlighting memories from each month. To help save you time, choose several photos from each month and focus on highlighting just those.

2009. First African-American President is inaugurated. Michael Jackson dies. H1N1 outbreak is deemed a global pandemic. You? Well, you are oblivious to it all. You just know you are loved. And that's exactly how it should be.

1978. First "test tube" baby is born in London. Diplomatic relations open between U.S. and China. Artificial insulin is invented. Me? Well, I was oblivious to it all. I just knew I was loved. And that's exactly how it should be.

Me Then–You Now by Deena Wuest. **Digital Supplies:** *Software:* Adobe; *Cardstock:* Michelle Martin; *Frames, notebook, and tabs:* Katie Pertiet; *Fonts:* Teen and Avenir.

THINGS i love

by savanna

kittens · lps · basketball · candy

@ge 9

God | Jesus | mom | dad | grandpa
grandma | cousins | kittens
dresses | Sunday School
Wednesday nights | sisters
brothers | telephones
elcrisity/lights | water
food | ice cream | oreos
hersheys chocolate
school | basketball
earth | rollerskating
volleyball | state fair
soccerball | golfball
sports | bowling
football | friends
family | home | air
chips | me/savanna
my room/Brooklyn's
candy | P.E. | music
recorder | flowers
pictures | computer
Jesus | pants | coats
jackets | hair brushes
great great grandma
great grandpa | pools
wiis | dolls | lpso | lps
polly pockets | hot tubs
water slides | cheerleading
puppy store | Big Time Rush
Selena Gomez | tony's pizza | TV
dog slide | movie theaters | bluejays

Things I Love @ Age 9 *by Deena Wuest.* **Digital** *Supplies:* Software: Adobe; *Cardstock and frames:* Katie Pertiet; *Font:* Avenir.

Capture Slang

Scrapbooking informal expressions of slang is not only entertaining, but it also points out details of a kid's age and generation. Scrapbook common slang terms, including the terms that left you scratching your head to figure out what they meant. To make even more sense of it, try defining those terms as well. Here, Laura Vegas showcases the key to her daughter's texting language.

Periodic Table for Text Messages *by Laura Vegas.* **Supplies** *Cardstock:* American Crafts; *Patterned paper:* Making Memories; *Journaling block and sticker:* Creative Imaginations; *Brad:* Making Memories; *Letter stickers:* Doodlebug Design; *Chipboard letters:* Scenic Route; *Chipboard accent:* KitoftheMonth.com; *Clips:* OfficeMax; *Periodic table folder:* Target; *Pen:* Slick Writers, American Crafts; *Adhesive:* EK Success, Plaid Enterprises and Therm O Web.

More Quotable Page Ideas

TRY THESE ADDITIONAL IDEAS OUT FOR "QUOTABLE KIDS" PAGES IN A SNAP:

 Where'd You Learn *That* **Word?** Scrapbook about the first time you heard a child use a word you know you didn't teach him.

 That's What He Said. Interview family members to record what they think are the kid's current expressions or catch phrases, and use the replies as journaling on a page.

 Texts in the Life of a Mom. Record the texts your kid sends you over a certain period of time (a day or a week) to show the typical communication.

 The History of Your/Our Slang. Compare the slang or expressions a kid uses at different ages. Or compare the slang or expressions you used at your child's age to show the differences in or commonalities of slang over the decades.

 A Day in the Life of a Chatterbox. Use a string of frequently said expressions or questions to create a border around a page or to create a custom background paper for a layout. **ck**

My Family *by Susan Weinroth.* **Supplies** *Cardstock:* American Crafts (brown and green), Bazzill Basics Paper (teal) and Die Cuts With a View (aqua); *Patterned paper:* American Crafts (orange), Bo-Bunny Press (green dot), Cosmo Cricket ("My Family" word block) and October Afternoon (pink and stripe); *Stickers:* Doodlebug Design; *Felt accents, rhinestone brads and rub-ons:* American Crafts; *Die-cut shape:* October Afternoon; *Scallop border and circle punches:* Fiskars Americas; *Font:* LTC Remington Typewriter; *Adhesive:* Fiskars Americas; *Other:* Thread.

Embrace *by Andrea Friebus.* **Supplies** *Cardstock:* American Crafts; *Patterned paper:* American Crafts and KI Memories; *Transparency frame:* Fancy Pants Designs; *Die-cutting machine:* Slice, Making Memories; *Journaling block:* Ella Publishing Co.; *Ribbon:* Home Shopping Network and Oriental Trading Company; *Brads:* Making Memories and Oriental Trading Company; *Ink:* Clearsnap; *Embroidery floss:* DMC; *Adhesive:* Therm O Web; *Other:* Felt, pen, flowers and buttons.

TIME-SAVING TIP:

To save time, Andrea used a Mad-Lib style journaling block to help her record her story on the layout.

DESCRIBE YOUR DAILY ROUTINE, WHETHER IT'S DRAB OR DAUNTING. LIST TYPICAL EXPERIENCES HOUR BY HOUR TO COMMUNICATE THE "EBB & FLOW" OF YOUR LIFE.

What We Do *by Laura Vegas.* **Supplies** *Patterned paper:* Fancy Pants Design; *Letter stickers:* Jillibean Soup; *Rub-ons and stickers:* Heidi Grace Designs; *Punch:* Stampin' Up!; *Pen:* American Crafts; *Font:* Old Remington; *Adhesive:* Creative Memories (pop dots) and Scrapbook Adhesives by 3L (tape runner).

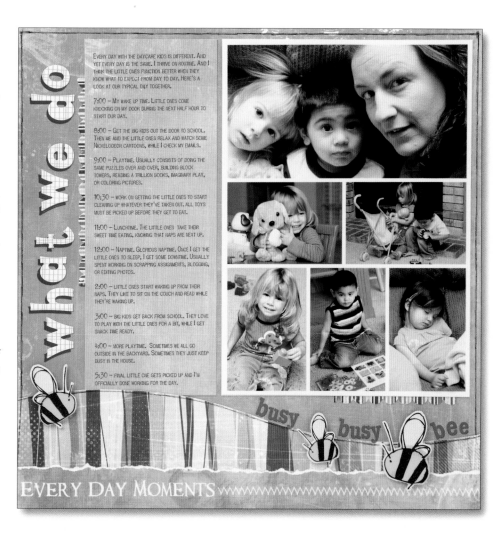

{ DESIGN TIP TO ADD OOMPH }
AND COLOR TO A TITLE

1. Select the same style of letter stickers in two colors.

2. Layer the sticker sets, adhering one sticker on top and slightly left for a shadow effect.

3. Adhere letters to layout.

{ HERE'S ANOTHER QUICK TRICK }

If a phrase rub-on won't fit existing space, simply cut apart each word, keeping the protective backing in place. Position your words as desired, remove their protective backing, and rub away, as Laura Vegas did with the phrase, "Busy, busy bee" on her layout shown above.

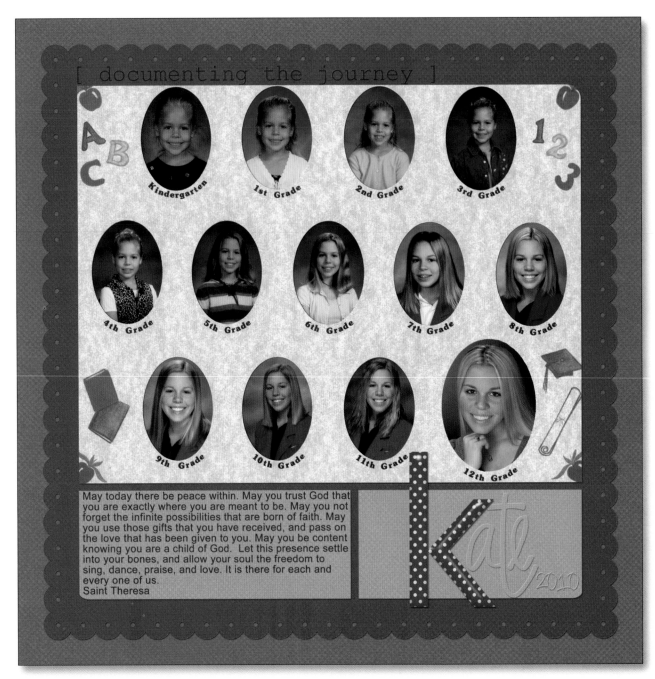

[documenting the journey]

Kindergarten   1st Grade   2nd Grade   3rd Grade

4th Grade   5th Grade   6th Grade   7th Grade   8th Grade

9th Grade   10th Grade   11th Grade   12th Grade

May today there be peace within. May you trust God that you are exactly where you are meant to be. May you not forget the infinite possibilities that are born of faith. May you use those gifts that you have received, and pass on the love that has been given to you. May you be content knowing you are a child of God. Let this presence settle into your bones, and allow your soul the freedom to sing, dance, praise, and love. It is there for each and every one of us.
Saint Theresa

Kate 2010

The Journey *by Angie Wagner.* **Supplies:** *School year frame:* AJ Phillips Publishing Co. **Digital supplies:** *Layered template:* Cathy Zielske; *Cardstock:* Katie Pertiet; *Word art and brushes:* Ali Edwards; *Letters:* Michelle Martin.

TECHNIQUE:

Not a fan of templates? You can still create this look by using an oval, square, or circle punch and placing your photos within the shapes.

Those Quirks

{ Dictionaries define "quirk" as a peculiarity of action, behavior, or personality; an idiosyncracy or mannerism. These quirks define who we are and where we came from. Which quirks define your family members? Capture these in your scrapbooks to create a more detailed picture of your family tree. }

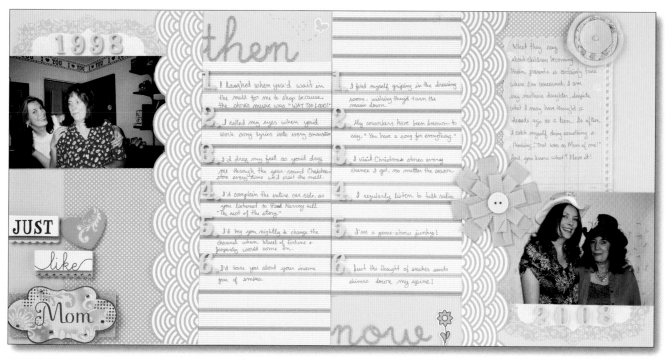

Then, Now by Megan Hoeppner. **Supplies:** Cardstock: Stampin' Up!; Patterned paper: American Crafts and Making Memories; Stickers: American Crafts, Little Yellow Bicycle, and me and my BIG ideas; Flowers: Pink Paislee and Prima; Pen: EK Success; Adhesive: Glue Arts.

X Have you ever caught yourself acting just like one of your parents? Today, you might be doing exactly what seemed so ridiculous when mom or dad did it back then. Compare these quirks like Megan Hoeppner did in her layout about her and her mom. Take a close look and you just might realize that you, too, are your mother's daughter.

Embellish
YOUR STORY

If you've walked through a scrapbook store lately (either in person or virtually), you'll undoubtedly agree that manufacturers create product for nearly everything imaginable. Take advantage! If you have an absent photo, use embellishments to tell your story. A tape measure and tree accent are the perfect visuals for Julie DeGuia's page about her growing children. And Christa Paustenbaugh's map paper and little houses represent her story brilliantly.

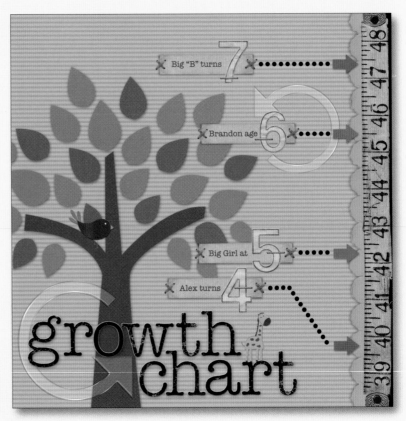

Growth Chart *by Julie DeGuia.* **Digital Supplies:** *Software:* Adobe; *Patterned paper:* Katie Pertiet and Lynn Grieveson; *Cardstock and journal strips:* Katie Pertiet; *Tape measure:* Lynn Grieveson; *Scallop strip:* Anna Aspnes; *Animal accents:* Mindy Terasawa and Pattie Knox; *Letters:* Katie Pertiet and Lynn Grieveson; *Acrylic arrow, brads and staple:* Pattie Knox; *Font:* American Typewriter.

On The Road Again *by Christa Paustenbaugh.* **Supplies:** *Cardstock:* Bazzill Basics Paper and Waussau; *Patterned paper:* Cosmo Cricket, Jillibean Soup, October Afternoon, Scenic Route, and Studio Calico; *Chipboard accents:* American Crafts and Maya Road; *Rub-ons:* Hambly Screen Prints; *Letter and number stickers:* Jenni Bowlin Studio and Sassafras; *Envelope:* Maya Road; *Button:* Making Memories; *Stamp:* Studio Calico; *Pearls:* Recollections; *Embroidery floss:* DMC; *Paint:* Craft Smart; *Ink:* Ranger Industries; *Adhesive:* Kokuyo, Plaid Enterprises, and Therm O Web; *Pen:* Sakura; *Font:* Times New Roman.

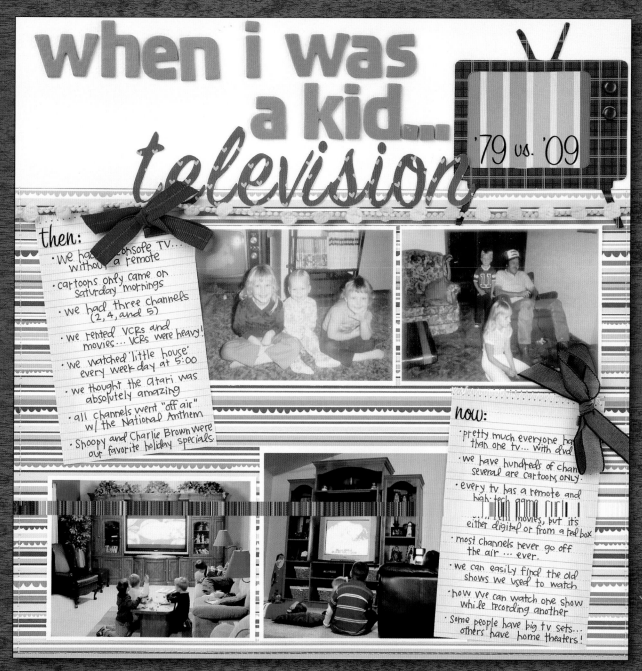

when i was a kid...
television
'79 vs. '09

then:
- we had a console TV... without a remote
- cartoons only came on saturday mornings
- we had three channels (2, 4, and 5)
- we rented VCRs and movies... VCRs were heavy!
- we watched 'little house' every week day at 5:00
- we thought the atari was absolutely amazing
- all channels went "off air" w/ the National Anthem
- snoopy and Charlie Brown were our favorite holiday specials.

now:
- pretty much everyone has more than one tv... with dvd
- we have hundreds of channels, several are cartoons ONLY.
- every tv has a remote and high-tech games.
- ... still rent movies, but it's either digital or from a red box
- most channels never go off the air ... ever.
- we can easily find the old shows we used to watch
- how we can watch one show while recording another
- some people have big tv sets... others have home theaters!

When I was a Kid by Wendy Sue Anderson. **Supplies:** *Cardstock, rub-ons, letters, and pen:* American Crafts; *Patterned paper:* Bella Blvd. and Cosmo Cricket; *Journaling blocks:* Jenny Bowlin Studio; *Brads:* Karen Foster Design and Making Memories; *Ribbon:* Imagination, K&Company, and May Arts; *Die cuts:* Making Memories; *Other:* Thread.

TIP: For a fun reference, compare electronics of today with those of years past.

Graduation

KINDER GARTEN

Where does time go? It seems like yesterday that my boy was graduating from Kindergarten. He was so nervous walking up to get his diploma from his teacher Mrs. Blamer. It was June 20th, 1997. There was a big banner hanging over the stage that said "Class of 2009". That seemed like such a long time away! And here we are in 2009 watching proudly as Thane graduates from high school. The time just flew by and my little boy has grown into a man. He is still the most amazing, wonderful son I could ever imagine. He has exceeded all of my dreams for him. I could not always be any prouder of who he has become. To me he will is all grown always be my little boy, my first born. At 6'3", he see the little up, but when I look (up) at him, I still sad to see smiling face from Kindergarten. I'm be happier 2009 is here so quickly, but I couldn't with where it has brought us! 06-09

CLASS OF 2009

Class of 2009 by Suzy Plantamura. **Supplies:** *Patterned paper:* American Crafts, Crate Paper, and Die Cuts With a View; *Letters:* American Crafts and SEI; *Stars:* Colorbök; *Border stickers:* Colorbök and Doodlebug Design; *Rub-ons:* Scrappin' Sports & More; *Fabric paper:* KI Memories; *Numbers:* Sassafras; *Pen:* EK Success; *Adhesive:* EK Success and Glue Dots International; *Other:* Rickrack.

 TIP: For a unique take on school photos, show several images throughout the years highlighting similarities and differences.

Then and Now by Kayla Aimee Terrell; Photos by Shannon Wright. **Supplies:** *Software:* Adobe; *Fonts:* Century Gothic and Rosewood.

THEN NOW

Senior Year of Highschool 2001

Senior Year of College 2006

When I think about it I smile. At 17 years old I was certain you were my soulmate. You were not so certain. In fact, as much as you cared about me, you just didn't see me as ever being anything more than your very good friend. So at 19 I decided to give it up and see if maybe I was wrong and someone else was actually my soulmate. At 22 you changed your mind. And then I had been away from you for so long, that this time I wasn't certain. But at 23 I was certain. And you were certain. And you asked me to be your wife. And I said yes.

Sometimes I read those journals written by my 17 year old self. The ones that insist that you are the one for me and lament you not knowing it. And I smile. **the wait was worth it**

TIP: Capture photos of loved ones in a similar pose over a timeline. For example, you could show your parents as they dated, were first married, and now as grandparents.

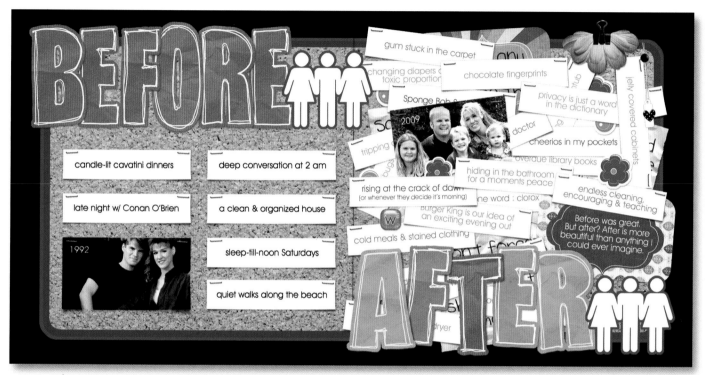

candle-lit cavatini dinners

deep conversation at 2 am

late night w/ Conan O'Brien

a clean & organized house

1992

sleep-till-noon Saturdays

quiet walks along the beach

 TIP: Create a layout about the way things were before your children or career to show how your life has changed.

Before Kids/After Kids by Deena Wuest. **Digital Supplies:** Software: Adobe; Patterned Paper and icons: Anna Aspnes; Cork board and jewelry tag: Katie Pertiet; Crumpled notepaper: Ali Edwards; Flowers and labels: Mindy Terasawa; Alphabet: Lynn Grieveson; Brads: Pattie Knox; Fonts: Avant Garde and CK Deena.

Use Those Leftover School Photos

I found these wallet-size school portraits at my mom's house years ago, and they've been sitting in a filing cabinet ever since. I finally realized they were absolutely perfect for creating a timeline. The small size of wallets allowed me to showcase several photos on my layout. This is a great way to represent several years on one layout.

It's OK by *Autumn Baldwin.* **Supplies:** *Patterned paper:* BoBunny Press and Three Bugs in a Rug; *Stickers:* American Crafts, KI Memories, and Making Memories; *Rub-on:* We R Memory Keepers; *Font:* Century Gothic; *Adhesive:* Scrapbook Adhesives by 3L.

Tell Many Stories

Do you just have too many stories to tell? That's where a "Family Stories" box like this one comes in handy. Each page is only 4" x 6" and comes together in a snap using one wallet-size photo, one journaling block, a scrap of patterned paper, and one small embellishment. Using this method, you can quickly record those family stories that start with "remember when . . ." without feeling pressured to make a whole layout for each and every one.

Remember When *by Autumn Baldwin.*
Supplies: *Cardstock:* Bazzill Basics Paper; *Patterned paper:* BasicGrey, BoBunny Press, Fancy Pants Designs, and Making Memories; *Recipe Box:* We R Memory Keepers; *Stickers:* American Crafts, Colorbök, and Making Memories; *Tags:* October Afternoon; *Rub-ons:* American Crafts and Fancy Pants Designs; *Adhesive:* Tombow.

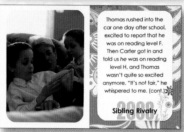

TRY IT:

Download a Microsoft Word template for the journaling boxes used for this project at *creatingkeepsakes.com/issues/September_2010*. Simply replace the text, title, and year; print on white cardstock; and trim along the lines. Add a wallet-size photo and you're nearly done!

Get creative with the "album" you use for this project. I used a chipboard recipe box, but you could use a board book, a standard two-up photo album, or 4" x 6" photo sleeves connected with a jump ring.

the FAIRY Princess

Nimi's been dressing up in Halloween costumes since 2005 and every year she's either a princess or a fairy!

STYLE

CHIC

epic adventures

2005   06   7   08   09

The Fairy Princess by Mou Saha. **Supplies:** *Cardstock:* Die Cuts with a View; *Patterned paper, letter sticker backings, and packaging:* Anna Griffin; *Stickers:* 7gypsies, Anna Griffin, and My Little Shoebox, *Decorative scissors:* Fiskars Americas; *Punch:* EK Success; *Embroidery floss:* DMC; *Pen:* American Crafts; *Adhesive:* 3M.

Don't Call it Fall, Call it Autumn *by Lisa Kisch.* **Supplies:** *Cardstock:* Creative Memories; *Patterned paper:* Creative Imaginations, Jenni Bowlin Studio, and Prima; *Die cuts:* Crate Paper; *Stickers:* American Crafts, BasicGrey, Pink Paislee, and Sassafras; *Buttons:* American Crafts; *Rub-on:* My Mind's Eye; *Adhesive:* Creative Memories.

DESIGN TIP

Create texture on your layout by adding trims, buttons, stickers, and die cuts to better illustrate the textures of the season.

DESIGN TIP

You can combine traditional colors for more than one season and have successful, eye catching designs—and it's okay to use non-traditional colors and accents on your layouts. In fact, it's a great solution for using product you already have on hand, just as Lisa Truesdell did by combining her fall photos with winter themed product.

Snowman *by Lisa Truesdell.* **Supplies:** *Cardstock:* Bazzill Basics Paper; *Patterned paper:* Cosmo Cricket and Crate Paper; *Die cut:* Elle's Studio; *Snowman and flower:* Cosmo Cricket; *Letters:* American Crafts; *Buttons and baker's twine:* Studio Calico; *Punch:* Fiskars Americas; *Font:* Times New Roman; *Adhesive:* Fiskars Americas; *Other:* Font and thread.

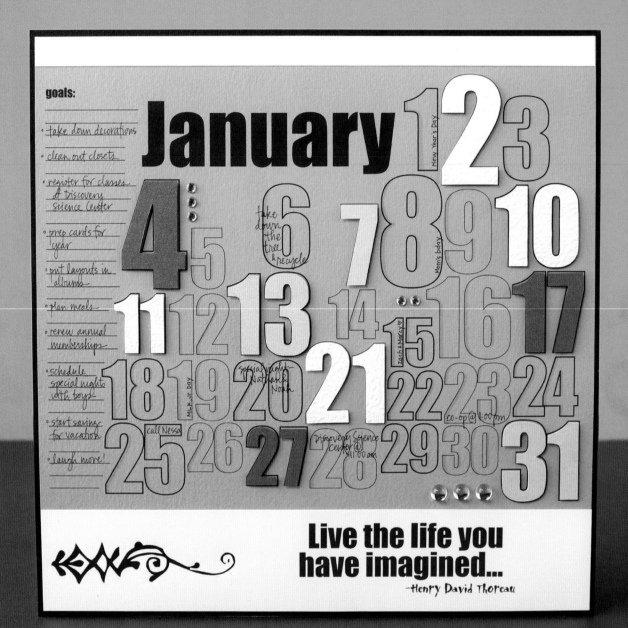

goals:

- take down decorations
- clean out closets
- register for classes at Discovery Science Center
- prep cards for year
- put layouts in albums
- plan meals
- renew annual memberships
- schedule special nights with boys
- start saving for vacation
- laugh more!

January 1 2 3 4 5 6 7 8 9 10 11 12 13 14 15 16 17 18 19 20 21 22 23 24 25 26 27 28 29 30 31

New Year's Day
take down the tree & recycle
Mom's b-day
Zach & Macy ♥
MLK Jr. Day
special night — Nathan & Noah
call Nessa
Discovery Science Center @ 11:00 am
co-op @ 1:00 pm

Live the life you have imagined...

—Henry David Thoreau

{ JANUARY }
by Amanda Probst

Make a list.

I don't know about you, but I always seem to need an extra column on my calendar to jot down things that don't fall on a given day. Life gets so crazy, I tend to think in terms of what I need to do during the week or the month to allow myself more flexibility. No doubt your life is busy too. Amid all the craziness, don't forget to live each day with intention.

Monthly Info:
Birthstone: Garnet
Flowers: Carnation, Snowdrop
Astrological signs: Capricorn
(Dec. 22–Jan. 19), Aquarius
(Jan. 20–Feb. 18)

Use dialog to tell the story

Getting someone else to do your journaling may not work for you. But that doesn't mean you can't capture his words on your page. For her "Career Aspirations" layout, Deena Wuest used a conversation she had with her son. Sometimes, the nuances of a conversation capture far more than the words do. It's those little nuances of her son's thoughtful pauses and Deena's silence that makes the journaling on this layout so poignant.

For her journaling, Deena introduced each part of the conversation with the name of the person speaking. But notice how she also created the journaling so that the words spoken by her are a different color from those spoken by her son. This makes the conversation effortless to follow; and the reader doesn't even need to pause to read who is speaking—allowing them to almost hear the conversation as it happened. How can you creatively capture a conversation on your next layout?

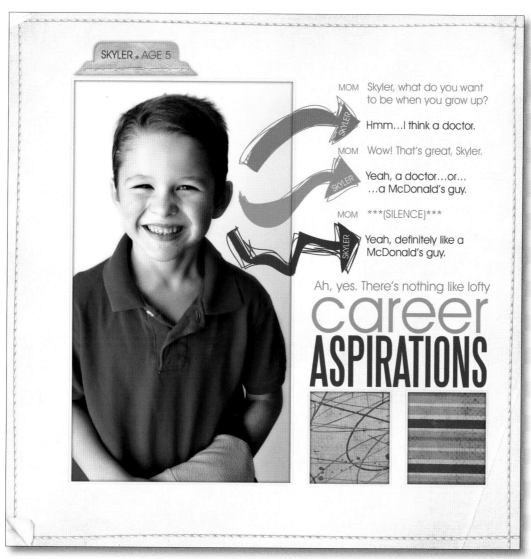

Career Aspirations by Deena Wuest. **Digital Supplies:** *Software:* Adobe; *Patterned paper and template:* Lynn Grieveson; *Arrows:* Jesse Edwards; *Fonts:* Avant Garde and Steelfish.

write about your family
from a reporter's
point of view

special report   special report   special report   special report

BREAKING NEWS BREAKING NEWS BREAKING NEWS
Preschooler recoils from pepperoni pizza

Researchers astounded the preschool community today by announcing the discovery of the only known four-year-old to not only dislike – but to actually be repelled by – pepperoni pizza.

The discovery was made on an ordinary Friday night, when the parents of the child, Catesby Pinney, suggested "pizza and movie night." Catesby responded with an unequivocal "no."

Catesby claimed to have no objection to at least four foods: peanut butter & jelly, hot dogs, chicken fingers, and pop tarts. When asked about any other sort of nutrition, he collapsed in terror.

The parents of the preschooler are baffled,

insisting that they have tried every trick to encourage him to eat adventurously – including animal-shaped sandwiches.

"I've heard of picky eaters before," said Catesby's mother, who asks to remain anonymous. "But this is embarrassing."

This is not the first time Catesby has declined food traditionally appealing to the under-five set. Apple pie, Chef Boyardee, and fish sticks are also on the ever-growing "no" list.

Catesby's little brother, Brooks, could not be reached for comment, as his mouth was stuffed with Catesby's portion of the pizza. 03-2007

materials patterned paper (American Crafts) • Courier, Featured Item, Times New Roman, and Traveling Type-writer fonts • *12 x 12 page by Elizabeth Woodford, Mt. Sterling, KY*

MT. STERLING, KY—

A Kentucky woman was astounded Friday by her 4-year-old's reaction to the suggestion that the family eat pepperoni pizza for dinner. The woman, who prefers to remain anonymous (although, if you really want to know her name, just look at the materials list), decided to scrapbook this strange occurrence—especially since she was in possession of a particularly amusing snapshot of the incident. The woman decided to write about the event from the viewpoint of a newspaper reporter, and she heartily encourages scrapbookers everywhere to give this writing technique a try.

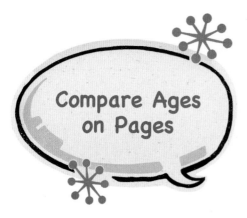

Compare Ages on Pages

As we grow, our language abilities do, too. Show the difference in developmental stages by comparing the same child's language at different ages, as Becky Olsen did on her layout below with her daughter's questioning ways. You could also ask the same questions of kids of different ages, and then scrapbook their answers as April Anderton did with her page at right (which was inspired by a video she took of the same topic). Both approaches make for entertaining layouts.

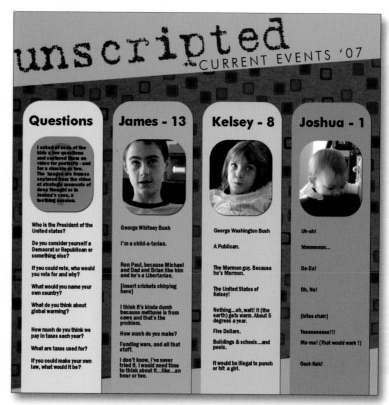

Unscripted *by April Anderton.* **Supplies** *Software:* Adobe Photoshop; *Patterned paper (altered):* Love Chocolate Paper Pack by Melissa Shupe; *Fonts:* Harting and Futura.

What Begins with Why? *by Becky Olsen.* **Supplies** *Cardstock:* Bazzill Basics Paper; *Patterned paper:* Cosmo Cricket, Crate Paper and October Afternoon; *Letter stickers:* American Crafts; *Buttons:* My Mind's Eye; *Embroidery floss:* DMC; *Pen:* Precision Pens, American Crafts; *Adhesive:* Therm O Web and Tombow; *Other:* Thread.

INTERVIEW with MEGAN CAMILLE {at 12}

Who is the smartest person in your family?
besides me?

What is your dad really good at?
having fun!

What can you do better than dad?
yell

How are you like mom?
We're both scared of dogs.

How are you different from mom?
I can rollerblade and she'll fall.

What did you and dad do together that you'll always remember?
He went on my 2nd grade field trip to the dinosaur museum.

If you could have one superpower what would it be?
mind reading.

What was the last chore you did?
cleaned bathroom sinks.

What is your favorite song?
Dream Big

What was the last movie you saw at a theater?
Alvin & the Chipmunks 3

What food would you like to eat every day?
Ham and Funeral Potatoes

If you could choose a different name, what would it be?
Melody

Is your room messy or clean?
clean.

What's your favorite restaurant food?
McDonald's French fries

If you had a million dollars, what would you buy first?
A Disneyland Vacation

What's your nickname and how did you get it?
Maggie — from Josh

What's your favorite holiday and why?
Christmas because everyone is happy.

What's your favorite cereal?
Cheerios with yogurt

What's your favorite TV show?
Castle and Dr. G

What vegetables do you like best?
Baby carrots (raw)

What's your favorite book?
The Hunger Games series

What's your favorite candy bar?
PayDay

Interview with Megan Camille by Wendy Sue Anderson. **Supplies:** *Cardstock:* Bazzill Basics Paper; *Patterned paper:* Jillibean Soup; *Butterfly accents:* Jenni Bowlin Studio; *Ribbon:* Berwick Offray; *Letter stickers:* SEI; *Die-cutting machine:* Provo Craft; *Die:* Ellison; *Font:* Small Type Writing Medium; *Other:* Cardstock and thread.

August 22, 2006

Will you still...

- call me mommy?
- skip?
- hold my hand?
- let me pick out your clothes?
- love babies, puppies & Lion King?
- sleep in a sleeping bag on Collin's floor?
- suck on your fingers at bed-time?
- sleep with four shredded blankies you call your babies?
- run into my arms + hug me when you see me?
- call Maggie "Doo-dah"?
- snuggle?
- love "girlie girl nights"?
- wave to Daddy at both doors?

Will you still do all these delight-ful things that are so *you* on the last day of kindergarten?

materials patterned papers (My Mind's Eye) • ribbon (SEI) • flowers (Bazzill Basics, Making Memories) • brads • *12 x 12 page by Aby Garvey, Edwardsville, IL*

why it's simple

ABY ORGANIZES HER SPACE AND HER THOUGHTS so she can capture those little moments that might otherwise get lost in her daily comings and goings. She keeps notepads stashed throughout her house (including the laundry room) and jots down ideas as they come. She stores the notebooks in a little bin until she has time to scrapbook. This layout is the result of Aby's musings about what life would be like when her daughter started school. "I captured my thoughts but didn't have time to create a layout," she says. "By the time I scrapbooked this page, many of the things on my layout had already changed." How does this process make scrapbooking easier? It allows Aby to write her journaling the moment inspiration strikes. No need to stare at a blank sheet of paper, trying to think of what to say!

type
tips

by Cathy Zielske

keep it classic

If the sheer number of typefaces available today seems overwhelming, take heart: there are only a handful of typefaces you really need to create timeless, readable scrapbook pages.

Times Roman, or variations thereof, is probably the single most usable, dependable and readable typeface out there for scrapbookers. It typically comes pre-loaded on your computer as part of the operating system or word processing application. There's a reason for this: it's a classic.

life lessons

big lessons learned from my little boy

It's amazing how as your mother, someone who is supposed to instruct *you* in the ways of life, I've learned so much about life from you. You're only five years old, Matthew, but already you've made such a big impact on my life. Here are just a few important things I've learned from you already. *Thanks little one.*

It's okay to feel proud, really damn proud in fact, for even the smallest of accomplishments.

Sometimes, thinking is just plain overrated.

Just because you may do things a little differently, doesn't mean you're doing it wrong.

Live in the now. And enjoy it.

Keeping things neat and clean isn't all it's cracked up to be. Making a mess can be equally as satisfying.

Don't be embarrassed or shy to love openly or deeply.

Everyone deserves a little respect. Even a five year old.

type tip use a serif font for classic readability

life lessons Margaret Scarbrough

serif

Times New Roman is a classic serif type face

Times Roman is a serif typeface. Serifs are the small thick and thin strokes found on the letterforms themselves. It's the style of type most used by magazines and newspapers because it can be read the fastest. In short, our eyes are used to serif type. It feels instantly familiar and recognizable, thereby making it easier to read.

Whether you have paragraphs of journaling, or a few lines, you can never go wrong with a classic serif typeface. Other serif typefaces to check out are: Goudy, Garamond, Janson and Caslon.

keep it modern

Helvetica is a common sans serif type face

Sans serif typefaces are the more modern, clean-lined members of the typographic world. Thin and thick strokes and flourishes are replaced with uniform lines and even forms. Helvetica is probably the most well known sans serif typeface.

Sans serif typefaces can lend a modern feel to a scrapbook page, however, they also can serve a neutral role as well. I use sans serifs frequently when I want to make a quieter, more subdued typographic statement.

People will often ask me, "Well, which style of type works best with what type of scrapbook page?" And I always answer, you can never go wrong with a classic serif, or a classic sans serif. Because it's true: classic faces will never date a scrapbook page, will be easier to read, and will never call undue amounts of attention to themselves. Other classic sans serifs typefaces to try out include Avant Garde, Arial, Verdana and Interstate.

Goudy
Garamond
Janson
Caslon

Avant Garde
Arial
Verdana
Interstate

his

hers

type tip use a san serif font to keep it modern

what do they say? Cathy Zielske

type it like a pro

If you want your journaling blocks to appear more polished and flow better, you've got to hop on the one-space-after-a-period bandwagon. I realize most of us learned to type with a heavy thumb on that space bar, but with today's proportionately designed typefaces, those two spaces add too much space between a period and the start of the next sentence. Using only one space creates a visual flow that you can't match by putting those two spaces in there.

Some scrapbookers think, "But those spaces signal the end of a sentence, and the beginning of a new one." I'm here to tell you that a period—and one space—signals the end of a sentence; that added space isn't needed to emphasize the point, so to speak.

Try doing your journaling blocks both ways. In one, use the two spaces, and in the other, use only one. Print them out and carefully analyze them side by side. Which one is easier to read and follow? Which one carries more flow and unity? Hopefully, you'll start to notice that the one with single spaces feels more cohesive.

It takes some practice to break the two-space habit, but it can be done. I did it years ago. If I can do it, so can you!

There is not enough closet space. The rooms are all just a bit too small. Three people cannot work comfortably in the kitchen. Storage space is almost nonexistent. Despite all these things, I love my house. It isn't just a house, it is our home. We have a flower garden that blooms with daffodils, iris, chrysanthemums and roses. We have bobcats and their babies who hang out on our property. We have quail that return every year to nest in the same pot of geraniums on the patio. Sunsets delight us almost every night. Our back patio is cool and welcoming, even on most summer nights. Our fireplace warms us in the winter. Photographs of the people and places I love adorn the walls. That too small kitchen has made countless meals for family and friends. Colorful quilts are on the beds. We have too many books and a ridiculously large music collection. We are comfortable, content and happy. Our children grew up here and thank goodness, still love coming back home. And perhaps, *that* is the most important thing of all.

type tip use only one space after a period

happy home Barbara Carroll

Of course, the most important things in life are not things. But as far as material possessions go, my camera would have to be at the top of my list. And really, to be fair, this thing goes beyond inanimate-object status for me. It's an amazing tool, one that helped me to learn and practice what would become one of my greatest skills. It's a means of self-expression, of creating. It is the backbone of a business that I have built out of practically nothing. And perhaps most importantly, it's a faithful record keeper, helping me capture over a year of my family's life, from the mundane to the monumental. It doesn't do all the work for me, nor would I want it to. But I certainly wouldn't be able to do what I do without it.

Soon, my precious camera will be usurped by an upgrade. Even sentimentality has to give in to technological advances sometimes, and there's just no ignoring the fact that I, and my business, have outgrown what this thing can do. But not once have I considered putting it up for sale. It's a good idea to have a back-up, sure. But even without that justification, I have a sneaking suspicion that I would just find it too hard to part with this one. Inanimate as it may be, we've been through a lot together. And it will always remain a prized possession, for sure.

type tip open up the leading

prized Angi Stevens

leading saves the day —and the eyes

Space between lines of journaling enhances the readability of the entire block of text. We call this space "leading" (led-ing). If you've given careful thought to and taken time writing down your memories, put the same care into how you present the information. Appropriate amounts of leading increases the ability of the eye to read what you've written.

You can choose a double space option in most word processing programs. This is a good place to start. Better yet, check and see if your word processing offers an "exact" line spacing option. Microsoft Word does. If you CAN choose exact line spacing, use this handy guide as a starting point:

Type Size	Leading Amount
10	18
11	20
12	24

readability tests

Long before you send your cardstock through the printer, conduct your own readability test. After composing your journaling, print out a test sheet on plain paper, and take a careful look at what you've got.

edit your journaling

Do you ever pour your heart out into what you are writing, and end up cramming too much text into a too-small space? Have you ever made the font a smaller size or tightened up the leading to get it to fit? Don't do it. All you'll have to show for your efforts is a journaling block that isn't inviting or easy to read.

This is where editing comes in handy. Even if you love every single word you've written, take a stab at cutting it down. I do this all the time when I'm journaling. First, I write whatever I want to say. Then I tighten up the text wherever I can.

Even if you feel you can't spare a single word, read through it carefully one last time. You'll probably find several things you can say more succinctly. Remember, give your words more room and they'll appear more important and be easier to read.

type tip keep it short and sweet, but meaningful

conversation Elizabeth Dillow

ask yourself:

• Are there any places with two spaces following a period?

• Are there any sentences that end with a one-word "orphan" on its own line? Eliminate orphans by shifting another word down so the orphan is no longer "lonely."

• Does your line length seem appropriate and easy to read? Four inches wide is an optimal line length to shoot for. Include even more leading for longer line lengths.

• Is your font easily read? Is your font size too small or too large?

Just because we say "thought bubble" doesn't mean you have to actually draw a cartoony-looking bubble thing on your photo and totally ruin your layout. Moon* added these amusing thoughts to pictures of her 3-year-old, sans bubbles. Narrate someone else's (or your own) thoughts using journaling strips, punched circles of cardstock, lined journaling stamps, or sticky notes.

materials patterned paper (American Crafts) • metal letters, acrylic paint (Making Memories) • Arial Narrow and Franklin Gothic Demi fonts • 8½ x 11 page by Moon Ko, Versailles, KY

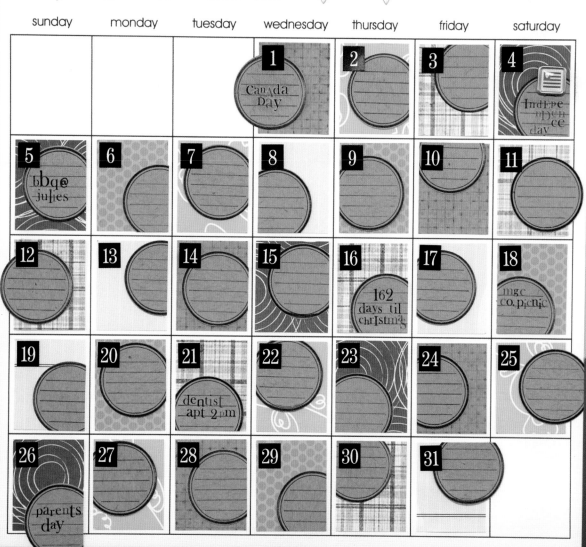

sunday	monday	tuesday	wednesday	thursday	friday	saturday
			1 Canada Day	2	3	4 Independence day
5 bbq@ julies	6	7	8	9	10	11
12	13	14	15	16 162 days til christmas	17	18 mgc co. picnic
19	20	21 dentist apt 2 pm	22	23	24	25
26 parents day	27	28	29	30	31	

{ JULY }
by Summer Fullerton

Use a journaling stamp.

I love how Summer made use of a journaling spot stamp for this calendar page! The random pattern of both the colored papers and the journaling circles gives this page such a feeling of joy and freedom.

Monthly Info:
Birthstone: Ruby
Flowers: Larkspur, Water Lily
Astrological signs: Cancer (June 21–July 22), Leo (July 23–Aug. 22)

Substitute handwritten journaling for printed journaling.

Create a hybrid layout by incorporating your own handwriting. Says Brittany, "Instead of typing my journaling on the template, I decided to print out the digital portion of my layout and journal by hand." *Note:* When you print out your digital page, hide the elements that you don't want to show, such as the sample text. (Simply click on the eyeball icon in the Layers palette to hide the selected layers.)

Oh, Baby *by Brittany Laakkonen.* **Supplies** *Software:* Adobe Photoshop Elements 2.0, Adobe Systems; *Digital page template:* Jen Caputo, www.creating-keepsakes.com; *Patterned paper:* Prima; *Digital patterned paper:* Katja Kromann, www.katjakromann.com; *Digital brushes:* www.twopeasinabucket.com; *Buttons:* foof-a-La, Autumn Leaves; *Chipboard letters:* Heidi Swapp for Advantus; *Ink:* Distress Ink, Ranger Industries; *Pen:* Zig Writer, EK Success; *Brads:* K&Company and Prima.

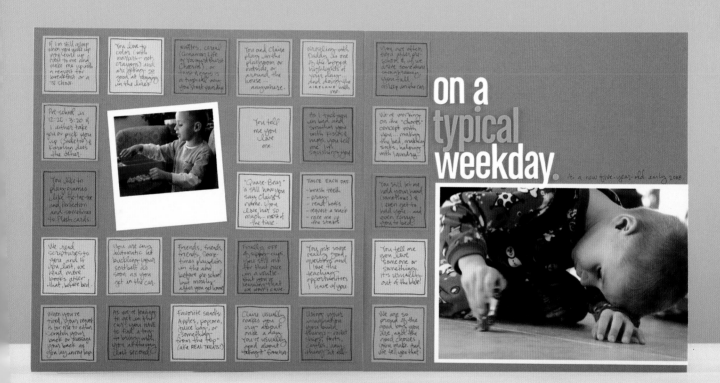

on a typical weekday.

As a new five-year-old, early 2008

WHEN YOU INCLUDE a lot of photos (or journaling blocks like those shown above), it's also a good idea to have a focal-point photo—a larger image that catches people's attention first. This will lend visual balance and help establish where you want the greatest emphasis.

Remember that when looking at sketches, each box doesn't necessarily need to translate into a photo. This layout design was perfect for an idea that I had in mind for Porter's album. In his scrapbook, I wanted to include a list of what a typical day is like in his five-year-old life before he attends all-day Kindergarten.

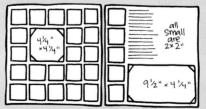

4 1/4" × 4 1/4"

all small are 2 × 2"

9 1/2" × 4 1/4"

On a Typical Weekday *by Becky Higgins.* **Supplies** *Cardstock:* Bazzill Basics Paper; *Foam letter stickers:* American Crafts; *Black pen:* Precision Pens, American Crafts.

BY BECKY HIGGINS

IT'S THE TRUTH

Why: To reflect on what honesty means to you, to impart your values to your family.

What role does honesty play in your life? When is it best to be totally honest? Have you ever been hurt by dishonesty?

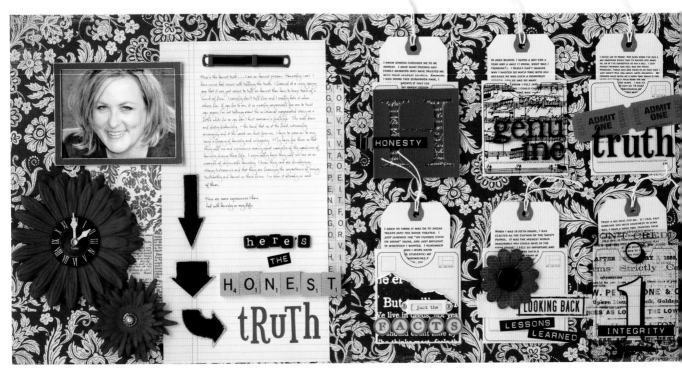

be completely honest
HERE'S THE HONEST TRUTH by Marci Leishman

Here's the Honest Truth by Marci Leishman. **Supplies:** Patterned paper: 7gypsies, Autumn Leaves, and Scenic Route; Chipboard frame, clock, arrows, letters and monogram: Advantus; Fastener: Magic Scraps Pockets and rub-ons: 7gypsies; Transparency and rub-ons: Daisy D's Paper Co.; Paper flower, gem, brads, and bookplate: Making Memories; Letter stickers: Chatterbox; Tags: American Tag; Acrylic letters: The Paper Studio and Doodlebug Design; Scrabble tiles: Mattel; Game-board letters: Li'l Davis Designs; Label tape: Dymo; Silk flowers: Tai Pan Trading; Punch: EK Success; Brads: Delish Designs; Button: Buttons Galore; Fonts: CK Becky and CK Regal; Other: Staples, tickets, and twill.

"HONESTY is the first CHAPTER in the the book of WISDOM ." —THOMAS JEFFERSON

justify your type

Fully justified type lends a structured flair to any journaling. You can use this easy but little-known technique in Adobe Photoshop Elements to create newspaper-style columns of journaling, to tell a long story on your page, or to create gorgeous home decor using your favorite quotations.

This is the *story* of a girl and a camera.

Actually, two girls. And a few cameras. And how we arrived here at this moment.

Like I said, this is the story of a girl. A girl who received her first camera in high school - the year 1991. It wasn't a nice camera, and it was shaped like a bar of soap, but it took the few photos that the girl ever wanted to take anyway. As the years passed, the girl took the camera with her on a mission, and with her on her honeymoon to San Francisco, where she took only 25 pictures.

Years passed, and she purchased a new camera - a digital camera, which she took with her on a once-in-a-lifetime trip to Brazil. She took only 12 pictures.

You see, the girl had not yet learned how important photos are. She had not yet learned that photos are life - that they are captured instants to be collected and cherished and smiled at and wept over as we - as only humans can - **remember**.

More years passed, and she purchased another new camera. Then one day, this girl had a baby - a daughter of her own. And now, with something to photograph, she took more pictures. When this beautiful daughter was six months old, the girl decided she needed some way to keep track of all these photos, and her love for scrapbooks was born.

As time went on, the girl grew to realize that photos are sometimes the only way we remember things, and that recording is a way to taste life twice. She carried her camera with her, and took many, many photos. She collected moments and stored them and printed them, and then took more.

The day came when the beautiful daughter picked up her first camera and held it to her eye. She held the pink camera in two small hands and looked through the window that millions have looked through, at life from behind a lens. And what did this beautiful daughter point her camera at, for her very first picture? Her mama, who was taking a picture, too.

she said

06.07

Paula Gilarde used one on her "B&A" layout, and I used one to create my quotation wall decor (both shown later). These tags are perfect for trying this fun (and simple!) technique on your next project.

Every now and then I have a really long story I'd like to tell, and I want the journaling to take center stage. By justifying the text (making sure to keep my paragraph box wide enough that I don't get too many hyphens at the end), I create a cool architectural style that allows the simple lines of the page to shine through, placing focus on the story I'm telling.

This Is the Story . . . *by Jessica Sprague.* **Supplies** *Software:* Adobe Photoshop Elements 6.0, Adobe Systems; *Printer:* Epson R1800; *Cardstock:* Bazzill Basics Paper; *Flourish die cuts:* me & my BIG ideas; *Chipboard circle:* Scenic Route; *Acrylic number stamps:* My Sentiments Exactly; *Ink:* Distress Ink, Ranger Industries; *Corner-rounder punch:* EK Success; *Mini brads:* Chatterbox; *Fonts:* Myriad, Adobe; Ma Sexy, www.dafont.com.

BY JESSICA SPRAGUE

the technique

You can have fun with this technique traditionally and digitally! Here's how:

traditional scrapbooking method:

1 Use a pencil to draw light vertical guidelines down the sides of your journaling area.

2 Hand journal, being careful to begin at the left guideline and spacing your words and letters so you'll either end with a word or a hyphen at the right-hand guideline.

3 Erase your guidelines to show off your "justified" journaling.

digital technique using Adobe Photoshop Elements:

1 Select the Horizontal Type tool and draw a text box on your document.

2 Type your journaling, then select the Horizontal Type tool again and highlight all of your text.

3 Type Ctrl+Shift+j to fully justify your paragraph of journaling. Print your journaling, or even add a stamp to the journaling block to decorate your text before printing.

VARIATION **1**
Create a framed quote with justified text.

Justified type doesn't have to be boring! By playing with the font sizes and adding in a couple of extra line breaks for the focal area of my text ("do what is in us"), I easily created a beautiful, dynamic wall hanging that's full of interest.

Quote Wall Decor *by Jessica Sprague.* **Supplies** *Software:* Adobe Photoshop Elements 6.0, Adobe Systems; *Printer:* Epson R1800; *Photo paper:* PremierArt Matte Scrapbook Photo Paper, Epson; *Digital patterned paper:* Living - Being Papers by Jen Wilson, *www.jen-wilsondesigns.com; Digital journaling stamp:* By Nancie Rowe Janitz and available as a free download at *www.creatingkeepsakes.com;* *Watercolor brush stamps:* Michelle Coleman, *www.littledreamerdesigns. com; Font:* VT Portable Remington, *www.dafont.com; Frame:* Michaels.

It is not our part to master all the tides of the world, but to **do what is in us** for the succor of those years wherein we are set, **uprooting** the evil in the fields that we know, so that those who live after may have **clean earth** to till.

VARIATION 2

Justify journaling in a shaped journaling tag.

Paula picked a fun, whimsical journaling tag to match the lighthearted feel of her layout. By justifying her journaling text within the tag, she created a perfect balance between the photos on the left of her page and the block of journaling and title on the right.

Pink *by Paula Gilarde.* **Supplies** *Software:* Adobe Photoshop CS2, Adobe Systems; *Cardstock:* Bazzill Basics Paper; *Patterned paper:* Adornit - Carolee's Creations (floral), BasicGrey (small dot), Daisy D's Paper Co. (plaid), KI Memories (pink flowers and dot) and SEI (colored dots); *Rub-ons:* Autumn Leaves; *Journaling brush:* Love Frames Brushes-n-Stamps by Jesse Edwards, *designerdigitals.com*; *Font:* Century Gothic, Microsoft.

VARIATION 3

Balance text within a circular journaling tag.

Combining different shapes on a layout based on a grid can be tricky, but Paula figured out an easy workaround. Says Paula, "I like the circular journaling shape and thought it would be an interesting addition to this grid. By justifying my journaling within the circle, I maintained the style of the square photos and the grid on my layout."

B&A *by Paula Gilarde.* **Supplies** *Software:* Adobe Photoshop CS2, Adobe Systems; *Cardstock:* Bazzill Basics Paper; *Patterned paper:* me & my BIG ideas; *Felt flowers:* American Crafts; *Chipboard letters:* Crate Paper; *Brads:* Jo-Ann Stores; *Rub-ons:* Doodlebug Design; *Digital journaling stamp:* By Nancie Rowe Janitz and available as a free download at *www.creatingkeepsakes.com*; *Font:* Century Gothic, Microsoft.

For me, journaling is easy. I write a lot—in notebooks and e-mails; on sticky notes, scraps of paper, concert programs, and ticket stubs. It's how I process thoughts and ideas and make sense of my life. Once I realized that journaling is the reason I care about scrapbooking, I quit worrying about photos and products and started viewing them as supporting players that add dimension to my writing passion.

Dog pants - Dog collars, carefully chosen to best flatter and complement the personality and coloring of the furry recipient.

Football minutes - Minutes that are much, much longer than "clock minutes." Actual length varies widely. Doctor's offices, washing machines, and moms ("Just a minute, honey,") also use this measure of time.

Pizza house, the - House on the dog-walking route where Moose, the chocolate lab, found a box with leftover pizza on the porch. On every walk thereafter, the location had to be thoroughly sniffed.

Rose saddeners - The little bugs that make rose buds sag and wilt before they've had a chance to bloom.

Jamie's Dictionary

Slow-pokins disease - Ailment suffered by customers of Jim's Café, where huge, heavy breakfasts are offered for $3.99. Symptoms include walking very slowly across the parking lot and taking more than five minutes to get into the car.

Senior citizen cheese - Free cheese distributed by the state welfare department every Thursday, to residents over 65. Gathered by grandparents and given to working mothers to turn into a staple diet of grilled cheese sandwiches for growing kids with endless appetites.

White money - Receipts that slowly replace the green money in your wallet. Representation of money you no longer have.

materials circle punch (Marvy Uchida) • Times New Roman and P22 Typewriter fonts • *8½ x 11 page*

CHAPTER 4:
Creative Journaling

Words simply aren't enough...sometimes I just sit & am amazed at how incredibly blessed I am...how very thankful. Pausing here to remember that...

SCRAPBOOKING IS ALL ABOUT taking creative license while preserving your photos and memories. Use that same creativity to focus on the presentation of your journaling with formats and techniques that not only enhance the look of your layouts, but make your journaling a highlight of every scrapbook page. Enhance the theme of a page by mixing fonts and styles within your journaling. Create a designated area for text with stamps, blocks, and backgrounds designed specially for journaling. Try breaking up journaling into strips, cutting it into shapes, or tucking it away with functional pull tabs. Or, add unexpected mediums such as paint, fabric, buttons, and more to embellish your themed journaling.

Outline fonts

Outline fonts are popular in print advertisements using both serif and sans-serif fonts. Use one on your pages to update the monogram, or try it on a title treatment over a patterned background or large photo. This font style looks particularly cool in white or a light color. **ck**

font watch

Talisman

Per

ype

Ne

A² by Lisa Brown. **Supplies** *Patterned paper:* Chatterbox; *Font:* 2Peas Cross Eyed, downloaded from *www.twopeasinabucket.com*; *Pen:* Uni-ball Signo, Sanford.

Milan

American Crafts • *www.americancrafts.com*
JustRite • *www.justritestampers.com*
KI Memories • *www.kimemories.com*
Technique Tuesday • *www.techniquetuesday.com*

fresh layers

I love creating in layers—combining both the obvious and the hidden treasures. Layering my digital *and* handmade designs on one page gives me so many wonderful options to work with!

note: Printing at home makes working with a layered project like this so easy. I used HP Photosmart printers to print my small circle photos and the background page.

BY C.D. MUCKOSKY

Beginnings *by C.D. Muckosky.* **Supplies** *Software:* Adobe Photoshop CS2, Adobe Systems; *Printer, ink and photo paper:* Hewlett-Packard; *Acrylic letters:* Heidi Swapp for Advantus; *Watercolor paints:* Prang; *Adhesive:* EZ Runner, Scrapbook Adhesives by 3L; Gloo, KI Memories; *Date stamps:* Amber Clegg, *www. scrapartist.com; Paint circles:* Ida, *www.catscrap.com; Stitches:* Jackie Eckles, *www.littledreamdesigners.com; Other:* Embroidery floss, graph paper and masking tape.

{ reversed-out journaling }

Nothing adds a graphic touch to a layout better than white type! This technique involves creating a solid fill of color and typing over it in white. When you print your document on white cardstock or photo paper, your printer will leave spaces where your letters are, allowing the white paper to show through and giving the illusion of white printed type. Here are some examples of this great technique!

The World's Smallest Jedi by Jessica Sprague. **Supplies** Software: Adobe Photoshop Elements 6.0; Printer: Epson R1900; Photo paper: PremierArt Matte Scrapbook Photo Paper, Epson; Cardstock: Bazzill Basics Paper; Patterned paper: American Crafts (background) and KI Memories (stripe); Chipboard letters: Heidi Swapp for Advantus; Nested star chipboard: Deluxe Designs; Font: Century Gothic (journaling) and Impact (title), Microsoft; Other: White acrylic paint.

A LARGE brown block is the home to my title (in a combination of type and chipboard letters) and fully justified journaling. The rounded corners and the way the block extends all the way to the edge of the page add interest to a basic, four-square grid page. I printed the journaling onto matte photo paper for a crisper edge to the lettering and a richer color to the brown block, then I trimmed it to size for my page.

BY JESSICA SPRAGUE

the technique

You can have fun with this technique traditionally and digitally! Here's how:

traditional scrapbooking method:

1. Add a large block of black or brown cardstock to your layout.

2. Use a white pen, such as a Uni-ball Signo from Newell Rubbermaid, or a white inkpad, such as the StazOn opaque inkpad from Tsukineko, with rubber or acrylic stamps to create white journaling and accents.

digital technique using Adobe Photoshop Elements:

1. Create a new blank document. With the Rectangular Marquee Tool, draw a selection on its own layer and fill the selection with black or another dark color.

2. Select your Horizontal Type Tool and set your font color to white.

3. Type your journaling, title or accent type in white. Print onto white cardstock or matte photo paper.

Note: You can easily achieve this same look in Microsoft Word. Simply create a text box, change the fill color to your desired hue, and type your text with a white font color.

variation 1:
Create a mini album with white text.

A premade, ring-bound mini book became home to a cool album-in-progress. Because I kept the template simple, I can take five minutes each year to add a photo and label, change the year, then print the pages to keep my album updated.

Spooks Mini Album *by Jessica Sprague.* **Supplies** *Cardstock and chipboard circle:* Bazzill Basics Paper; *Digital patterned paper:* Fairy Dreamer Kit by Katie Pertiet, *www.designerdigitals.com; Digital photo frame (black):* Grunged Up Photo Blocks No. 2 by Katie Pertiet, *www.designerdigitals.com; Patterned paper (stripe):* Cosmo Cricket; *Letter stickers:* American Crafts; *Scallop-oval punch and oval punch:* EK Success; *Font:* Impact, Microsoft (year) and Sidewalk, *www.dafont.com* (label).

variation 2:

Create an informal look with white script text.

You can also create a more informal look with reversed text using a script font in your journaling and title. Marcia Bettich also created white-pen pumpkin designs to emphasize the white text in the layout.

You & a Pumpkin Patch Adventure *by Marcia Bettich.* **Supplies** *Software:* Adobe Photoshop Elements 6.0; *Patterned paper:* Samantha Rose Paper Pack by Katie Pertiet; Color My World (Free Digital Kit June 2007) by Rhonna Farrer, *www.twopeasinabucket.com;* Lov-e-ly Paper Pack by Jesse Edwards; *Flourishes:* 2nd Hand Titles {Love} Brushes-n-Stamps and On the Edge Flourishes by Katie Pertiet; *Transparencies:* 3M; *Paint pen:* Sharpie, Newell Rubbermaid; *Felt shapes:* Fancy Pants Designs; *Ribbon:* American Crafts; *Chipboard letters:* Heidi Swapp for Advantus, *Fonts:* Century Gothic, Microsoft; CK Classic, *www.scrapnfonts.com; Other:* Thread. *Note:* Unless listed otherwise, all digital elements are from *www.designerdigitals.com.*

Forest for the Trees *by Noel Culbertson.* **Supplies** *Software:* Adobe Photoshop Elements 5.0; *Cardstock:* Bazzill Basics Paper; *Patterned paper:* Scenic Route; *Lace paper:* KI Memories; *Flowers and journaling block:* Making Memories; *Foam letters:* American Crafts; *Printed tape:* Prima; *Stamp:* Impress Rubber Stamps; *Brad and ink:* Stampin' Up!; *Font:* Arial, Microsoft.

variation 3:

Use reversed text to add extra color.

Noel Culbertson used reversed text on a green background for her title and journaling strips. By putting white text on a green background, she was able to add an extra element of color—the green—which brings out another color in her photos and papers.

mason,

whoo could resist

that sweet little

face of yours?

{not me}

WHOO

materials letter stamps (EK Success) • patterned papers (Making Memories, My Mind's Eye) • other stamps (BasicGrey, Hampton Arts) • stamping ink (Clearsnap) • chipboard letters (K&Company) • chipboard heart, photo corners (Heidi Swapp) • metal charms (Imaginisce) • flowers (Creative Imaginations, Heidi Grace, Petaloo) • rub-ons (Fancy Pants) • embroidery floss (DMC) • buttons • brads • 12 x 12 page by Andrea Friebus, La Habra, CA

Trusty tools are versatile.

Looking for a budget-conscious, creative way to add titles and text to your pages? Forget about saving your pennies for a large-format printer, and take a tip from Andrea: pull out your letter stamps!

More versatile than letter stickers and rub-ons, stamps are portable and can go anywhere on a page—in any size or color. "I love that they are a cute alternative to handwriting," adds Andrea, who turns to this handy little stamp set from EK Success on layout after layout.

a few little tidbits about you

You were such a drooly baby

As a baby you loved to play with mommy's hair. While you nursed, as I held you around the house. Even now at 2.5, you still do. When we're reading books or you're feeling kindof sad or when we're just having some snuggle time.

You wear me out most days

I definitely wouldn't describe you as a quiet child.

The way you say 'ours' is my favorite. It's more like 'errs.' That and the way you use the word 'actually' in sentences (and correctly at that) at age two and a half.

You adore your Grandpa McCance

I'm so glad your eczema is under control. As a baby is was such a hard thing to watch you go through, now the little spots you have behind your knees and on your legs are so manageable. It's such a blessing that you've grown out of it like you have!

You think Thomas the train, horses, your new big boy Diego 'unner-wears' and tractors are **SO** cool.

materials patterned papers, die-cut shapes (My Mind's Eye) • brads • corner rounder
• Cambria font • 8½ x 11 page by Rebecca Cooper, Raymond, AB, Canada

exploring
laughter
giggles
smiles
tasting
touching
love
playing
photographs
and a floor full of toys..

cole . 9 months

materials ribbon (KI Memories, Li'l Davis Designs, Offray) • buttons (Autumn Leaves) • machine stitching • Times font • *12 x 12 page*

No Kids Allowed

TECHNIQUE TIP

Ria Mojica saves time by editing and printing her photos in batches. She also uses standard size photos to avoid spending time cropping, which allows her to complete pages faster.

DESIGN TIP

Use a white or black pen for more than just journaling—create a hand-drawn frame around a photo or journaling spot to help draw the eye to that part of your layout.

No Kids Allowed *by Ria Mojica.* **Supplies:** *Cardstock:* Bazzill Basics Paper; *Patterned paper:* Kiki Art; *Stickers:* Scenic Route; *Rub-ons:* 7gypsies; *Pen:* Ranger Industries; *Adhesive:* 3M.

2009 Summer Vacation *by Lisa Pate.* **Supplies** *Software:* Adobe Photoshop Elements and Adobe Lightroom; *Patterned paper:* Ocean Solids Paper Pack by Andrea Victoria; *Month tabs:* Tabbed Dates by Katie Pertiet; *Clock:* Clock Parts Elements by Katie Pertiet; *Photo arrangements:* Photo Clusters No. 17 by Katie Pertiet; *Text overlay:* All You Need Overlays No. 05 by Katie Pertiet; *Letter stamps ("Road Trip"):* Messy Stamped Alphabet No. 02 Brushes and Stamps by Katie Pertiet; *Stitching:* Stitched by Anna White No. 01 by Anna Aspnes; *Word art ("Summer Vacation"):* Hello Summer Hand Drawn Brushes by Ali Edwards; *Brad:* Brad Bonanza by Pattie Knox; *Circle text:* Memories Circles No. 01 Brushes and Stamps by Art Warehouse; *Distressing:* Worn Page Edges No. 02 by Lynn Grieveson; *Font:* Arial.

TIME-SAVING TIP:

Lisa Pate created two folders on her computer to house her digital elements. One folder is for kits and embellishments, and the other is for papers. Each item is saved as a thumbnail so Lisa can look through them and find the perfect accent or paper to complete her project.

TITLE TECHNIQUE:

If you're creating a travel layout, search the Internet for fonts with a similar look or feel of the signs as your destination.

Snippets of San Francisco *by Maggie Holmes.* **Supplies** *Cardstock:* Prism Papers; *Patterned paper:* Making Memories (blue), Scenic Route (orange) and Studio Calico (turquoise); *Rub-ons:* Hambly Screen Prints; *Stamps:* Hero Arts; *Buttons and ink:* Papertrey Ink; *Brads:* Making Memories; *Stickers:* Studio Calico; *Letter stickers:* American Crafts (black) and Making Memories (orange); *Decorative tape:* Creative Imaginations (white) and Studio Calico (brown/black and green/blue); *Transparency accents:* Little Yellow Bicycle; *Scissors:* Provo Craft; *Punch:* Fiskars Americas; *Pens:* Zig Writer, EK Success; Slick Writers, American Crafts; *Adhesive:* Mono Vellum, Tombow; Zots, Therm O Web; Dot 'n' Roller, Kokuyo.

Group your journaling with pictures of the same subject. Maggie grouped her photos into sections based on the different places they visited on a trip. She also put related journaling next to each photo grouping. Maggie says, "This makes the layout organized. It's easy for a reader to follow our travels by using grouped photo collages rather than including one huge journaling block for all the pictures."

Like Valentine's, there wasn't much fanfare for St. Patrick's Day growing up. My mom, though, did pop green popcorn (still not sure how she did that) & serve green food on occasion. I definitely remember remembering to wear green &, in my younger days, trying to sneakily wear green so that others would think I wasn't & try to pinch me. I, then, of course, "got" to pinch them in turn & think highly of myself for being so cool.

green popcorn & pinch -ing

Yeah. I was weird. I'm going to blame it on that green popcorn.

{ GREEN POPCORN & PINCHING }

by Amanda Probst

Let your text be your embellishment.

Call me odd, but this is one of my favorite layouts. I love how the word "green" just jumps out at you and how perfectly the stamp goes with the whole idea. Sometimes you just don't have the pictures you need to tell a story. In those cases, play around with your text. It can be just as visually interesting.

tell a story

ADD COLOR AND STYLE TO HANDWRITTEN MEMORIES by sprinkling a few decorative words throughout your journaling block. Here Margaret selected four Flair Designs word stickers and filled in the details with a standard black pen.

materials word stickers (Flair Designs) • patterned paper, letter stickers (Cloud 9 Design) • metal clip (Making Memories) • calendar • staples • 8½ x 11 page by Margaret Scarbrough

get in shape

START WITH A FULL SHEET OF WORD STICKERS (still on their original backing), and cut them into a simple shape. To create this oversize accent, Margaret printed a large number "1" on plain printer paper and trimmed it into a template. She traced her template on the back side of a Making Memories Word Fetti sheet; then she clipped out the shape and added it to her layout using dimensional adhesive.

happy happy birthday, happy happy birthday, happy birthday sweet hoonie, happy birthday to you! your very first birthday was celebrated here at home (in California) with nearby family. i made an upside-down pineapple cake and virgin strawberry daiquiris. there were lots of presents to open, a big balloon (in the shape of a number one) and the relaxing sounds of the creek in the background. may 2007

materials word stickers (Making Memories) • buttons (Autumn Leaves) • metal embellishment (K&Company) • ribbon • Baskerville and Plantagenet Cherokee fonts • *8½ x 11 spread by Margaret Scarbrough*

layered type effects

Simple words can become both meaningful and magical when you begin experimenting with font, color, spacing, alignment and the orientation of various parts of your message. Whether you're creating a bold title treatment or adding design flair to the words of your favorite quote, all you need is some attention to detail paired with a little Photoshop know-how!

Grateful, Joyful, Thankful *by Jessica Sprague.* **Supplies** *Software:* Adobe Photoshop Elements 6.0; *Printer:* Epson R1900; *Photo paper:* Premium Presentation Paper (Matte), Epson; *Cardstock:* Bazzill Basics Paper; *Patterned paper:* Cosmo Cricket (dot) and My Mind's Eye (brown and green); *Flower stickers:* K&Company; *Punches:* EK Success (circle and corner rounder), Martha Stewart Crafts (scallop circle) and Marvy Uchida (scallop square); *Chipboard photo corner:* Tattered Angels; *Fonts:* Century Gothic, Microsoft (journaling); You Are Loved, Internet (title); *Other:* Wooden circles.

A LARGE TITLE TREATMENT balances out the large photo on this page, while an overlapping edge ties the two pieces together. I played with size, orientation and color in the title, and my journaling text (set in the same font and color as it appears in the strips below it) doubled as a textural background behind everything. Simple to do but stunning!

note: I use Epson's Premium Presentation Paper (Matte) when I want true-color title effects like these. The paper is bright white and treated to provide great color. It's available in letter size at most office-supply stores.

BY JESSICA SPRAGUE

the technique

You can have fun with this technique traditionally and digitally! Here's how:

traditional scrapbooking method:

Layer type by using stamps, rub-ons, alphabet stickers, chipboard letters or handwriting in new ways:

1. Rotate your paper 90 degrees and create some of the letters vertically.

2. Choose letters in a different color for a highlight.

3. Try squeezing lines of letters together for graphic appeal.

4. Use large letters on part of a word (see the "ful" in my "Grateful, Joyful, Thankful" layout on page 242).

digital technique using Photoshop:

1. Create a new blank document larger than your journaling or title block will be. Select the Horizontal Type Tool, then type the first part of your first word.

2. When you reach the point where you'd like to change size, font or alignment, hold down the Shift key and click (twice if you're using Elements 6.0) to set a new cursor and create a new layer of type.

3. Finish typing each part of your title onto separate layers, then use the Move Tool to rotate, resize and reposition the layers. Use the Horizontal Type Tool to recolor or change fonts.

variation 1:

Add a layered-type title to a photo.

When you're working with a large photo with a good amount of open space, consider using it to hold your title and journaling. Notice how the layered-type treatment on Tiffany Tillman's layout emphasizes the title. Says Tiffany, "I wanted my text and title to complement each other and layer over the photo. I really enjoy using this technique to draw the reader into my layout."

Whistleblower *by Tiffany Tillman.* **Supplies** *Software:* Adobe Photoshop CS3; *Cardstock:* Bazzill Basics Paper; *Patterned paper:* My Mind's Eye; *Brads:* Making Memories; *Journaling spot and clear flower:* Heidi Swapp for Advantus; *Square punch:* EK Success; *Epoxy sticker:* Love, Elsie for KI Memories; *Fonts:* Georgia, Microsoft (journaling) and Impact, Internet (title). *Idea to note:* Tiffany opened her photo and printed a second copy as a mirror image.

variation 2:

Set a quote on a card.

You can really practice your typography skills by setting a quote in varying weights and sizes using one or two fonts. Print it out on double-sided matte "presentation paper" (a little lighter than photo paper, with truer color than plain cardstock). Use a pretty ribbon to wrap the results up with an envelope. It makes a wonderful, simple gift with a striking visual message.

Thank You Card Gift Set *by Jessica Sprague.* **Supplies**
Software: Adobe Photoshop Elements 6.0; *Printer:* Epson R1900; *Photo paper:* Premium Presentation Paper (Matte), Epson; *Tree graphic: www.istockphoto.com; Circle tag:* Heidi Swapp for Advantus; *Stick pin:* Heidi Grace Designs; *Fonts:* Myriad Pro, Adobe; P22 Cezanne, Internet; *Other:* Velvet ribbon and envelopes.

variation 3:

Layer text over your page title.

Maggie Holmes's page title also serves as the starting phrase for each sentence of her journaling. To visually convey this connection, she layered her entire journaling block over her page title. Maggie remarks, "I love this technique. I like to layer different words, dingbats or other brushes. Putting them each in their own layer makes it so easy to move things around and change colors or sizes until you're happy with the overall design of the page."

Grateful For *by Maggie Holmes.* **Supplies**
Software: Adobe Photoshop CS2; *Patterned paper and brads:* Making Memories; *Buttons:* Autumn Leaves and Daisy D's Paper Co.; *Stickers:* GCD Studios; *Label sticker:* FontWerks; *Pen:* Slick Writers, American Crafts; *Fonts:* Cairo and Type Embellishments One, Internet.

Journaling cards are all the rage—and it's no wonder. They provide a convenient, lined space to add handwritten journaling to a page, and the right design can dress up even the worst penmanship. But did you know that you can create custom journaling cards in Microsoft Word? Instead of buying every journaling card under the sun, you can quickly and easily make your own in a variety of colors, styles, shapes, and sizes.

Here's how:

1. Open a new Word document.

2. To create the border, go to **Insert > Picture > AutoShapes**. On the **AutoShapes** palette, select **Basic Shapes > Rounded Rectangle**; then draw a box by clicking and dragging.

3. Double click the **Rounded Rectangle** to bring up the **Format AutoShape** palette. On the **Colors and Lines** tab, choose a **Fill Color**, **Line Color**, and **Line Style**. Click **OK**.

4. To add journaling lines, go to **Insert > Text Box**. Inside the **Rounded Rectangle**, draw a slightly smaller text box with **No Fill** and **No Line**.

5. Click in the text box, and press **Enter**. Then hold down the **Shift** and **Hyphen** keys until the entire text box is filled with lines. *Note: Adjust the line spacing by changing the font size.*

6. Highlight the lines, go to **Format > Font**, and choose a color from the **Font color** drop-down menu.

7. To add an image above the lines, insert another text box sized to the same width as your **AutoShape**. Double click the text box to bring up the **Format Text Box** palette, and choose a **Fill Color** and **Line Color**.

8. Type a word or dingbat in the new text box. Highlight the type, go to **Format > Font**, and choose a font style, size, and color.

9. Print your journaling card on cardstock, and cut it out. Use a corner rounder to round the bottom corners.

materials vinyl letters, letter stickers (American Crafts) • WM Aquatic font • 8½ x 11 page by Celeste Smith, West Hartford, CT

TRY THIS:

- Create circles, arrows, squares, or stars using AutoShapes.
- Type your actual journaling (instead of lines) inside the shape.
- Try a dashed or other line style to create the shape.
- Change the color of your journaling lines or the fill color of your text box to get a different look.

SPOOKY

by Amy Williams

Spice up an album made with traditional supplies by adding photo sleeves between the pages. This is especially effective for chipboard mini albums—simply cut any photo sleeve down to fit the size of your album. And since photo sleeves can be cut using standard paper trimmers, you'll be able to add photos to your album in a jiffy.

FRESH TIP

Use pre-printed journaling cards for Amy's fresh tip: use a few uncropped cards on your album pages for journaling, then cut others apart to create neat spaces for captioning your photos.

Supplies: *Album, patterned paper, chipboard, and rub-ons:* Cosmo Cricket; *Ribbon:* BoBunny Press; *Stamps:* Making Memories; *Other:* Ink and wiggle eyes.

BOO TO YOU

YIKES! 2003

This Year Personalities really came into play when picking costumes. A Rock Star and Two Princesses — So Right on!

PRETTY PRINCESSES

Katy=Cinderella Cambree=Sleeping Beauty Marinne=Rocker

MAKE YOUR OWN PHOTO SLEEVE MINI ALBUM

To start, you'll need:

- a blank chipboard book bound with binder rings
- several divided photo sleeves (available in bulk)

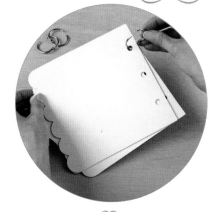

1. Open binder rings and remove from book.

2. Cut photo sleeves to fit using paper trimmer.

3. Align holes. Thread rings through holes and close.

on-the-spot *journaling*

Journaling blocks, also known as "journaling spots," are all the craze right now! But I often find myself stumped on how to incorporate them into my pages. To help, I challenged myself to come up with fun ideas for journaling blocks. Let's see what *you* can create.

CUT journaling blocks in half and use them to frame a photo.

Two *by Jennifer McGuire.*
Supplies *Journaling blocks:* Maya Road; *Die-cut number:* Cricut, Provo Craft; *Patterned paper:* Bo-Bunny Press; *Buttons:* Autumn Leaves; *Other:* Cardstock, thread, adhesive dots and string.

BY JENNIFER McGUIRE

SEW three sides of a journaling block to a cardstock block of the same size to create a pocket for photos.

Big Day by Jennifer McGuire. **Supplies** *Journaling block:* Scenic Route; *Star punches:* Fiskars; *Rub-ons:* American Crafts; *Gems:* Hero Arts; *Other:* Cardstock and thread.

TURN a journaling block sideways and use the lines as stems for flowers.

First Day by Jennifer McGuire. **Supplies** *Journaling block:* Maya Road; *Flowers:* Doodlebug Design; *Scallop-edge paper:* Bazzill Basics Paper; *Font:* CK Jessica, *www.scrapnfonts.com; Other:* Cardstock, string, thread and permanent pen.

ENHANCE lines on a journaling block with stitching.

Kay by Jennifer McGuire. **Supplies** *Journaling block stamp:* Close To My Heart; *Tag:* K&Company; *Flourish stamp and mini buttons:* Hero Arts; *Ink:* ColorBox Fluid Chalk, Clearsnap; *Other:* Cardstock, thread and beaded chain.

EMBELLISH a journaling block frame with glitter and stickers for added fun.

Yooo Hooo!! by Jennifer McGuire. **Supplies** *Journaling block:* American Crafts; *Glitter:* Doodlebug Design; *Dimensional stickers:* K&Company; *Stamps:* Hero Arts; *Ink:* StazOn, Tsukineko; *Other:* Cardstock.

USE a journaling block for the address block on an envelope.

Envelope *by Jennifer McGuire.* **Supplies** *Journaling block rub-on:* Hambly Studios; *Stamps, note cards and gems:* Hero Arts; *White pen:* Ranger Industries; *Other:* Ribbon and googly eyes.

try it yourself!

Want to check out journaling spots for your own use? Try these:

AMERICAN CRAFTS	**MAYA ROAD**	**SANDYLION**	**UPSY DAISY DESIGNS**
www.americancrafts.com	www.mayaroad.com	www.sandylion.com	www.upsydaisydesigns.com

These Are the Days by Kim Watson. **Supplies:** *Cardstock:* Bazzill Basics Paper; *Patterned paper:* American Crafts, Close to My Heart, Fancy Pants Designs, Prima, and SEI; *Brads, embossing powder, and ink:* American Crafts; *Metal accents:* Making Memories; *Leaves:* Prima; *Chipboard:* Jenni Bowlin Studio; *Stickers:* Jenni Bowlin Studio, Pink Paislee, and Studio Calico; *Lace and tickets:* Cocoa Daisy; *Stamps:* Croxley Stationery and Prima; *Rub-ons:* Lily Bee Design; *Pen:* Sakura; *Adhesive:* American Crafts, Scrapbook Adhesives by 3L, Therm O Web, and Tombow; *Software:* Adobe; *Other:* Acrylic paint, doilies, jute, and thread.

The Perfect End by Cindy Tobey. **Supplies** *Cardstock:* Bazzill Basics Paper; *Patterned paper:* K&Company (map), My Mind's Eye (dot) and October Afternoon (cloud); *Rub-ons:* Love, Elsie for KI Memories; *Ribbon:* Making Memories (pink) and Mrs. Grossman's (yellow); *Brads:* Queen & Co.; *Stickers:* American Crafts (letters) and Love, Elsie for KI Memories (button); *Buttons:* Autumn Leaves and Fancy Pants Designs; *Journaling notepaper and paint:* Making Memories; *Marker:* Sakura; *Adhesive:* 3M, Glue Dots International and Tombow.

Products for Your Journaling

Pick up a few of these journaling products to scrapbook your next vacation, or take them along with you when you travel!

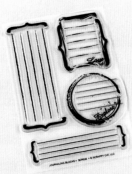 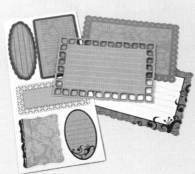 

Journaling Blocks Clear Stamps
Scrappy Cat
ScrappyCatOnline.com

Zinnia
Little Yellow Bicycle
MyLYB.com

Memory Block Stamps: Jot It Down and Wire Bound
Stamping Bella
StampingBella.com

little Emmie
is a bright
spot in my life.
She is always so
happy to see me
and makes me
feel loved. I take
pride in her everyday
accomplishments
and look forward
to more Emmie time.

OUR SWEET EMMIE

materials patterned papers, journaling card, rubber flower (October Afternoon) • velvet ribbon, letter sticker, metal tag rims, tag maker (Making Memories) • notch and die cutting tool (BasicGrey) • laser ruler (Westcott) • ribbon iron (Pebbles Inc.) • labeler, labeling tape (Around The Block) • craft knife, cutting mat (Doodlebug) • dauber, paint, sander (Close To My Heart) • *12 x 12 page by Wendy Smedley, Centerville, UT*

Place your photos and journaling inside a brush.

Joanna enlarged her brush to hold her photo and journaling (she used the .png file). Joanna comments, "A thought bubble was a perfect fit for my partial list of Harper's words and phrases . . . to indicate the fact that she talks a lot! I've used journaling boxes before, but this was the first time I used a large brush. It's a handy technique because it made my page design go very quickly."

Talkative *by Joanna Bolick.* **Supplies** *Software:* Adobe Photoshop Elements 5.0; *Cardstock:* Bazzill Basics Paper; *Craft knife:* Fiskars; *Fonts:* 2Peas Fancy Free, *www.twopeasinabucket.com;* Donata, Internet; Impact, Microsoft; *Digital brush:* Think About It Brush Set by Erica Hernandez, *www.twopeasinabucket.com. Idea to note:* Joanna hand cut the title using the Impact font as a guide

Christmas

Snow

Living in Indiana, you can never count on having a white Christmas. This year was different, and it was absolutely wonderful!

12/25/2000

Grandpa & Grandma Brown's

materials patterned papers (Love, Elsie; Making Memories) • chipboard word (Scrapworks) • letter stickers (Making Memories) • felt snowflakes (American Crafts) • 11 x 8½ page by Louanna Stiner, Indianapolis, IN

Dual-Tip Pen + Decorative Journaling Stamp

This acrylic journaling stamp gave me enough space to document my daughter's personality, yet it's small enough to let my photo take center stage. I saved time by using both ends of my dual-tip pen—a handwritten title is easy when you use a multitasking writing utensil.

try this!

Instead of using black stamping ink, look for a color that complements your overall design; then write your words in black so they'll really stand out.

materials journaling pen (EK Success) • journaling stamp, letter sticker, rhinestone brads (Making Memories) • patterned paper (SEI) • chipboard snowflakes (Autumn Leaves) • letter rub-ons (American Crafts) • stamping ink (Stampin' Up!) • *12 x 12 page by Elizabeth Dillow, Arlington, VA*

Frame and label stamps are a great way
to add a spot of journaling to a layout.

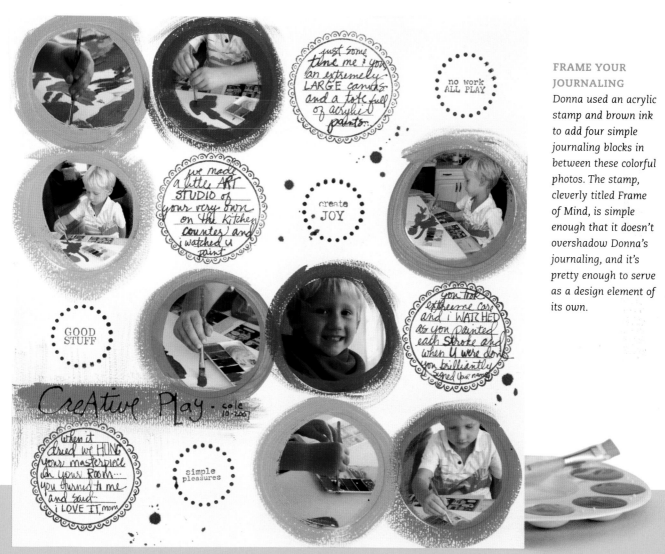

**FRAME YOUR
JOURNALING**
*Donna used an acrylic
stamp and brown ink
to add four simple
journaling blocks in
between these colorful
photos. The stamp,
cleverly titled Frame
of Mind, is simple
enough that it doesn't
overshadow Donna's
journaling, and it's
pretty enough to serve
as a design element of
its own.*

materials stamps (Fontwerks, Red Lead) • stamping ink (Tsukineko) • acrylic paints
(Delta Technical Coatings, Making Memories) • circle punch (Marvy Uchida) • *12 x 12 page by
Donna Downey, Huntersville, NC*

january
01 new year's day
07 emma turns 6
february
14 stan sends gifties for valentine's day
23 great grandma rusk in art show
march
14 torrey's knocked out tooth came in
19 emma's kangaroo farm field trip
20 up to laconner to see the daffodil fields
25 torrey at young authors conference
april
09-11 surprise trip to seattle with girls for spring break
17, 30 up to roozengaarde to see tulips
may
09 torrey's state park field trip
11 mother's day & silly pictures
24 made homecoming signs for stan
june
06 stan comes home from 5th six month deployment
19 last day of school
24-30 vacation to yellowstone & the ranch
july
02 torrey turns 8 & we close on our new house
19-21 noel at c.h.a.
august
01-06 grandpa gene & grandma linn visit
15 emma lost her 2 front teeth
september
02 first day of school
5-7 camping at camano island state park with fuentes
25 stan turns 33
october
11 pumpkin patch with the family
23 torrey's rock quarry field trip
november
10 stan speaks at the veteran's day assembly
14 our 9 year anniversary
27 family thanksgiving at our house
december
09 torrey gets glasses, lots of snow & sledding
23 noel turns 32
25 family christmas at our house
30 stan hit by drunk driver

i heart this
life 2008

I Heart This Life *by Noel Culbertson.* **Supplies** *Software:* Adobe Photoshop Elements 6.0; *Patterned paper:* Hoopla: Oh Happy Day by Paislee Press Designs; *Stamps and elements:* Hoopla: Oh Happy Day, Happy as a Lark Kit and Sociologie Kit by Paislee Press Designs; *Frame:* Labeled Frames + Clipping Masks by Paislee Press Designs; *Fonts:* Decker and You Are Loved.

SAN FRANSISCO TREATS

october'07

STONEHOUSE
CALIFORNIA
OLIVE OIL

THE FERRY BUILDING
SAN FRANCISCO 94111
415 765 0405

ORDER ONLINE
stonehouseoliveoil.com
800 865 4836

LULU PETITE
GASTRONOMIC DELIGHT

BOUDIN
SOURDOUGH

CITIZEN CAKE

Being the self-proclaimed foodie that I am, I always look forward to eating out on a trip. San Fransisco didn't let me down one bit! It's definitely a bonus when I get to go somewhere with fresh seafood, and it was everywhere in SF. I was able to try a delicious cracked crab dinner that was so meaty and spicy. I kept seeing Boudin clam chowder everywhere so my last day I took the trolley back down to the Pier to get a breadbowl full. So satisfying. I also loved walking through the market at Pier 1 and seeing all the fresh food the boutiques had to offer. In Chinatown I picked up a huge bag of freshly made fortune cookies to bring back to share at work. And then there is Ghiradelli Chocolate... what trip to SF would be complete without indulging in Ghiradelli?! It was definitely a city that kept my stomach very full and happy!

San Francisco Treats by Kelly Purkey. **Supplies** *Cardstock, patterned paper, stickers and rub-ons:* American Crafts; *Stamps:* Hero Arts; *Ink:* Memories, Stewart Superior Corporation; *Punches and decorative scissors:* Fiskars Americas; *Buttons:* Hero Arts; *Font:* American Typewriter.

materials letter rub-ons (American Traditional Designs) • decorative rub-ons (Sassafras Lass) • Photoshop (Adobe Systems) • 12 x 12 page by Peg Manrique, Essex Junction, VT

fill it in

DRESS UP A DESIGN. Use rub-ons to add color and depth to a plain stamped image, whether it's a regular stamp-and-ink design or a digital stamp, like Peg's. Peg printed a retro design on her white background cardstock, then dressed it up with colorful pops of personality. She selected playful rub-ons that illustrated her daughter's youth and energy, adding standard black letter rub-ons into the mix as well.

Rub-on Tips

You don't have to rub a magic lamp to uncover the secrets to using rub-ons; designer Celeste Smith has uncovered them for you. Follow these simple tips, and your rub-on wishes shall be granted!

- **SURFACE SAVVY.** Most rub-ons will adhere to any smooth surface (paper, glass, chipboard, etc.). For best results, make sure your surface is clean and dry before applying.

- **TRANSFER TIP.** As you apply your rub-on, the image will get lighter on the transfer sheet. This lets you know that it's adhering.

- **FIND YOUR CENTER.** When applying large or long rub-ons, it's best to work from the middle out. This will help prevent your image from moving off center as it adheres.

- **TAKE IT SLOW.** After applying your rub-on, slowly lift your transfer sheet to ensure that it has completely adhered. If an area doesn't stick, reposition the sheet, and continue rubbing.

- **SEAL THE DEAL.** Position your transfer sheet over an adhered rub-on, and smooth with a flat, spatula-like tool to smooth out bumps, seal the image, and avoid lift. This is known as burnishing.

- **SMART PACKAGING.** Every sheet of rub-ons is packaged with a backing sheet, which protects the fragile images from scuffing. Once you've opened your rub-ons, staple this sheet to the rub-on sheet to ensure they stay together and your rub-ons stay intact.

- **RUB REMOVAL.** Rub-ons generally aren't permanent, so don't fret if you end up changing your mind about the placement of one. To remove, gently scratch it with your fingernail first. If that doesn't work, pat it with tape, and it should come off. If all else fails, cover it with another element, and no one will be the wiser.

storytelling
shortcuts

Go by Michelle Alynn Clement. **Supplies** *Patterned paper, felt shapes and journaling card:* Fancy Pants Designs; *Letter stamps:* Hero Arts; *Ink:* StazOn, Tsukineko; *Date stamp:* Making Memories; *Chipboard letter stickers:* American Crafts; *Dimensional globes:* Magic Scraps; *Other:* Staples, paint, watercolor pencils, sandpaper, buttons, journal page, embroidery floss and cardboard circle.

MICHELLE created this whimsical layout as the title page for an album about a trip she won to France. For her photos, Michelle used the index prints so she could document all the great times and people she met through **"thought bubble" style journaling** stemming out from her main photo.

MICHELLE'S EASY-ACCENTS SOLUTIONS

No circle stamp? Michelle didn't have one either, so she used the edge of a cardboard tube from an empty roll of Glue Dots. Just brush paint around the edge and voila . . . an impromptu circle stamp.

BY VANESSA HOY

May

A Beautiful rainbow

Addie's sealing day

Aunt Amy comes to visit

Taft turns 6
Jenna is party planner!

Mom's b-day (42)

Kerry goes to hospital
Mom gets to visit!

Trip to Utah

Wendy's new studio

A day at doodlebug

Dogwood tree blooms

Sunday walks

Kitchen sink baths

Clark loves soccer

Bridal showers

Dad's b-day (41)

Ashli marries Michael

Bday Bucket of Balls

Friday night lettuce wraps

Mom color class at BPS

Dad 3rd cruise climb!

07 highlights

materials patterned papers (Bo-Bunny, Making Memories) • chipboard letters (Making Memories, Pressed Petals) • letter stickers (Doodlebug Design) • velvet flowers (Maya Road) • ribbon • brads • Century Gothic font • *12 x 12 page by Stacy Julian, Liberty Lake, WA*

She was a skater girl, she said 'see ya later,' or something like that, right? Well, after many years

of flooding our tiny little backyard to make our own rink, this year, we just said, "no!" and guess what? The kids found a new place to

skater *girl*

february

never ever flood our yard again!

go: the school! Now tell about a rink. Goodbye, 2-skate backyard Hello, Chelsea Heights! We'll

materials chipboard letters, tag (Making Memories) • mini brad (American Crafts)
• Amelie font • 8½ x 11 page by Cathy Zielske, St. Paul, MN

love is an escape

Love can transport us to another world. What better way to take a break from reality than by escaping for a few minutes or hours to a more exciting—or more relaxing—life?

at the park with {harry potter}

The way I see it, it's not actually neglect. Sure, we pretty much ignore our kids for two or three days when a new Harry Potter book comes out, but we ignore them at fun places, like the park. So that's ok, right?

Scott and I love Harry Potter. Years ago in Memphis, we started checking out the books on tape and listening to them in the car while we drove around the city, trying to calm crying babies. Scott read book 4 out loud to me while I made cookies to give as Christmas gifts for our neighbors. As each subsequent book has been released, we've taken turns reading it aloud to each other, spending the better part of three days immersed in J.K.'s world. The final book was released on a Friday night, and Saturday morning found us at the park, hoping the kids would play for a few hours so we could read as much as possible. That weekend we read while they watched movies, we read while they ate snacks, we read after they went to bed. We hated to see the book going by so fast, but we hated even more when we had to stop reading in order to take care of daily life. We loved being able to share the stories with each other and we can't wait until the kids are old enough that we can share the series again as a family. 8.08.

Autumn says that the best part about her obsession with Harry Potter is sharing it with her husband. "We don't have that many common interests, so I was excited when we watched the first movie together and he decided he wanted to read the books as well," she says. "I've been trying to incorporate more of the two of us into my scrapbooks, since they are so heavily dominated by pages about my kids."

materials lace paper (KI Memories) • ric rac (May Arts) • letter stickers (American Crafts) • Optima font • 8½ x 11 spread by Autumn Baldwin, Spanish Fork, UT

Sometimes it is a tragedy

and then becomes fantasy,

science fiction,

and then a biography...

At times it is a comedy,

and others it is a drama.

The story of us.

Even with all of this change,

it is still our story,

and it is the story of us.

The Story of Us *by Becky Olsen.* **Supplies** *Cardstock:* Bazzill Basics Paper (white) and Cornish Heritage Farms (journaling strips); *Patterned paper:* Cosmo Cricket and Lily Bee Design; *Scalloped punch:* Stampin' Up!; *Ribbon:* Prima; *Flowers:* Studio Calico; *Embroidery floss:* DMC; *Adhesive:* Scotch ATG, 3M; *Other:* Vintage trim and thread.

Remember that time a few years ago, you went into the skateboard shop in a bid to prove that although you were almost 30 you were still young & hip?

And the guy working there {who you claimed was only a few years younger than you} said, I think it's really cool when old dudes still ride."

And then do you remember how much I laughed when you came home and told me that story?

And do you also recall how I stopped laughing when you smirked and said, "I'm okay with it, babe, because when I start to feel like I'm getting old, I just remember that I will always be younger than you.

very funny, **PUNK**, very funny.

Use Your Strength as a Starting Point

Cheryl is a funny lady—one who easily sees the humor in a picture or story. (She admits her family's silliness makes humor simple to spot.) It only makes sense, then, for Cheryl to use this strength to her advantage as she approaches her journaling. "I write like I speak," she says, "and I have been told by family members and friends that when they read some of my journaling, they can totally hear me saying the words that they are reading." Now that's a scrapbooking legacy.

materials photo turns (7gypsies) • Joyful Juliana and Planet Benson 2 fonts • 8 ½ x 11 page by Cheryl Overton, Kelowna, BC, Canada

I REMEMBER FASCINATION WITH KITES AS A YOUNG BOY, ESPECIALLY AT THE BEACH. I HAD A GAYLA FLAMING EYEBALL KITE THAT I JUST LOVED. THINGS CAME AROUND FULL CIRCLE THIS SUMMER WHEN ANDREW WOULDN'T STOP TALKING AND ASKING "DADDY, WHEN ARE WE GOING ON THE BEACH TO FLY A KITE?" WE ENDED UP FINDING AND BUYING KITES AT THE STORE AT OCEAN LAKES RESORT. MUCH TO MY SURPRISE, THERE I FOUND MY CHILDHOOD FASCINATION, THE GAYLA FLAMING EYEBALL KITE. THE DATE ON THE WRAPPER SAID 1976! NATHAN AND ANDREW THOROUGHLY ENJOYED OUR TIME FLYING KITES ON THE BEACH, AS DID I. I HOPE THE FUN WE ENJOYED TOGETHER STAYS IN THEIR HEARTS FOR A LONG TIME TO COME

JUNE 2007

Happiness never decreases by being shared.
Buddha

Hand the Pen Over to the Husband (or Aunt, or Best Friend)

Letting someone else do the journaling isn't abdicating responsibility; it's just plain smart. Not only are you relieving the pressure on yourself to do it all, you're also giving the gift of a different perspective to future generations. To make it easier on your assistant, provide guidelines, as Michelle did: "This time I gave him some journaling lines using rub-on stitches. Tried to keep him in line!"

materials patterned paper (American Crafts) • die cut (My Mind's Eye) • rub-on stitches (Die Cuts With a View) • brads (Making Memories, Queen & Co.) • *12 x 12 page by Michelle St. Clair, Fuquay-Varina, NC*

Natalie

kept her embellishments to a minimum so she could feature as many photos of this kite-flying experience as possible. Notice how she placed both her **title and journaling elements on the swirls** in the center of her layout.

NATALIE'S SECRETS FOR A GREAT MULTIPHOTO LAYOUT

- Make your own paper swirls—Natalie created these fun kite-string embellishments by freehand cutting her paper. ("I'm not much of a measure-and-sketch girl," she admits.) Notice how the paper swirls perfectly mimic the kite images in her photos.
- Trim premade embellishments (such as these crystal swirls) to fit your design. Don't be afraid to alter accents to make them fit your layout.

Kite Strings *by Natalie Call.* **Supplies** *Patterned paper:* Fancy Pants Designs; *Letter stickers:* Making Memories; *Rub-ons:* Scenic Route; *Crystal swirls:* Prima.

Annette creates a similar layout every year

with **the same questions for her children.** What a wonderful way to document what changes and what remains the same from year to year!

ANNETTE'S INTERACTIVE JOURNALING TRICK

- Use lined paper to make it easier for children to write their answers.

Fifth *by Annette Pixley.* **Supplies** *Patterned paper:* Creative Imaginations; *Chipboard:* Junkitz; *Stickers:* American Crafts and EK Success; *Pen:* American Crafts.

GET SHAPED TEXT WITH PHOTOSHOP

It's easy to shape your text using Adobe Photoshop. Just choose your font style and size, then type each line as a separate layer. Next, highlight each line (one at a time) and click on the "Wrap Text" icon. Here, Elizabeth used the "Rise" and "Wave" options.

I Promise by Elizabeth Kartchner. **Supplies** *Patterned paper:* BasicGrey (yellow) and October Afternoon (apples); *Rub-on:* Hambly Studios; *Chipboard frame:* Love, Elsie for KI Memories; *Stamps:* October Afternoon; *Ink:* StazOn, Tsukineko; *Sticker labels:* Scenic Route; *Chipboard heart:* Heidi Swapp for Advantus; *Heart brads:* Making Memories; *Font:* Love Ya Like a Sister, *www.dafont.com*; *Software:* Adobe Photoshop, Adobe Systems; *Other:* Date stamp and paper clip.

Journaling Design

It's time to tap into your inner child—Sesame-Street style—and start looking at everything with shapes in mind. With a little spark of imagination and just a few added touches, basic shapes like squares, triangles and circles can be transformed into journaling designs that not only catch the eye but also fit the theme of the layout. Don't forget about more complex shapes like stars, hearts and flowers. They, too, can be used for unusual theme- shaped journaling.

WHAT I DID: For the "shape" on this birthday layout, I transformed a triangle into a party hat by adding a scalloped border along the bottom and a flower cut from patterned paper to the top. If you prefer to use your handwriting rather than your computer for journaling, create a shape and pencil in journaling lines as a guide for evenly spaced lines.

Celebrating One
by Allison Davis. **Supplies** *Cardstock:* Bazzill Basics Paper; *Patterned paper and letter stickers:* KI Memories; *Ink:* ColorBox Fluid Chalk, Clearsnap; *Word stickers:* Making Memories; *Circle stickers:* Heidi Grace Designs; *Font:* Arial, Microsoft; *Pen:* Zig Memory System, EK Success; *Other:* Craft wire.

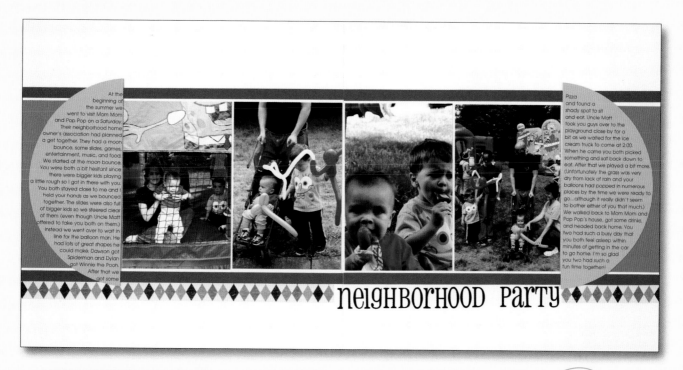

At the beginning of the summer we went to visit Mom Mom and Pop Pop on a Saturday. Their neighborhood home owner's association had planned a get together. They had a moon bounce, some slides, games, entertainment, music, and food. We started at the moon bounce. You were both a bit hesitant since there were bigger kids playing a little rough so I got in there with you. You both stayed close to me and I held your hands as we bounced together. The slides were also full of bigger kids so we steered clear of them (even though Uncle Matt offered to take you both on them.) Instead we went over to wait in line for the balloon man. He had lots of great shapes he could make. Dawson got Spiderman and Dylan got Winnie the Pooh. After that we got some

Pizza and found a shady spot to sit and eat. Uncle Matt took you guys over to the playground close by for a bit as we waited for the ice cream truck to come at 2:00. When he came you both picked something and sat back down to eat. After that we played a bit more. (Unfortunately the grass was very dry from lack of rain and your balloons had popped in numerous places by the time we were ready to go...although it really didn't seem to bother either of you that much.) We walked back to Mom Mom and Pop Pop's house, got some drinks, and headed back home. You two had such a busy day that you both fell asleep within minutes of getting in the car to go home. I'm so glad you two had such a fun time together!!

NEIGHBORHOOD PARTY

DAWN HAGEWOOD placed her photos between two large half-circles of text. How'd she do it? "I drew a circle in Microsoft Word to use as a guide," she explains. "I created two text boxes and added journaling in both. Then I deleted the original circle before printing out my text." After printing the journaling, Dawn used her Curvy Cutter by EK Success to cut out the circle halves.

Neighborhood Party *by Dawn Hagewood.* **Supplies** *Cardstock:* Bazzill Basics Paper; *Patterned paper and letter stickers:* Mustard Moon.

Thanks, Easter Bunny! *by Connie Tomasula.* **Supplies** *Patterned paper:* Rusty Pickle; *Rub-ons:* Doodlebug Design; *Ribbon:* May Arts; *Brads:* Lasting Impressions for Paper; *Fonts:* DW Dingbats (bunny clip art), *www.twopeasinabucket.com*; Hot Chocolate (text), Internet; *Other:* Vellum.

^ wrapped text made easy

Getting your journaling to wrap around an accent can be frustrating. I know I've printed try after try before achieving a journaling box that's just right. That's why I love Connie's layout. The Easter Bunny accent is actually a dingbat she printed onto white cardstock and cut out. Here's how to simplify your journaling wraps:

1 Type your text.

2 Add a dingbat accent in your text document and use the text wrap feature for a perfect fit.

3 Print the dingbat onto a separate sheet of cardstock. Cut the image out, then adhere it over the dingbat on the journaling block for nice dimension.

summer is

feasting on watermelon for breakfast, lunch and dinner ○ fresh flowers from the farmers market ○ running through the fountain at Tualatin Commons at 8 o'clock at night ○ hearing the ice cream truck 5 blocks away and convincing your sister to buy you a popsicle ○ cruising around the neighborhood on your scooter ○ lathering up with sun screen ○ and many back yard water fights all in the name of staying cool

{ SUMMER IS . . . }
by Summer Fullerton

Make your own definition.

Journaling doesn't have to be difficult. Simply list everything that comes to mind when you think of summer. Easy. By the way, I love how Summer matted the photos to look like Polaroid shots and added detail to the title with stamps and embossing powder. Fun!

materials label (Dymo) • letter stamps • acrylic paint • stickers • *12 x 12 spread by Jennifer Davis, Woodruff, WI*

journal around a photo block

Do you ever add that last touch to a layout, sit back, and smile contentedly, then realize you've missed something important? Oh yeah, journaling! It's kind of like making Kool-Aid and forgetting the sugar, or leaving the peanut butter out of peanut butter cookies. But luckily, you don't have to start completely over when you neglect to journal. No matter how "finished" your layout is, you can almost always journal along the edges of something: a photo collage, an oversize photo mat, even the layout itself. This technique isn't just for the forgetful, however: Jennifer planned in advance to border her photos with descriptive words.

journal vertically—
one word on each line

To emphasize each individual word of your journaling—which is especially effective when you're quoting a kiddo—print each word on its own line. Call attention to the most important words by changing their size, color, font, or a combination of these. (But first you may want to seek permission from King Kyla. We hear she's got some pretty specific preferences.)

"The time has come, my little friends, to talk of other things. Of shoes and ships and sealing wax, of cabbages and kings."
—*Walrus in Disney's* Alice in Wonderland

FOLLOW YOUR HEART
DREAM
YOU CAN DO ANYTHING

I
don't
want
to
be
a
princess...

I
want
to
be
a
KING

~Kyla
March 2007

conversations w/ kyla

materials Stemma patterned paper (Masterpiece Studios) • chipboard letters (Heidi Swapp) • rub-on letters (KI Memories) • rhinestones (Westrim Crafts) • stamping ink • Century Gothic and CK Lovenotes fonts • *12 x 12 page by Lea Lawson, Missoula, MT*

journal between
patterned paper strips

Looking for a new way to incorporate journaling onto a layout? Try Joey's trick. Run a series of patterned paper strips behind an oversize photo; then jot down your thoughts in the in-between spaces. Joey cut her strips into varying lengths and widths for an eclectic look; it also saved her time (no need to measure!). This is her first-ever landscape-oriented layout.

> "The space between your heart and mine is a space we'll fill with time."
> —*Dave Matthews Band*

carefree and happy as

you give in to your instincts

and bolt for the water.

Perfect weather, perfect place,

makes for the most perfect of days.

Castaway Cay- May 2006

Family Disney Cruise

beach

materials patterned paper (Crate Paper, Scenic Route Paper Co.) • flower brad (Making Memories) • gem stars, brad, paper clip (KI Memories) • star button (All Dressed Up) • rub-on letters • stamping ink • *11 x 8½ page by Joey Whittaker, West Jordan, UT*

journal on a real
library card

Well, this isn't a real, real library card—but it looks like one! Debbie gathered two old photos of her son with his dad and paired them with some of Davey's own words written on a library card. To reflect the playful theme of the photos, Debbie chose bright and engaging paper colors that (gasp!) don't appear anywhere in the photos themselves. And you know what? It works! For extra fun, she cut her title letters from a sheet of patterned paper.

"You can discover more about a person in an hour of play than in a year of conversation."
—Plato

materials patterned paper (Junkitz, Leaving Prints, My Mind's Eye) • buttons (American Crafts) • library card (Boxer Scrapbook Productions) • chipboard accent (BasicGrey) • ribbon (Making Memories) • paper clip • 12 x 12
page by Debbie Hingston, Lynnwood, WA

each one of you
are such a blessing
in my life. I
honestly and truly
dont know where
I would be with
out you! I am
so grateful for
the beautiful
gift of you.
Love you guys!
xoxo, mommy

CHECK PLEASE

Requesting the check just got a lot more fun thanks to this journaling tip provided by Ginger John of Glitz Design. Record your memories on a blank bill for a fresh, found-items approach. It will give your layout lots of character. Various receipt forms can be found at your local office-supply store. This is definitely an idea to check out!

Gift by Ginger John for Glitz Design. **Supplies:** *Patterned paper:* Glitz Design, Graphic45, and Pink Paislee; *Stickers:* Glitz Design and Jenni Bowlin Studio; *Rub-ons and die cut:* Glitz Design; *Button and pearl accents:* Jenni Bowlin Studio; *Pen:* Bic; *Adhesive:* Ranger Industries and Tombow; *Other:* Acrylic paint, cardboard, guest check, lace flower, ledger sheet, mirror, rhinestones, staples, vintage card, and sheet music.

buttoned up

Even something as fun as homemade buttons can help tell your story! This layout contains five random facts about each of my family members right now, and the page is decorated with a scattering of random little buttons to echo that theme.

BY C.D. MUCKOSKY

5 about Five *by C.D. Muckosky.* **Supplies** *Patterned paper:* BasicGrey; *Printer and photo paper:* Hewlett-Packard; *Labels:* 7gypsies; *Felt circles:* Fancy Pants Designs; *Transparency:* 3M; *Clear buttons:* Autumn Leaves; *Floss:* DMC; *Adhesive:* Aleene's Tacky Glue, Duncan Enterprises; Glue Dots International and hot glue gun; *Paint and eyelets:* Making Memories; *Old proof-sheet frames:* Christina Renee, *www.christinareneedesigns.com; Pens:* Sakura (journaling) and Sharpie, Newell Rubbermaid (on button); *Other:* Beads, cheesecloth, clay, duct tape and twine.

by Amanda Probst

Ask your kids.

This is something I started doing last year: asking my kids what it was they wanted to learn in the coming school year. It's informative and quite fun! To make it a bit more "official" this year, we typed up the lists. I mounted them on a cookie sheet turned magnetic display board and added Shrinky-Dink artwork the boys had drawn as magnets.

can i, mom?

Can I go outside?

Can you help me get dressed?

Can I roll around in the snow?

Can you zip my boots?

Can I stay out for two hours?

Can I help Dad clean the driveway?

Can I come inside?

(time elapsed getting ready: 30 minutes.)

(time elapsed outside: 15 minutes.)

Nicole used paint dabbers in five different ways on this fresh layout: to distress the edges of her photo and a clear acrylic heart, to add two-tone color to white vintage buttons, to colorize her journaling strips, to transform a plain white paper frill into a colorful border accent, and to ink the "faq" stamp that appears in the lower-right corner of her photo.

materials acrylic paint (Ranger) • patterned papers (Collage Press, Scenic Route, SEI) • paper border (Doodlebug) • stamp (Studio Calico) • vinyl letters (American Crafts) • acrylic heart (Heidi Swapp) • scallop punch (Fiskars) • buttons • Typenoksidi font • *12 x 12 page by Nicole Harper, Elyria, OH*

You always want to be the kid with the toy that makes all the other kids jealous (at least I did, growing up). Thanks to Grandma Kathy and her gift of stomp rockets, the boys have achieved this coveted-toy status. The neighborhood kids love coming over to find out who can send a rocket furthest. Currently, I hold the record. *Carter, March 2008*

Stomp Rocket *by Autumn Baldwin.* **Supplies:** *Cardstock:* Bazzill Basics Paper; *Stickers:* American Crafts; *Journaling page:* Making Memories; *Circle cutter:* Creative Memories; *Font:* Optima; *Adhesive:* Avery and Scrapbook Adhesives by 3L; *Other:* Chipboard.

world views

PHOTO VALANCE

I've been blessed with opportunities to travel to some of the most spectacular areas of the world. Because each country represents a life-changing moment, I wanted to create something that not only celebrated each locale but also allowed for easy expansion so that I could continue to document the places I visit in the future. As I was musing over these requirements while staring out my studio window, the answer suddenly came to me: a new window valance!

STEP ONE
Print photo on fusible inkjet fabric sheet. Cut out, leaving 1/8" border.

STEP TWO
Press photo onto fabric. Sew edges to secure.

STEP THREE
Stamp title on leftover fusible inkjet fabric. Press onto fabric. Sew edges to secure.

MATERIALS

fabrics (Amy Butler, LakeHouse Direct Fabrics, Moda Fabrics) • fusible inkjet fabric sheets (June Tailor) • buttons (Autumn Leaves) • bookplate (BasicGrey) • flowers (Prima) • calendar stamp (Fontwerks) • journaling card (7gypsies) • doodling template (Chatterbox) • alphabet stamp set (Her o Arts) • StazOn ink (Tsukineko) • eyelets (Making Memories, Dritz) • Crop-A-Dile (We R Memory Keepers) • curtain rod • shower curtain hooks • brads • embroidery floss • quilt batting • thread

mckenna's family

CHILDREN'S ART QUILT

One afternoon, the girls talked me into covering the counter with newspaper, tying on their aprons, and squeezing out colorful blobs of acrylic paint for them to use. As they painted, I watched McKenna create page after page. Suddenly, I realized that she was painting our portraits! She laid them out on the deck to dry exactly as you see here, and the idea for this quilt was born.

Scan children's art and resize to desired size. Print on inkjet fabric sheet, leaving at least 1/2" border on all sides. Remove paper backing from pictures.

MATERIALS

fabrics (FreeSpirit) • sew-in inkjet fabric sheets (June Tailor) • bias tape (Wrights) • grommets (Dritz) • Crop-A-Dile (We R Memory Keepers) • quilt batting • thread

all my love

CANVAS WALL HANGING

Creating art for your home doesn't require a degree in oil painting or a huge investment in supplies. But it does require a willingness to play with the products you already have in new ways. This project is a great example. Break it down into steps, and build each layer to make the subjects literally pop right out of the design. Start by choosing a color palette; then pull out paper, paint, ribbon, buttons, fabrics, and other goodies, and pile them in front of you. As you work, play with placement and texture until you have a design you like. Don't limit yourself or your creativity. Remember, "You're perfect just the way you create!"

MATERIALS

stretched canvas (Michaels) • patterned papers (Crate Paper) • word stamps (Heidi Swapp, Inkadinkado, Limited Edition Rubber Stamps) • StazOn ink (Tsukineko) • chipboard flourishes (Maya Road) • ribbon (Offray) • acrylic paint • dictionary pages • canvas • clothespin • felt • buttons • embroidery floss

PLAY WITH POSTCARDS

Wait a minute, Mr. Postman! Before you run off with that batch of postcards, please leave a few behind for scrapbooking. Postcards make excellent scrapbook additions, whether you're adding them to a page with photos or using them as the photos. And, as Suzy Plantamura's page illustrates, they can also be a source of instant journaling. She took the message from the back of one of her cards and used it as the sentiment on her layout for a unique perspective on her trip.

Greetings from Hawaii *by Suzy Plantamura.* **Supplies:** *Patterned paper, borders, and chipboard:* GCD Studios; *Stickers:* American Crafts, Doodlebug Design, K&Company, and Making Memories; *Straight pin:* Maya Road; *Staples:* Making Memories; *Fonts:* Courier, Franklin Gothic Book, and Lucida Calligraphy; *Adhesive:* EK Success and Scrapbook Adhesives by 3L; *Other:* Trim.

Fabulous Fashion Finds

Just look at all of the cool bargains you girls have been able to find ever since you started managing your own fashion budgets! Up until now, you would pick clothes off the rack without even looking at the price tag. More often than not, I was shocked by the prices of some of the clothes you picked out. But now, armed with your trusty prepaid debit cards and a fixed budget, you have become true bargain hunters!

Shirt, $5@H&M

Ed Hardy Purse, $60@TJMaxx

Sequined high-tops, $18@Justice

Purse, $20@TJMaxx

Shirt, $15@H&M

Ed Hardy Jacket, $35@TJMaxx

Sweater, $15@H&M
Necklace, $9@Forever21

Dress, $29@Target
Belt, $12 @Charlotte Russe

Shirt, $7@TJMaxx
Cardigan, $12@Delia's

Boots, $20@Macy's

Fabulous Fashion Finds *by Brigid Gonzalez.* **Digital Supplies:** *Software:* Adobe; *Patterned paper:* Vector Jungle; *Grunge frames:* Anna Aspnes; *Fonts:* Bleeding Cowboys and Chalkduster.

Mid pleasures and palaces though we may roam, be it ever so humble, there's no place like home.

—JOHN HOWARD PAYNE

Always leave enough room in your life to do something that *makes you happy*, satisfied, or even joyous.

—PAUL HAWKEN

Dreams are like stars—you may never touch them, but if you follow them, they will lead you to your destiny. —UNKNOWN

Sometimes the QUESTIONS ARE COMPLICATED and the ANSWERS ARE SIMPLE.

—DR. SEUSS

Gratitude is not only the *greatest of virtues*, but the *parent* of all others.

—CICERO

Family means putting your arms around each other and *being there.*

—BARBARA BUSH

"*Mistakes* are the portals of *human discovery.*"

—JAMES JOYCE

A **best friend** is someone who makes you **laugh**, even when the jokes aren't **funny**.

—KERMIT THE FROG